COMPREHENDING
CULTS

The Sociology of
New Religious Movements

Lorne L. Dawson

Toronto   Oxford   New York
Oxford University Press
1998

Oxford University Press
70 Wynford Drive, Don Mills, Ontario M3C 1J9
http://www.oupcan.com

Oxford New York Athens Auckland Bangkok Bogotá Buenos Aires
Calcutta Cape Town Chennai Dar es Salaam Delhi Florence
Hong Kong Istanbul Karachi Kuala Lumpur Madrid Melbourne Mexico City Mumbai
Nairobi Paris São Paulo Singapore Taipei
Tokyo Toronto Warsaw
and associated companies in Berlin Ibadan

Oxford is a trade mark of Oxford University Press

Canadian Cataloguing in Publication Data

Dawson, Lorne L.
 Comprehending cults : the sociology of new religious movements

Includes bibliographical references and index.
ISBN 0-19-541154-4

1. Cults – Sociological aspects. I. Title.

BL60.D387 1998   306.6'919   C98-931495-2

Copyright © Oxford University Press Canada 1998

Cover Design: Sonya Thursby/Opus House
Text Design: Brett Miller

1 2 3 4 - 01 00 99 98
This book is printed on permanent (acid-free) paper å.

Printed in Canada

To the memory of Donald R. Dawson and my first
and most important lessons in curiosity,
critical insight, and independence.

Do not think that I have come to bring peace to the earth: I have not come to bring peace, but a sword.

For I have come to set a man against his father, and a daughter against her mother . . .

Whoever loves father or mother more than me is not worthy of me; and whoever loves son or daughter more than me is not worthy of me; and whoever does not take up the cross and follow me is not worthy of me. Those who find their life will lose it, and those who lose their life for my sake will find it.

Matthew 10: 34–9 (New Revised Standard Version)

Faith is better than knowledge if it works; but knowledge is better if faith be only an escape from knowledge.

Philip Rieff, The Triumph of the Therapeutic. New York:
Harper and Row, 1968, p. 98.

Table of Contents

Acknowledgements

Parts of Chapter 1 are drawn from Lorne L. Dawson, 'Constructing "Cult" Typologies: Some Strategic Considerations', *Journal of Contemporary Religion* 12 (3): 363–81, and reprinted with the permission of the journal. Parts of the Introduction and Chapter 3 are drawn from Lorne L. Dawson, 'Who Joins New Religious Movements and Why: Twenty Years of Research and What Have We Learned?' *Studies in Religion* 25 (2): 193–213, and reprinted with the permission of the journal. Parts of Chapter 6 are drawn from Lorne L. Dawson, 'Anti-Modernism, Modernism, and Postmodernism: Struggling with the Cultural Significance of New Religious Movements', *Sociology of Religion* 59 (2): 131–56, and reprinted with the permission of the Association for the Sociology of Religion, Inc.

In writing this book I have benefited greatly from the comments and assistance of Jim Richardson. I would also like to thank Euan White and Phyllis Wilson of Oxford University Press for their encouragement and patience.

Introduction

Why I Wrote
This Book

Two prominent local newspapers lay on my desk when I decided to write this book. The headlines read, '48 Found Dead in Doomsday Cult' and '50 from Quebec Cult Found Slain'.[1] On Tuesday, 4 October 1994, the members of a small new religious movement, called the Order of the Solar Temple (*L'Ordre du Temple solaire*), committed mass suicide by shooting or asphyxiating themselves and burning their homes to the ground, almost simultaneously, in three different places (Morin Heights, Quebec, and the villages of Cheiry and Granges-sur-Salvan in Switzerland).[2] On Wednesday evening I tuned in to ABC's popular and award-winning news commentary program 'Nightline'. Characteristically, the host Ted Koppel was already interviewing three 'cult experts' about the Solar Temple tragedy. I hoped to gain a better understanding of what happened, but to my dismay, though not to my surprise, two of the 'experts' in question were drawn from the American anti-cult movement, and the third was a Canadian journalist. Over the next half hour Mr Koppel asked the usual questions: What could make someone end their lives in this way? How could someone come to join such a group in the first place? What do we know about the mysterious leader of the cult? Just over a year earlier he had posed the same questions to similar 'experts' trying to explain the stand-off and eventual massacre of the Branch Davidians, under David Koresh, in Waco, Texas. The answers to these questions this evening seem as pat and pre-programmed as they did a year earlier. They are largely devoid of specifics and are speculative and polemical. We are informed, with few direct references to the actual beliefs and practices of the Solar Temple, that the group is like all other 'destructive' and 'apocalyptic' cults. In passing, one of the 'experts' makes specific reference to two other new religious movements, the Unification Church of Reverend Sun Myung Moon and John-Roger's MSIA (pronounced Messiah). Curiously though, neither group has ever been associated with either violence or suicide. Nevertheless, these experts assure us that the members of such dangerous cults are recruited through deception and the sophisticated use of techniques of 'mind-control'. The cunning and charismatic leaders of these groups exploit the psychological weaknesses and idealistic aspirations of their recruits, it is implied, in order to satisfy their own desires for material wealth and power. Yet, these experts acknowledge, we really do not know much about this cult leader or his followers. By the end of the interview, those viewing the program had probably had the prejudices that most Canadians and Americans harbour against 'cults' confirmed. These prejudices have been reinforced by the sheer reiteration of the pejorative observations and charges favoured by the media for the last twenty years. Little real insight has been obtained into the circumstances leading to the Solar Temple tragedy or the nature of cult activity in contemporary Western society.[3]

Listening to these 'experts' I could not help wondering whether other viewers would not be dissatisfied with such superficial responses. Might they not ask why we seem to know so little about these groups, especially in the wake of the Jonestown massacre of 1978 and the Koresh débâcle, or how these groups can continue to ply their trade if their sins are so transparent. In fact, much of the recent public debate over cults ignored the substantial and growing body of academic literature on the beliefs, practices, failings, and significance of cults (i.e., what sociologists prefer to call 'new religious movements'). A large body of empirical information and explanatory insights, directly pertinent to the issues at hand, can be found in this literature and in the broader literature of both the sociology and the psychology of religion.

Part of the blame for the misunderstanding and ignorance about contemporary religious cults rests with the academic community itself. To be sure, commendable efforts are being made by true experts like Eileen Barker, James T. Richardson, Thomas Robbins, David G. Bromley, and many others (e.g., Bromley and Richardson, 1983; Barker, 1989; and Bromley and Hadden, 1993) to refute publicly some of the more suspect claims of anti-cult organizations like Citizens Freedom Foundation, the Cult Awareness Network, the Council on Mind Abuse, and American Family Foundation.[4] And yet the diverse and disparate nature of the results of the scholarly investigation of new religious movements has frustrated the development of a more widespread understanding of the phenomenon. Broadly speaking, the voluminous information available tends either to survey the stated beliefs and practices of individual groups or collections of groups, without substantial reference to the relevant insights of the social sciences,[5] or it concentrates on specific sociological or psychological concerns related to the study of religion or cults, in a manner that hampers public dissemination.[6] In all regards, some very fine work has been done. But the scholarship on most aspects of new religious movements has reached a certain obvious maturity and more synthetical work is needed.[7]

My objective here is to provide a fairly comprehensive introduction to the insights gained, from decades of social scientific study, into the nature of cults and the controversy surrounding them. I will examine such social-scientific questions as the reasons for the recent growth in the size and number of new religious movements, what we know about who joins such religions and why, the charge that converts to cults are 'brainwashed', what may cause some cults to become violent, and what these groups indicate about the future of religion and culture in general in North America. These are the questions most commonly asked about cults.[8]

Now any introduction to the study of new religions is faced with the proverbial problem of 'the chicken and the egg'. On the one hand, how can we critically understand any of the new religions without some prior knowledge of the social-scientific insights into such groups? On the other hand, how can we fully understand the social-scientific discussions of these groups without some prior knowledge of some specific new religions? There is no sensible way to avoid the pitfalls of this dilemma other than by working simultaneously at both tasks. To that end the reader should try to complement this analysis by reading some of the many good case studies available about a variety of new religions, ranging from such prominent groups as Theosophy (e.g., Campbell, 1980), Scientology (e.g., Wallis, 1977), the International Society for Krishna Consciousness or Hare Krishna movement (e.g., Rochford, 1985), the Unification Church or Moonies (e.g., Barker, 1984), the Jesus Movement (e.g., Richardson, Stewart, and Simmonds, 1979), and the Rajneesh Foundation (e.g., Carter, 1990), through to such less conspicuous groups as spiritualism, Eckankar, Nichiren Shoshu, Vajradhatu, UFO cults, and various New Age and neo-pagan groups (see, e.g., Ellwood and Partin, 1988; Melton, 1992a; Miller, 1995; and the many relevant studies cited in these books and in the bibliography of this book). As with any religion, we should not pass judgement on any aspect of these groups without at least a rudimentary awareness of their concepts of the divine or transcendent, their views of human nature, their beliefs about death and the afterlife, and their definition of the good life.[9] Seen in broader historical, social, and cultural context, the new religions of recent times do not always appear to be so new. Moreover, many of the seemingly irrational aspects of contemporary cult life appear more reasonable, comprehensible, and socially significant than one might expect.

In writing this book it is not my intent to offer an apologia for cults, in either a religious or a sociological sense. I will attempt, however, to replace suspicion and misinformation with a greater knowledge of the facts (as best we know them) and a measure of sympathetic understanding. I will concern myself equally with the 'good, the bad, and the ugly', while striving to delineate the very real limits of our knowledge as well. I maintain no pretence to being definitive in my discussions, since the phenomena under study and the relevant literature are so vast and complex.

Most people are aware of cults only through the pervasively negative reports encountered in the media. So let us return to where we began and attempt to understand the cults better by exploring this negative reaction and its impact on the academic study of new religions. Before we can begin to talk about cults in a more balanced manner, it is necessary to correct the image of exotic and dangerous 'otherness' that pervades the public perceptions of these new religions.

The Hostility towards Cults

'Nightmare Tales—Why People Join Violent Cults' is the headline of an article on cults in a recent issue of a national news magazine.[10] In the first paragraph we are plunged into a gruesome account of a young woman's experience of extreme abuse, as a child and a teenager, at the hands of a Satanic cult. By the end of the second paragraph we are informed of the following 'facts': thousands of people join some 3,000 cults each year, 'dozens' of these cults (police sources say) are violent, and cults can take control of people's minds and brainwash them. Then the article quotes a 'former professor of psychiatry', who says that those of us who stand by and let it happen are no better than the 'regular white middle-class people [who] helped the Nazis murder six million Jews'. In the next two paragraphs we are treated to a recounting of the bloody Manson Family murders and the mass suicide of over 900 members of the Peoples Temple at Jonestown. With our fading memories of these tragedies sufficiently refreshed we are told: 'To lure people into their dark world both violent and nonviolent cults often prey on people who are emotionally confused or distraught.' Then another psychiatrist tells us, 'Cult members actually suspend their rational thought processes to do whatever the group leader asks of them—even if it involves murder or suicide.' As in the propaganda about drugs to which many of us were exposed as teenagers in the sixties and seventies, it is suggested that all this tragedy can grow disastrously 'out of a simple flirtation with something different or unknown'. From youthful experimentation with marijuana, heroin addiction follows. From experimentation with alternative religious views, one runs the risk of becoming a zombie enslaved to an imbalanced and immoral cult leader. When you are so enslaved, as several more stories of ex-cult members relate, you will lose all your material goods and savings to the greed of the cults. Unless, of course, you are as lucky as Treva Mailer, whose parents loved her enough to hire a deprogrammer from California to kidnap her and return her to reason.

This kind of journalistic account of cults is common (Jorgensen, 1980; Bromley, Shupe, and Ventimiglia, 1983; Van Driel and Richardson, 1988; Beckford and Cole, 1988; Lippert, 1990; Selway, 1992; Barker, 1993; Richardson, 1996). I would have been less surprised, though, if the article in question had appeared at the height of the cult scare in the 1970s and early 1980s. Instead, it was written in 1993, in wilful ignorance, it would seem, of two decades of academic study of new religious movements. Admittedly, the article is about 'violent cults', and much of what it says, in that limited regard, is a matter of record. The Manson Family committed terrible murders. But did the group of drifters 'in love' with Charles Manson constitute a cult? Not by the reckoning of most qualified scholars. In general, given the language used, only the most careful and determined of readers could keep from falsely identifying the charges levelled at violent cults with all cults. The article panders to our worse fears and unfounded prejudices on the basis of a few aberrant cases. A similarly biased and simplistic treatment of almost any other issue, like the question of drugs mentioned above, would be met with ridicule—especially by journalists. Through the course of this book it will become apparent that the results of investigations by social scientists into new religious movements not only fail to substantiate, but usually refute, most of the suppositions of this and so many other popular accounts of cults.

As Eileen Barker (1993: 204–8; 1995: 299–300) has pointed out, we must realize that journalists face considerable constraints of time, space, and competition in fashioning their stories about new religions. They are necessarily guided by the commercial demand to attract readers, and they often lack expertise in the subject (see, e.g., Jorgensen, 1980; Lippert, 1990; Beckford, 1994). But as other subjects continue to be newsworthy, a marked improvement can usually be detected in the quality of the reporting and commentary. Such does not appear to be the case (with rare exceptions) when it comes to cult stories. As Van Driel and Richardson (1988: 37) summarize their longitudinal and comprehensive analysis of print media: news about cults in America 'although not uniformly negative, can best be described as "a stream of controversies" with little attention to the history or human side of the new religions.'

In the end, does it matter that the media continue to get things wrong? The answer depends, of course, on how much one values an honest treatment of any public issue, but especially that of alternative religions. In this regard, a social psychological study undertaken by Jeffrey Pfeifer (1992) is instructive.

Pfeifer randomly assigned 98 undergraduates to three different groups and gave each group the identical scenario to read: a description of a young man who joins a group and is exposed to its indoctrination process. In its details the scenario was modelled on the charges of brainwashing commonly levelled at new religious movements (see Chapter 4). In each case, however, each group of students was given a different label for the group in question. One was told they were reading about a man joining the Moonies (i.e., the Unification Church), another about a man joining the Marines, and the third, a man entering a Catholic seminary to become a priest. Afterwards, each participant filled out two questionnaires, the first about the scenarios they had read, and the second about their opinions and knowledge of cults. The results revealed that the participants overwhelmingly preferred the term 'brainwashing' for the experience of a man joining the Moonies, yet not for a man joining the Marines or the Catholic priesthood (70.9 per cent, 44.12 per cent, and 29.41 per cent respectively). Though the scenarios were all the same, more neutral terms like 'resocialization' were preferred for the latter two possibilities. The participants also considered the man joining the Moonies to be less happy with life before joining the group, less intelligent, and less responsible than the man joining the Marines or the Catholic priesthood. The man joining the Moonies was also more likely to be rated as having been coerced into joining, less able to resist indoctrination, and less free to leave, and it was felt that he was treated less fairly. Similarly, 82.42 per cent of the participants described the average cult member in negative terms, the rest giving neutral descriptions (no positive descriptions were recorded). Clearly, the mere introduction of the label 'cult' produced a significant skewing of the participants' evaluations of the situation. Yet the second questionnaire revealed that 82.2 per cent of the participants admitted that they had never talked to a cult member, known a cult member, or been a cult member; 91.67 per cent said they were basing their opinions on media reports. How the media has treated cult phenomena, then, certainly seems to have had some telling consequences.[11]

Such findings have been corroborated by other studies. In her excellent analysis of the Unification Church in Britain, *The Making of a Moonie: Choice or Brainwashing*, Barker (1984: 2–3) makes similar observations, based on a survey of the views of the control group used in her research. A recent random national sample of 1,700 Americans found that, despite a long tradition of freedom of religion (enshrined in the First Amendment of the American Constitution), 73 per cent supported the idea of legislation that would prohibit the conversion of teenagers to cults (Bromley and Breschel, 1992). Likewise, in many recent court cases involving new religions, the jurors have shown a surprising disregard for the constitutional protection of religious freedom (see, e.g., Richardson, 1991, 1992; Robbins and Bromley, 1993; Anthony and Robbins, 1995). And a study for the University of Colorado school of journalism by Stewart Hoover (1994: 2–6) acknowledges that the media probably contributed significantly to the sad demise of the Branch Davidians at Waco by reinforcing the conception of David Koresh as a mere terrorist and not a religious leader open to theological debate and persuasion. Agreeing with Hoover, Richardson (1995a) argues more generally that the FBI was emboldened to override the advice of its own behavioural experts and to proceed with the drastic measures that ultimately led to the loss of lives at Waco by the highly negative and unrealistic conception of cults that had gained currency in the United States as a result of the media's reliance on press releases from anti-cult organizations (see also Jones and Baker, 1994).

And indeed, much of the strength of the popular and media prejudice against new religious movements does stem from the success of the anti-cult movement (Shupe and Bromley, 1980, 1994). An organized response to the newly emergent religious alternatives on the American scene began to take shape in the mid-1970s. It had its origin in numerous grass-roots reactions to the new religions. Most of these anti-cult groups were composed of the distraught relations of young adults who had joined these unconventional religions. Some groups were also organized by members of the fundamentalist Christian right to defend their vision of the religious culture of America. The former groups sought the return of their children or siblings to conventional life; the latter often envisioned themselves to be struggling with the minions of Satan. By the mid-1980s these anti-cult groups had become a movement in their own right, and an element of professionalism emerged as permanent staff were hired, efforts were co-ordinated, full-time 'deprogrammers' began to ply their trade, and concerted legal actions were launched against various cults (see Richardson, 1991; Anthony and Robbins, 1995). Soon, when the media sought ready information on cult activities, they began to turn to the Citizens Freedom Foundation, Love Our Children Inc., the Council on Mind Abuse, the Cult Awareness Network, and dozens of other anti-cult organizations. Governments, however, at least at the federal level, have refrained from formally recognizing or assisting these groups, arguing that they are special-interest groups and purveyors of opinion, not substantiated and legally documented claims. In spite of this denial of legitimacy to the anti-cult movement, the academics who study cults played no significant role in advising the various government officials involved in the Branch Davidian stand-off and conflagration, or the media covering the story. For the most part, academics continue to be left largely out of the popular information loop.[12]

Responding to the Suspicions of the Public

The public controversy over cults poses unique problems for sociologists of religion and for religious studies scholars. In the study of new religions, unlike most other areas of academic endeavour, scholars often find themselves pitted against an active opposition to their findings. Every day, in and out of class, I encounter evidence that the anti-cult movement has brought about what Shupe and Bromley (1980: 242) call the 'symbolic degradation' of cults. But to sustain the image of 'deviance' associated with new religions, the anti-cult movement must, paradoxically, keep the cult threat alive. Cults must continue to be seen as undesirable and dangerous in all regards, and also as more pervasive and influential than commonly thought. In response, most sociologists, historians, psychologists, and religious studies scholars involved in the study of cults have striven to disseminate more neutral explanations of cult activity. First and foremost, they have sought to replace the very word 'cult', with all its pejorative connotations, with such terms as 'new religions', 'marginal religious groups', 'emergent religions', and 'new religious movements'. As we will see in the next chapter, the term 'cult' has a legitimate academic pedigree, but its popular meaning has been so distorted by popular usage that the term 'new religious movements', or as commonly abbreviated NRMs, has been widely substituted in academic discussions, as it is in this book (see Richardson, 1993a). On occasion, though, I will use the term 'cult' to evoke the kind of fear and suspicion that is an irreducible part of the dialogue to which this book is contributing. Moreover, there is reason to hold to the distinction between cults and other forms of religious organization, which may be new as well, like sects (see Chapter 1). This important distinction tends to be blurred by the more generic classification of NRMs. It should also be noted that the designation NRM has another limitation, namely that not all NRMs are so new (depending on how that is gauged), nor are they all movements. In any event this book was not written with any illusions about achieving some ideal terminological consensus.

The controversial nature of the study of new religious movements poses other difficulties as well. Recognizing that the public distrusts the way that the cults portray themselves, many NRMs have tried to foster social-scientific interest in their groups in hopes of countering the misinformation and prejudice of the anti-cultists and the media (Barker, 1993: 197–8; 1995). They have used the social sciences to court legitimacy. And the social scientists in turn have sought cordial relations with NRMs in order to establish and maintain the rapport necessary to conduct their research. In the face of the anti-cult movement, however, this rapport is easily misinterpreted as evidence of the covertly apologetic purpose of this research. Students of NRMs are burdened, then, with a double necessity to appear impartial, and their only real protection against accusations of bias is the depth and quality of their knowledge of these groups.[13]

Given these and other difficulties inherent in the study of NRMs, we need to keep a number of things in mind.

First, contrary to the tendencies of the media and the anti-cultists, we must guard against lumping all new religious movements together. Anti-cult literature is fond of casting aspersions on 'cults', in general, as if they were in essence all the same. But as leading sociologists of new religions stress, amongst the many thousands of cults there is great diversity. Despite some similarities, these new religions have different conceptions of our origins, development, and future. They propose different explanations of our existential plight, and they offer different programs to alleviate our woes. They mobilize and organize different resources, in different ways, with different immediate and distant consequences. They may even be responding to different situations, needs, desires, and constituencies (Beckford, 1985: 60).

Of course, some generalizations about these groups are warranted, especially in the attempt to understand new religious movements as a social phenomenon. Nevertheless, almost any generalized statement about so diverse and complex a subject as NRMs is subject to notable exceptions. Often the real theoretical challenge is to provide a systematic reason for the variations inevitably encountered. It is a platitude and yet none the less true that the more we learn about NRMs, the more we realize how much is left to learn.

One significant distinction initially emerges when we try to generalize about the new religious life in our midst. NRMs seem to divide into two groups. On the one hand, there are the more traditionally oriented religions that tend to stress communal life and exclusive commitments. On the other hand, there are religions that are more oriented to modernity and that tend to be non-communal and open to segmented and plural commitments. I am speaking of a continuum of possibilities and not two exclusive categories, and in Chapter 6 we will see that even this generalization is useful only to a point, beyond which it can be crucially misleading. However, it is useful to think of NRMs in terms of this distinction. The Unification Church, Krishna Consciousness, and most Christian fundamentalist groups lean to the traditional end of this continuum, while Theosophy, Scientology, and most religio-psycho-therapeutic groups lean towards the modern end.[14] The proclivity stressed normatively by any NRM affects the way its origins are to be explained, who is recruited to it, what joining means for converts, and how we judge its significance and future development. The latter judgement depends as well on how the signs of secularization are read. Are the loss of traditional religious authority and the decline of involvement in organized religion that are now so characteristic of our societies a sign of the end of religion or of its transformation? Much depends on the answer.

Second, the new religious movements that have attracted so much recent attention in North America and Europe are unique neither in history nor in these societies: 'They have had counterparts in earlier times and they continue to have them in other regions of the world' (Beckford, 1985: 25). There is something new and yet not so new about the cult activity we are studying. Likewise, these groups are both 'North American' and foreign to North America at the same time. They are a curious and potentially important blending of the cultural traditions of the East and the West and of past and present elements of different cultural heritages.

Third, we must be careful not to indulge in 'reductionistic' analyses of these groups. The social-scientific study of religion confronts a unique methodological difficulty. It strives to make objective, empirical, and logical sense of a subject that is highly subjective, claims to be non-empirical in its essence (i.e, it is 'spiritual'), and is often purposefully paradoxical in its basic premises and practices (for example, many religions, like Christianity, Islam, and Hinduism, claim that one can win ultimate freedom only by complete surrender to the will of God and his or her chosen agents). In the face of this rudimentary dilemma, and to protect scholarly claims to objectivity, most students of religion opt for 'methodological atheism' (Berger, 1967). It is not the function of social scientists to resolve matters of ontology or theology; that is the concern of philosophers and theologians. Setting aside the question of the truthfulness of the claims of any religion, the function of social scientists is merely to record and explain those aspects of religious life that are susceptible to empirical research. In practice, however, matters are rarely so straightforward. Attempts to explain elements of religious life may depend on implicit assumptions about human nature and the nature of the world that are contrary to the fundamental assertions of the religious. In fact, as Hamnett (1973), Johnson (1977), and others have argued, the methodological stance of the sociology of religion seems to be covertly founded on a rather inconsistent assumption: religion is good for society and yet the beliefs of religions are a problem to be explained. For most sociologists, belief in the supernatural is implicitly erroneous. Consequently, in seeking to explain religious phenomena, sociologists often seem to be actually explaining the phenomena away. Where once there were religious processes, there are now merely social, psychological, and even biological processes. In the last analysis, however, since social scientists cannot adequately resolve ontological issues (like whether the supernatural exists or not), there is often no sound reason to place more value in the accuracy of some scientifically derived explanations of religious phenomena than in some religious explanations of the same phenomena.[15]

So, in order to avoid being too reductionist, this study will be guided by two methodological principles. First, an effort will be made to treat the doctrines of new religious movements seriously, though with caution. As Geoffrey Nelson (1984) and others (e.g., Wilson, 1982a; Bateson and Ventis, 1982; Stark and Bainbridge, 1985, 1987) have argued, we must to some extent acknowledge that new religious movements grow out a desire to satisfy certain 'spiritual' needs of humanity that have a reality and importance independent of our other social and psychological needs. Likewise, part of the impetus for their existence stems from the logical and practical elaboration of religious beliefs and practices in order to satisfy these needs.

Second, in a similar vein an effort also will be made to remember that much of religious life is like the rest of life. Religious choices, like other choices, are made on the basis of a reasonable calculation of apparent benefits and costs. Contrary to a strong inclination in the social sciences and the public in general, there is no a priori reason to assume that religious activities are primarily irrational. Rather, we should look for evidence of a reasonable exchange of investments and sacrifices by the convert to a cult in return for rewards and satisfactions provided to the convert by the group. This is a point I have argued at length elsewhere (Dawson 1988, 1990, 1994a), as have others of note recently (e.g., Gartrell and Shannon, 1985; Stark and Bainbridge, 1985, 1996; Neitz, 1987; Iannaccone, 1990; Durkin and Greeley, 1991; Stark, 1991; Stark and Finke, 1993; Stark and Iannaccone, 1993; Iannaccone, 1995; Young, 1997).

In our society the practice of law, education, politics, economics, and daily business are guided by two related and basic assumptions: (1) people are predisposed to be rational, and hence once they become aware that they are behaving irrationally, they will try to adjust their beliefs, attitudes, and actions; (2) in explaining the actions of others it is logical to assume that their behaviour is rational until a reason is given for thinking otherwise. Such assumptions introduce a necessary measure of economy into the processes of explaining and understanding social life. They stop us from falling prey to an infinite regress of impractical speculations about the 'real' causes or motivations of other people's actions. In the study of new religious movements, as in the rest of the social sciences, we have no reason to assume in advance that this profitable explanatory dictum no longer holds. As with every other aspect of life, however, we must try to see how the actions of cult members make sense in context. No action can be deemed rational or irrational in ignorance of the circumstances and perspectives of those taking the action (Weber, 1949; Blumer, 1969).

To comprehend and eventually explain the acts of others, sociologists must first seek to understand the definition of the situation (that is, the meanings and interpretive processes) that others have fashioned for any given state of affairs. Part of the definition of the situation, in this context, is the evident interest of most of humanity in some kind of spiritual element in their lives. Contrary to popular opinion, a methodological focus on the rational character of people's judgements in no way excludes this possibility. As the philosopher Nicholas Rescher (1988: 9) observes, reason 'recognizes the utility and appropriateness of our *higher* (aesthetic and affectively social and even *spiritual*) values. The realm of rationality is as large and comprehensive as the domain of valid human concerns and interests.' Reason and religion are not necessarily antithetical, in principle or in fact (see Weber, 1963). Thus, 'in addition to the oft repeated insight that people who want to do good work in [the] area [of NRMs] must be able to overcome personal religious commitments, it must be added that it is equally important that people be able to overcome their lack of faith. One need not be a believer, but one must understand how belief is possible' (Stark and Finke, 1993: 123).

This approach neither overlooks nor factors out of consideration the affective component of religious actions. In most popular and many academic accounts of new religious movements, however, this affective component receives ample if not unwarranted attention. Here an effort will be made to correct the balance, so to speak, by highlighting some grounds for perceiving the 'relative rationality' of seemingly irrational or sometimes even unsavoury behaviour.

Fourth and lastly, I would like to stress that part of the reason for studying new religious movements is that they are mirrors of our society as a whole and the scientific study of religion in particular. 'The new religious movements often serve as spiritual inkblots: reports of movements may tell us more about the observers than about the observed' (Stone, 1978a: 42). Our individual and collective reactions to religious innovations reveal much about our self-understanding (Beckford, 1985). Hence, a better understanding of NRMs should pay dividends in increased self-understanding, both individually and collectively.

Chapter One

What Are
New Religious
Movements?

The Emergence of the 'Cults'

New religious movements or 'cults' first emerged into prominence in the 1960s and early 1970s. They became the focus of some public alarm and heightened media attention after the mass murder-suicide of 914 followers of the Peoples Temple, under the leadership of Jim Jones, at Jonestown, Guyana, on 18 November 1978 (see Reiterman and Jacobs, 1982; Chidester, 1988). This tragic and shocking event unleashed more than a decade of popular, journalistic, and academic study of the new religions. Seen as spin-offs of the counter-culture of the sixties, for some people these groups herald the possible disintegration of our traditional Judeo-Christian culture and perhaps even the beginning of the age of false prophets foretold by the Bible as a sign of the end of days. For others, the tragedies of Jonestown, the Branch Davidians at Waco, the Solar Temple, and Heaven's Gate are aberrations. They call attention, however, to the ground swell of a new and seemingly different spirituality that is infiltrating our supposedly ever more secular society. Whether good or bad, a sign of degeneration or regeneration, the religious life of North Americans is clearly changing and the birth of new religions provides a unique opportunity for scholars of religion to witness and trace the changes in unprecedented detail.

Twenty years after Jonestown, it is clear that only a small fraction of the population of the United States or Canada has ever been involved with a new religion.[1] But the cultural impact of these new religions would seem to be of much greater consequence. The religious landscape and consciousness of Americans have been irreversibly changed and a new spiritual pluralism established.[2] The denominational accommodation between Protestantism, Catholicism, and Judaism that shaped personal and collective identities in the period of prosperity immediately after the Second World War (Herberg, 1955; Wuthnow, 1988) has been fractured permanently by the sheer number of ever more conspicuous religious alternatives. After the sixties, in the evocative words of Robert Wuthnow (1988: 152), 'it was as if the bits of mosaic that had given shape to the religious topography had been thrown into the air, never to land in exactly the same positions as before.'

In the last few decades North Americans have witnessed the dramatic growth of such alternative forms of Christian expression as Mormonism, 'independent churches' (i.e., non-denominational congregations), groups founded in the ethos of the sixties counter-culture (e.g., the Family and other 'Jesus freaks'), and a plethora of other evangelical, fundamentalist, charismatic, and Pentecostalist 'churches' (e.g., Balmor, 1989). Even more dramatically, many Americans have turned from their Christian heritage altogether to become involved with a multitude of imported or innovated new religious movements. The latter new religions can be divided roughly into four sets: (1) groups associated with various Asian traditions of philosophy, devotion, meditation, and magic, such as Transcendental Meditation, Divine Light Mission, International Society for Krishna Consciousness, Rajneesh Foundation (now known as Osho Foundation), Nichiren Shoshu (also known as Sōka Gakkai), and Vajradhatu (which now also calls itself Shambhala); (2) groups associated with the American 'human potential movement' in popular psychology, such as Erhard Seminar Training (or est), Scientology, Psychosynthesis, and Silva Mind-Control; (3) groups associated with various forms of occult revival, such as Wicca, Feraferia, and the Church of Satan; and (4) groups that think their salvation depends on contact with UFOs and aliens, such as Bo and Peep, which developed into Heaven's Gate, Understanding Inc., and the Aethurius Society. Our primary concern is with these new kinds of religious life, both the imported and innovated groups, and not so much the new religious movements rooted in Christianity. Most particularly, the focus is on the substantial and established groups that have emerged within the first two of these categories, like Scientology, Krishna Consciousness, and the Unification Church.

The last group mentioned, the Unification Church of Reverend Sun Myung Moon (pronounced Sun-Young-Moon),[3] calls attention, however, to an important qualification to all our dealings with NRMs. Many of these groups are strongly committed to the ongoing synthesis of different religious traditions and elements of the religious and the secular worlds. Hence they do not readily fit into any convenient analytic groupings, and care must be taken to respect the individuality of these groups.

To give another example, although Scientology was born in the United States, it involves a composite of elements drawn from the American human potential movement and the Hindu and Buddhist religious traditions. The Unification Church, imported to North America from Korea, is essentially Christian. Yet it would be misleading simply to group the Moonies along with other unusual Christian groups, because the Reverend Moon revised the Christian gospel in the light of his own revelations, and the revisions bear the marks of his Korean background, with its Confucian and shamanistic elements. But these non-Christian elements are not sufficient to warrant classifying the Unification Church as simply another Asian import, like Krishna Consciousness.

This blending of cultural and religious legacies makes simple classification of many of these groups very difficult. But that is also the feature of many of these groups that makes it very important to understand them. These new religions both reflect and embody larger processes of cultural integration, transformation, and globalization (Robertson and Chirico, 1985; Bromley and Busching, 1988; Wuthnow, 1988; Beyer, 1994), which are slowly but surely altering the character of North American society. Modern mass media, rising levels of education, and changing immigration and economic patterns are ushering in a new era of cultural and religious pluralism, one that is bringing the East to the West almost as fully as the West was once visited upon the East by imperialism and Christian missionaries. It is likely, as many sociologists suggest (e.g., Tiryakian, 1967, 1972; Hammond, 1987; Robbins and Bromley, 1992), that NRMs provide sheltering enclaves in which social innovations and experiments are taking place. Some of these innovations could well spread to the larger culture. In any event, the cumulative effect of the very existence of such opportunities for lifestyle experimentation is bound to alter the self-understanding and values of future generations. These are themes to which we will return in Chapter 6.

At this juncture, it is time to pose two more fundamental and preliminary questions: What is the essential nature of religion as a social phenomenon? and, What constitutes a cult? To discuss the nature, operation, social significance, and future of NRMs requires some understanding of the nature of religion and its role in contemporary society. This is the subject matter of the sociology of religion as a whole, and its findings cannot be summarized here. Fortunately, it is not necessary to try, since much of the debate over the nature and the future of religion in North America is reproduced in a recent clash of two theoretical paradigms (Warner, 1993). An understanding of the fundamentals of these two perspectives and the interpretive options they entail helps clarify many of the issues raised by the study of NRMs.

As to the nature of cults or NRMs, recourse will be made to what sociologists call church-sect theory. To know what a cult is we must be able to distinguish it from other forms of religious organization. Sociologists have devised the church-sect typology to help them make these distinctions. A brief examination of this classic approach will allow us to specify an adaptation best suited to making sense of the welter of new religious activity.

Religion and Its Continuing Significance

The first of the two theoretical paradigms of the nature of religion that I intend to use to frame our discussions of NRMs is derived from the seminal writings of the American sociologist Peter Berger (e.g., 1967, 1969), in particular his book *The Sacred Canopy* (1967). The second paradigm is associated with the almost as influential, yet much more recent, work of the American sociologists of religion Rodney Stark and William Sims Bainbridge (1985, 1987), which has been developed further in the writings of Roger Finke and Rodney Stark (1992), Stark and Finke (1993), Stark and Iannaccone (1993), and elsewhere.

Berger's theory of religion offers an account of the most essential social grounds of religious belief and practice; his theory is repeatedly called upon, explicitly and implicitly, to explain the rise, spread, features, and demise of NRMs. The logic of his theory tends to suggest, though, that contemporary society is destined to become ever more secular. Hence neither old nor new religions are likely to have much importance in advanced industrial societies.

Stark and Bainbridge, and Finke and Stark, argue against the permanent disappearance of religion. Taking explicit account of NRMs, they advance a theory that is similar to Berger's in some respects yet crucially different because it breaks with the tendency to equate progress towards more rational forms of social management and organization with the demise of religion. The resultant theory provides alternative criteria for assessing the nature, appeal, and success or failure of various kinds of NRMs. A close reading of the divergent theoretical paradigms of Berger and of Stark and his colleagues reveals some interesting points of convergence, however, which may well point the way to an even better understanding of NRMs.[4] We will be discussing these points when we return to some of the issues raised in this chapter in Chapter 6.

Berger's Theory of Religion

Berger's highly influential theory of religion grew out of his earlier and equally important work with Thomas Luckmann on the social construction of reality (Berger and Luckmann, 1966). Building on a masterful synthesis of the insights of most of the foundational thinkers of contemporary social science (Karl Marx, Emile Durkheim, Max Weber, George Herbert Mead, Sigmund Freud, Max Scheler, Karl Mannheim, Alfred Schutz, and many others), this theory begins with the startlingly simple premise that 'every human society is an enterprise of world-building' (Berger, 1967: 3). The world we live in, the world as perceived by humans, is constantly being created and re-created by us through a 'dialectical process' that has three aspects: 'externalization, objectivation, and internalization'. Our thoughts become embodied in the things we make and the things we do in the world—they are externalized. Once in the world, these products of our thought (e.g., machines, art forms, and institutions) take on an independent existence as objects of our awareness—objectivation occurs—and they act back upon us, shaping and changing our behaviour and our further thoughts. We internalize the lessons of living in the world of these objects (physical, social, and cultural), adapting ourselves in thought, word, and deed to the presumed requirements of 'reality'. We are the creators of our world, but we are in turn shaped by our creation and become one of its objects. We become the passive subjects of our creation, in part because we simply are not fully aware of the extent or nature of our creativity. Our lack of awareness stems in large measure from the fact that the creativity in question is a collective undertaking. World-building is a social process, and as such it is so complex and dispersed as to defy the ready comprehension or control of any individual or group.

Berger argues that human participation in the dialectic of world construction is an 'anthropological necessity'. Unlike other animals, humans are born 'unfinished'. Since our biological programming is deficient, to survive we must complete our natures by learning how to function in our environment. To this end we have created culture. Culture is the truly 'natural' world of humans, and it stands protectively between individuals and the forces of nature. The problem is that, as a product of the dialectic, culture is also inherently unstable. It is subject to constant flux and change as the conditions of collective life change. Thus, Berger proposes, we are eternally trapped between a biologically given imperative to secure a stable and hence safe environment through culture and the inherent instability of the cultures we create. This is the human predicament.

Religion is the ultimate response to this predicament. To understand how this is so, more must be said about the dialectical process of constructing a world. The success of a culture in providing a stable environment for human development 'depends upon the establishment of symmetry between the objective world of society and the subjective world of the individual' (Berger, 1967: 15). When symmetry is achieved between the subjective and objective definitions of reality, that is, the definitions of the individual and the group, the institutions of society and the roles these institutions prescribe for individuals strike us as 'factual' and hence as 'coercive'. We think that we must abide by the dictates of society, its traditional ways of doing things, because these ways are seen as the dictates of reality itself. Under such conditions people do not merely perform their assigned roles in social life, they freely identify with these roles. They seek what another sociologist, Ralph Turner, calls 'role-person merger'—they become their roles—and in the process they impart great stability to the received social order. Human activity becomes very regular and predictable, providing practical and psychological reassurance to everyone about their own and other people's behaviour. Hence, under ideal circumstances, which are never actually achieved, most aspects of the social order should come to be 'taken for granted'. The relatively stable human environment that results is what Berger calls a 'nomos', a meaningful world order.

The collective effort to fashion this *nomos* is 'totalizing'. The more encompassing and integrated the meaningful world order, the greater the stability and satisfaction. In fact, however, the *nomos* does not embrace all the discrete experiences of individuals. Ultimately it cannot do so. On the margins of life 'anomie', an anxiety-inducing sense of normlessness, is waiting. In the everyday experience of dreams, death, defeat, and the unexpected, we are repeatedly threatened with separation from the social world and hence the loss of meaning. In Berger's words (1967: 23), 'every *nomos* is an edifice erected in the face of the potent and alien forces of chaos.' Religion seeks to provide the 'ultimate shield against the terror of anomie' (1967: 25) by supplying the most effective legitimation of the social order. Religious myths, rites, doctrines, and practices seek to assert the merger of the *nomos* and the cosmos. The social order, in Berger's words, is 'cosmosized' and rendered 'sacred'. The social order is no longer a human construct, subject to change, but a divinely given order subject to the will of the gods (or other supernatural forces) alone. The gods may choose to act through their human intermediaries, but the world is no longer a merely human creation. In such a world, any attempt to deny the order that the religiously sanctioned society imposes is an act of evil as well as madness (Berger, 1967: 39). Of course, it must be remembered that Berger is speaking hypothetically about the earliest stages of human social development. There has been no real mass awareness of the creative role of humans in the construction of the world until modern times. Rather, as best we can tell, the gods evolved hand in hand with society from the beginning. Historically, 'forgetfulness' is the normal state, and 'awareness' is the modern aberration brought on by philosophy, science, and technology.

In a world where the human microcosm has been conceptually merged with the natural macrocosm, where social roles become the mimetic reiterations of cosmic realities, through the mediation of the supernatural the experience of anomie is crucially ameliorated. It is not eliminated, since death, nightmares, and unanticipated twists of fate persist. But these events are given a meaning in light of some larger divine scheme, whether through reference to the will of a supreme God, the struggle of supernatural forces of good and evil, or the consequences of karma. This meaningfulness allows individuals to maintain hope and endure suffering. The promise of ultimate order provides comfort, and more, it ensures that individuals will continue to willingly sacrifice themselves and their own selfish interests for the benefit and survival of the group, the social system, and the culture. The price of this security, for the society and its individual members, is 'alienation', or the forgetfulness spoken of above. For the illusion of world-building to work, humans must 'forget' their own creative role in the dialectic. They must become estranged from their own responsibility for the nature and fate of their society. To recollect and reappropriate one's creative role would be to call into question the objectivity of the social order and hence the veracity of the ultimate meaning attributed to life. In Berger's theory, then, every society must strike some balance between the evils of anomie and alienation. Anomie can only be staved off at a certain price in alienation, while the reduction of alienation means a certain increase in the anomie that must be tolerated.

Of course, the complexities of Berger's theory of religion and of the social circumstances it seeks to explain are much greater than this brief summary can convey. In fact, religions exist, for example, in dialectical relationship with what Berger calls 'plausibility structures'. As systems of religious beliefs and practices provide conceptual justifications for social institutions (that is, groups and activities), in the course of human history social institutions have provided in turn what might be called material justifications for religious beliefs and practices. The sheer power and viability of any social system lend credence to the truth and utility of the religious system associated with it. Conversely, the military defeat or social disruption of a society often (but not always) discredits the religious ideology of the society. This rule of thumb, like all others, is subject to important exceptions. Judaism, for example, is one of several religions from around the world that managed to fashion a new ideology of hope and salvation out of military defeat and social disruption (for example, during the Babylonian exile and, later, the Diaspora). In this case, a *nomos* was developed from the notion and imagery of the redemptive suffering of the children of God.

Although Berger's theory is meant to provide only broad guidelines for the comprehension and assessment of the nature and social functioning of religion, it has decisively influenced the academic study of religion in general and the study of NRMs in particular. Since the 1960s, discussions of the emergence of NRMs have tended to lean heavily on the ideas of Berger. Some of this influence has also come by way of another major aspect of Berger's theory of religion, namely, his theory of the process of secularization. Thus, before the nature of Berger's influence can be explained, this theory of secularization must be sketched and contrasted with that of Stark and colleagues. The debate over the possible cultural significance of NRMs has been framed largely in terms of these alternative approaches to secularization.

Berger's Theory of Secularization

For the first time in history many humans, especially members of the advanced industrial West, live in largely non-religious societies. Our societies have been becoming increasingly secular since at least the middle of the nineteenth century. This process of secularization is the overriding feature of religion in the modern world, and hence the backdrop to all contemporary research in the sociology of religion, in particular the study of NRMs. Berger defines secularization quite simply as 'the process by which sectors of society and culture are removed from the domination of religious institutions and symbols' (1967: 107). For most scholars there is little doubt that secularization has occurred, and as Berger's popular theory of religion suggests, it is commonly thought that this social development represents a highly significant break with the dominant pattern of human history. There is ample debate, however, about the precise nature, causes, and prospects of secularization. Berger's arguments on these counts have helped to fashion the view of secularization that has been most prevalent in sociology for the last several decades. But this prevailing view presents only one set of interpretive possibilities for the explanation of the nature and significance of the new religions that have emerged since the 1960s. The alternative reading of the situation by Stark and his colleagues suggests another set of interpretive possibilities that is stimulating renewed debate about the truth of secularization and the present and future significance of NRMs.

In a manner that is now conventional, Berger sees secularization beginning with the rise of industrial society. More specifically, following the line of analysis first developed by Max Weber (1958a, 1958b), Berger links the secularization of society to the processes of 'rationalization' crucial to the establishment and operation of a capitalist and industrial economy. From the seventeenth century onwards, as the economic and then the political spheres of activity in society were liberated from religious tutelage, religious systems have been compelled to adapt to a new social structure. Specifically, Berger argues that religions must adapt to two new environmental 'realities'.

First, in its 'peculiarly modern form' religion has become a matter of choice; religious orientations are no longer the legitimating requirements of society so much as the preferences of individuals or nuclear families. Religion has undergone what sociologists call 'privatization' (Berger, 1967: 133–5). In the modern world, as Berger ruefully remarks (1967: 134), 'religion manifests itself as public rhetoric and private virtue. In other words, in so far as religion is common it lacks "reality", and in so far as it is "real" it lacks commonality.' Seen as a private matter, a matter of individual choice, religious beliefs and practices do not support a truly common universe of meaning for the members of society, and thus the traditional task of religion has been severely ruptured.

Second, while religions must struggle with the new 'reality' of privatization, they must also cope with the new 'reality' of 'pluralism' (Berger, 1967: 135–8). Religious choice is possible because the religious monopolies of the past (such as the nearly universal rule of the Catholic Church in Europe until the sixteenth century) were broken by the Protestant Reformation and the relativizing effects of the increased exposure of the West to the cultures of India, the Far East, and Africa (see, for example, Campbell, 1980; Fields, 1981; and Tweed, 1992).

The two processes of privatization and pluralism went hand in hand, and whatever the causes, for the purpose at hand the main point is that by the nineteenth century religious allegiances had become largely voluntary, especially in North America, and a competitive market for these allegiances had emerged. In Berger's words (1967: 138), this means that 'the religious tradition, which previously could be authoritatively imposed, now has to be *marketed*. It must be "sold" to a clientele that is no longer constrained to "buy".' Religious institutions have become marketing agencies and the religious traditions consumer commodities.[5]

This pronounced shift in the basic social circumstances of religious organizations has far-reaching consequences, Berger believes, for the both the structure and the ideologies of Western religions. In order to compete in the new religious market-place, religions must rationalize their efforts. To this end, like the other institutions of modernity, religious organizations have become increasingly bureaucratic. An unanticipated consequence of this bureaucratization is that religious groups have become ever more similar in form and functioning. As in other markets, the pressures of competition have led religious organizations to seek to mute the harshness of competition by forming cartels. To gain competitive advantage, small organizations attempt to open channels of communication and strike agreements with other religions in order to apportion and stabilize the market share of each organization. This situation is reflected in the shift to denominationalism in the nineteenth and early twentieth centuries, and Berger sees it continuing in the strong ecumenical movement and merger of many American Christian denominations since the Second World War (see, e.g., Wuthnow, 1988: 71–99).

The products of religion fall prey to similar homogenizing pressures. In economic terms, under such market conditions products are subject to standardization and marginal differentiation. With the consumer in the driver's seat each organization tries to fashion a product that meets the same consumer preferences. A competitive edge is maintained through the development and preservation of marginal differences in style and approach and the minimizing of any real differences in substance. As it is with toothpastes and cars, so it is becoming with religions. Likewise, in matters of substance and style, the product must conform to the dictates of its new institutional location—the private sphere. Religions that place a priority on satisfying the needs characteristic of private life, such as matters of sexuality, marriage, child rearing, and family norms and activities, gain a competitive advantage. Or so it is thought. Moreover, so do the religions that offer a product 'consonant with the secularized consciousness' of inhabitants of advanced industrial states, for example, conformity with the findings of science.

The net result, Berger laments, is that in the pluralistic competition of many look-alike religions the plausibility of all is undermined as the content of each is relativized. The religious beliefs that support a *nomos* 'are "deobjectivated", that is, deprived of their status as taken-for-granted, objective reality' (Berger, 1967: 151). The veracity of religious claims becomes a matter of subjective consciousness and conviction alone. In conclusion, Berger (1967: 153) proposes, two options seem to confront religions in the conditions of the modern world:

> They can either accommodate themselves to the situation, play the pluralistic game of religious free enterprise, and come to terms as best they can with the plausibility problem by modifying their product in accordance with consumer demands. Or they can refuse to accommodate themselves, entrench themselves behind whatever socio-religious structures they can maintain or construct, and continue to profess the old objectivities as much as possible as if nothing had happened.

For most religions, of course, the reality lies somewhere in between these two extremes. And in ways that Berger did not foresee (and perhaps could not have foreseen in the mid-1960s), other new options have arisen. Many NRMs (such as Krishna Counsciousness) refuse to accommodate themselves to the secular order of modernity, but they do not construct and maintain the same old objectivities. Others, like Scientology, fashion new modes of accommodation while reconfiguring the very nature of the religious market-place itself. In any combination, we get a radicalization of the conditions of religious life compared to the conventions of denominational Christianity dominant in North America. Some groups tend to become more totalistic in the commitments demanded, while others become more diffuse in their demands and more consumer-oriented. In other words, we get movement towards the division of types of NRMs mentioned in the Introduction.

Berger was clearly disturbed by these developments, and *The Sacred Canopy* has been read largely as a prognosis of religious demise as a whole, although its author may not have meant to create that impression (see Berger, 1969). In details and tenor, this pessimistic vision of the prospects of religion has exerted a marked influence on social-scientific attempts to account for both the emergence and the social significance of NRMs.

Stark and Bainbridge's Theory of Religion

Stark and Bainbridge (1985, 1987) have formulated a theory of religion, with specific reference to the study of NRMs, that takes this pessimistic reading of the future of religion as its point of departure: 'At least since the Enlightenment,' Stark and Bainbridge note (1985: 1), 'most Western intellectuals have anticipated the death of religion as eagerly as ancient Israel awaited the messiah. . . . But, as one generation has followed another, religion has persisted.' In response, Stark and Bainbridge have sought to fashion a simple, deductively structured theory of religion that explains this persistence while duly acknowledging that secularization is, for the moment, 'a major trend in modern times' (1985: 1). To this end they sound a theme that is increasingly being repeated in the literature: many scholars may be mistaking the secularization of certain traditional forms of religious life for 'the doom of religion in general' (p. 3). To make clear sense of their innovative view of secularization, we must first clarify the basic elements of their theory of religion.

Stark and Bainbridge's theory of religion grows out of the combination of four simple premises. The first is that any meaningful discussion of religious phenomena must ultimately be anchored in a definition of religion that acknowledges the pivotal role of the 'supernatural'. Religions, they argue (1985: 5), 'involve some conception of a supernatural being, world, or force, and the notion that the supernatural is active, that events and conditions here on earth are influenced by the supernatural.' Some scholars are inclined to see many phenomena and processes in this world as religious, even though they lack any explicit reference to the supernatural (for example, the fanatical cult of personality surrounding the Communist Chinese leader Mao Tse-tung in the 1960s, or the life-consuming commitment of certain radical environmentalists). But, in the last analysis, these phenomena and processes are still only deemed to be like 'religions' by virtue of the comparison made with certain past and persisting forms of activity that explicitly do refer to the supernatural, practices that unquestionably are 'religious' in the eyes of almost everyone (see Dawson, 1987).

The second premise of Stark and Bainbridge's theory is the oft-repeated maxim that 'humans seek what they perceive to be rewards and try to avoid what they perceive to be costs' (1985: 5). Stark and Bainbridge claim that it is this simple utilitarian adage that accounts reasonably for most human action, including religious acts.

The third premise is that the rewards people seek are often scarce, in both an absolute and a relative sense, and that throughout human history some of the most desired rewards seem to be things that are not readily available at all, like life after death or an end to suffering.

The fourth and last premise is that in the absence of some real rewards, people often create and exchange what Stark and Bainbridge call 'compensators'. By compensators they have in mind promises of reward at some later time or in some other place. These compensators range from the specific to the highly general. When a parent promises a future trip to the amusement park to a child in exchange for chores done around the house now, a specific compensator is being invoked. The promises of a happy life, knowledge of the meaning of life, or immortality, which are common to the religions of the world, are obviously very general. These most general of compensators can be provided only, Stark and Bainbridge assert, through the assumption of the intervention of some supernatural agency.

Combining these four simple premises, Stark and Bainbridge (1985: 8) then propose that religions should be viewed as 'human organizations primarily engaged in providing general compensators based on supernatural assumptions'. Hence they see little reason to be pessimistic about the future of religion. For history suggests that

> so long as humans intensely seek certain rewards of great magnitude that remain unavailable through direct actions, they will be able to obtain credible compensators only from sources predicated on the supernatural. In this

market, no purely naturalistic ideologies can compete. Systems of thought that reject the supernatural lack all means to credibly promise such rewards as eternal life in any fashion. Similarly naturalistic philosophies can argue that statements such as 'What is the meaning of life?' or 'What is the purpose of the universe?' are meaningless utterances. But they cannot provide answers to these questions in the terms in which they are asked. (1985: 7–8)

Implicitly, like Weber and Berger before them, Stark and Bainbridge are positing that humans inherently need to live in a meaningful world and that neither the wonders of modern science nor the material abundance of advanced industrial societies has displaced this need and the consequent quest for supernatural reassurances. The configuration of the possible reassurances offered, of course, is another matter. Religion, in their opinion, is changing, not dying.[6]

Stark and Bainbridge's Theory of Secularization

Secularization, in the sense Berger proposes, is indeed happening. But Stark and Bainbridge introduce an important qualification to their acceptance of this fact. Continuing the economic imagery introduced by Berger, they propose (1985: 429–30) that secularization is a constant element of all 'religious economies', and not a unique attribute of the contemporary world. The process of secularization is part of the primary dynamic of religious economies, a self-limiting process that engenders religious renewal, and not the sheer demise of religion. Properly understood, secularization refers to the periodic collapse of specific and dominant religious organizations as a consequence of becoming more worldly, more accommodating to the non-religious aspects of their cultural contexts. Contrary to Berger (and most other sociologists), in this more limited sense secularization should not be confused with the loss of the need for general supernatural compensators. The reverse is true. It is the failure to provide sufficiently vivid and consistently supernatural compensators that accounts for the decline of established religions.

In the modern era, the spread of an increasingly scientific and rationalistic world-view has pushed magic (one of the more specific forms of supernatural compensators) out of religion and forced the dominant traditional religions into a full-scale retreat from their essential principles. But the existential questions persist, and hence so does the demand for the kind of totalistic and ultimately unconfirmable responses provided by religions in the past. Commenting on this state of affairs, Stark and Bainbridge (1985: 434) note:

The conception of the supernatural [sustained by the dominant contemporary traditions] . . . has receded to a remote, inactive, almost nonexistent divinity. We see bishops and theologians denouncing as mere superstition the notion of a god 'up there'. Does a god who is not 'up there' plausibly preside over heaven and offer triumph over death? Many of the most prestigious denominations offer mixed signals at best in answer to this question. Such religions have reached the point where they can no longer offer the quality of general compensators that has been the historic *raison d'être* of religions. They offer little solace to the bereaved, to the dying, to the poor, or to those who seek to understand the enigmas of existence.

When religions ossify in this way, when their rituals and beliefs become dead and hollow formalities disconnected from any moving personal experiences, there are two possible socio-religious responses: revival and innovation. Stark and Bainbridge associate the revival option with the formation of what sociologists call sects. They associate the innovation option with the formation of cults. In broad form, sects tend to be splinter groups from mainstream traditions that are seeking to revive what they think to be the original or pure spirit of the religious tradition they are rebelling against. Cults signify the introduction of a more unconventional mode of religious expression, one that tends to depart altogether from the dominant traditions of the churches that are being secularized. This distinction is discussed more fully below; here we are simply interested in sketching the crucial links that Stark and Bainbridge forge between a more limited conception of secularization and the processes by which new religions are created.

Writing almost twenty years after Berger, Stark and Bainbridge have witnessed the unprecedented decline in the 1960s and early 1970s of the size and social influence of the liberal Protestant denominations that dominated North America for centuries—such as Anglicans and Episcopalians, Presbyterians, Methodists, Congregationalists, and Lutherans. They have also seen that this decline coincided with the rise, on what might be called the religious right, of more conservative and experiential forms of Christianity (such as Pentecostalism, Charismatic Renewal, and evangelicalism in general; see Roof and McKinney, 1988; Wuthnow, 1988) and the rise, on the religious left, of NRMs (such as Scientology and Krishna Consciousness). Many of the resultant sects and cults were and will continue to be short-lived and inconsequential. But as Stark and Bainbridge are fond of repeating, Christianity, Islam, and Buddhism all began as cults.

To test at least partially whether these developments are linked, Stark and Bainbridge (1985: 444–8) tallied the locations of sect and cult headquarters in the fifty US states (in the absence of accurate state-by-state membership figures) and showed strong negative correlations between the locations of churches and cults on the one hand, and between sects and cults on the other. It seems that where cults abound, conventional churches are weakest; and where either sects or cults abound, the other tends to be absent. The latter observation suggests that cults and sects are not just interchangeable responses to secularization. They would seem to have different constituencies, and hence their presence may mean different things. Sects, it should be noted, are not actually correlated strongly with church decline; in fact, they seem to thrive in the same environments where churches persist. This leads Stark and Bainbridge (1985: 445) to speculate that 'sect formation is, in part, a response to early stages of weakness in the general compensators provided by the conventional churches. Cult formation tends to erupt in later stages of church weakness, when large sectors of the population have drifted away from all organizational ties to the prevailing faiths.' Cult formation reflects then, they think, 'the efforts of the unchurched to become churched' (1985: 444). Most interestingly, Bader and DeMaris (1996) recently provided significant empirical corroboration of these findings. Using a sample of 12,415 subjects from the National Survey of Families and Households in the United States, they confirmed that the strength of conventional religious organizations in the subject's area is strongly correlated with the likelihood of cult and sect membership. Where conventional religions are weak, cults, but not necessarily sects, are strong.

Predictably perhaps, the highest rates of cult activity seem to be on the west coast of the United States, particularly in California, and in the sunbelt (New Mexico, Nevada, and Arizona). Those are places to which large numbers of people have migrated in this century, severing their past religious affiliations. On the other hand, as one might expect, the Deep South and parts of the Midwest remain strongholds of sectarianism and conventional church membership (Stark and Bainbridge, 1985: Chaps 6 and 9).

Commenting on the value of their theory, Stark and Bainbridge conclude (1985: 455):

> We do not posit a steady-state religious economy in which cults immediately make up deficits in conventional religious affiliation. We argue only that, to the degree a population is unchurched, there will be *efforts* to fill the void. Most such efforts will be abortive. . . . Only once in a while will an effective, rapidly growing cult movement appear. We cannot predict accurately *when* that will happen. But we think we can say *where* this is apt to happen and *why*.

One does not have to accept all aspects of their theories of religion and secularization to see the utility of their views in trying to understand NRMs. The same can be said of Berger's theories. In conjunction, the theories of Berger and of Stark and Bainbridge set the broad context for understanding NRMs in three ways.

In the first place, they guide our understanding of the most fundamental nature of NRMs. Whether or not secularization will ultimately prove to be a permanent condition leading to the near-disappearance of all forms of religion, the evidence discussed in this chapter, in Chapter 2 (on theories of why NRMs emerged), and in Chapter 3 (on who joins NRMs and why) supports the view that the rise of NRMs is symptomatic of some sociocultural resistance to recent secularizing trends. Berger's discussion of secularization helps us to see the religious context of the sixties in which NRMs proliferated. His analysis of the human conditions that require the creation and extension of a sacred canopy clarifies and reinforces Stark and Bainbridge's presumption of a continued need for supernatural compensators.

Second, Berger's theory also alerts us to the reason why many NRMs display totalizing tendencies, namely the desire to influence, even control, all aspects of the lives of their followers. The attainment of a condition of religious monopoly may no longer be possible, but it may remain the normative expectation of many of even the most marginal religious group. After all, that expectation is historically rooted in the dominant social function of religion itself. In general, the interpretive frameworks provided by Berger and by Stark and Bainbridge begin to unravel the mystery of why some people turn to NRMs, without presupposing some abnormality or deviant motivation. These theories get us thinking about the context of exchange in which NRMs exist. In every religion, after all, there is an exchange of commitments between individuals and groups, an exchange of sacrifices and benefits, which in most cases can be reasonably delineated and assessed.

Third, it seems that an awareness of these theories sets our options for discerning the social and cultural significance of NRMs and their future. As mentioned above, if Berger is right, NRMs may only be emblematic of the last gasp of religion in the advanced industrial world. Or—and this may amount to the same thing—they may only represent the final triumph of a modern commercial and consumer ethic in the affairs of humanity. From this vantage point, religion has been reduced to just another product to be matched with the private needs and desires of individual consumers. As such, its relative importance has been greatly diminished and the prospects for the survival and growth of most NRMs are not bright (see Wilson, 1976, 1988). Alternatively, if, as Stark and Bainbridge suppose, the rise of NRMs is a sign more of a changing of the guard than of the end of religion, the prospects of at least some NRMs may be brighter than our generation can foresee. And finally, in Chapter 6 we will see that the situation may well be even more complex. For there is a third possibility: many NRMs may be engaged in the process of adapting religion to the conditions of the modern world but in ways that ensure rather than diminish their continuing cultural significance.

Churches, Sects, and Cults

To organize information about the diverse religious practices of the world in a way that would permit comparisons across time and cultures, sociologists have tried to categorize different types of religious activity according to the dominant form of social organization within which the activities occur. This process of categorization, which is known as church-sect typology, provides us with the insights we need to understand what kind of religious organization or form of religious life cults belong to.

The first distinction between churches and sects was drawn by Max Weber in 1904 (Weber, 1958a). But it is best known in the form elaborated by his colleague Ernst Troeltsch in 1911 (Troeltsch, 1931). Over the years this Troeltschian dichotomy of churches and sects has been broadly accepted and developed in myriad ways, creating a confusing array of types and subtypes of religious organizations. It is out of this process, though, that the concept of 'cults' emerged, and in recent years, with the proliferation of NRMs, many scholars have tried to frame a sub-typology of different types of cults (e.g., Campbell, 1978; Bird, 1979; Robbins and Anthony, 1979a, 1987; Wallis, 1984; Lofland and Richardson, 1984; Beckford, 1985; Anthony and Ecker, 1987; Robbins, 1988). For the purposes at hand, we do not need to survey all the permutations of church-sect-cult typologizing; neither do we need to debate the merits of specific typologies nor of church-sect-cult typologizing as a whole. There is no working consensus in sociology about any of these matters.[7] Nevertheless, some understanding of the procedure and its options is useful in a study of NRMs.

In the first place, a grasp of the basic elements of church-sect-cult typologizing equips us with a language for simply talking about different types of religious activity in a coherent and readily identifiable manner. As the standard of reference in the sociology of religion, a knowledge of church-sect-cult typologizing is fundamental to the specification of a working definition of cult or NRM (that is, as opposed to other forms of religious organization). Second, a brief survey of some of the main developments in church-sect-cult typologizing serves a heuristic purpose. By highlighting the diverse classifactory possibilities, such a survey emphasizes the multitude of modes of religious expression encompassed by the notion of NRMs. It also accentuates the many different ways in which essentially the same phenomena can be conceptualized from different perspectives. When one is dealing with so diverse a phenomenon as NRMs, there is little that is obvious or given. Third, in the process of deriving various typological options, students of NRMs have acquired some fundamental insights, both empirical and theoretical, into the nature and development of different religious organizations. These insights have helped to shape the discourse about NRMs in the social sciences. Thus, since some kind of conceptual scheme must inevitably be used to sift and sort the welter of data available about NRMs, it is best to use these insights to advantage from the start. Through the selective discussion and integration of some of these insights, a minimal analytical framework will be fashioned for this book. But a commitment to any one of the existing typologies, with its assumptions about NRMs, will be minimized.

As framed by Troeltsch, with the Christian tradition in mind, the church-sect dichotomy is commonly described as follows. Churches are organizations into which people are born and baptized as infants. Membership is involuntary. Sects are voluntary organizations to which people usually convert, frequently as the result of very emotional experiences. All kinds of people usually can and do belong to churches, churches are inclusive, and their membership is heterogeneous. Sects tend to be much more homogeneous in their membership, drawing disproportionately from the underprivileged. This situation often reflects the fact that sects are created by schisms within a church that is aligned with the dominant social structure. The beliefs and practices of sects, then, tend to be more radical and ethically stricter than those of churches, and they constitute an act of protest against the values of the rest of society. Sects tend to be exclusive; that is, individuals must meet and maintain certain clear requirements to belong. Sectarians consider themselves to be an elect, and those who contravene the group's precepts are subject to expulsion much more readily than in the case of churches. The leaders of churches are usually hired or appointed on the basis of special educational qualifications. They operate within a hierarchical and impersonal administrative structure. Sectarian leaders tend to be charismatic, and sects tend to have smaller, more democratic, and personal organizational structures. In theology and liturgy, churches are inclined to be dogmatic and ritualistic. Sects are more inspirational, volatile, and even anti-ritualistic.

In the years since Troeltsch formulated his contrast between churches and sects, two other typologies of religious organizations have won favour amongst practising sociologists: those of J. Milton Yinger (1970) and Bryan

R. Wilson (1970). Using two parameters, Yinger formulated a sixfold typology of religious organizations as a whole. Focusing on one criterion, Wilson has proffered a sevenfold subtypology of sects themselves. These perspectives have influenced almost all later attempts to devise typologies of religious groups. In this brief summary of the views of Yinger and Wilson, it must be remembered that each typology is based on theoretical arguments and empirical evidence that cannot be described adequately here.

In order of decreasing inclusiveness (and hence increasing exclusiveness) and decreasing attention to the social integration of members (over against the satisfaction of personal needs), Yinger distinguishes between the following types of religious organizations: the 'universal church' (e.g., the Roman Catholic Church); the 'ecclesia', that is, the established national church (e.g., the Church of England or the Suni faith of Saudi Arabia); the 'denomination' (e.g., Baptists or Presbyterians); the 'established sect' (e.g., Jehovah's Witnesses or Christian Science); the 'sect' (e.g., Pentecostalists or the Worldwide Church of God); and the 'cult' (e.g., the Unification Church or Scientology).

The last of these distinctions, of course, adds the sole truly new category to church-sect typology and the focus of our attention.[8] As mentioned above, cults are on a continuum with sects, and compared to churches, they share much in common with sectarian forms of religion. But cults are more concerned with the satisfaction of individual needs and desires. They usually lay claim to some esoteric knowledge that has been lost, repressed, or newly discovered, and they offer their believers some more direct kind of ecstatic or transfiguring experience than traditional modes of religious life. In comparison to the established faiths, cults tend to 'offer a surer, shorter, swifter, or clearer way to salvation.' They offer a more 'proximate salvation' and, in principle, one more readily attained by more people. 'In new religions,' Wilson explains, 'there is prospect of spiritual abundance' (Wilson, 1982b: 17, 20). Cults, however, often display no systematic orientation to the broader society and usually they are loosely organized. They are almost always centred on a charismatic leader and are subject to disintegration when the leader dies or is discredited (see Miller, 1991). Not surprisingly, then, the vast majority of cults are short-lived and small.

In those respects most of the cults studied in any depth during the recent controversy about NRMs are actually atypical. Scientology, Krishna Consciousness, and the Unification Church, for example, are relatively long-lived and relatively large. Accordingly, many of their features are rather sect-like. They are more highly organized and are more ideologically and practically sophisticated in their relations with the larger world. And except in the case of the Unification Church, they have managed to survive the death of their charismatic leader. Originally, though, each of these groups displayed markedly the traits of a cult. Moreover, they continue to display many cult-like attitudes and practices, such as the emphasis on esoteric teachings and the satisfaction of individual needs. Perhaps, then, yet another category should be added to church-sect typology, that of 'established cult'.

Let us return to our general consideration of church-sect typologies. As noted, Wilson differentiates between types of sects; following Max Weber, he thinks we should make sense of religions in light of their manifest function: they offer paths to salvation. Accordingly, he distinguishes sects in terms of the supposedly deviant responses to the world generated by their answers to the question: 'What shall we do to be saved?' (Wilson, 1970: 36–40). Sects that view the world and its institutions as evil and believe that salvation can be had only as a result of a profound change in oneself, he calls 'conversionist' (e.g., Salvation Army and Pentecostalists). Sects which 'declare that the world is evil, and that the only prospect of salvation is the overturning of the world by supernatural action' he calls 'revolutionist' (e.g., Jehovah's Witnesses and Christadelphians). Those groups which recognize that the world is evil and seek salvation by withdrawing from it he calls 'introversionist' (e.g., Hutterites and Exclusive Brethren). Groups that seek salvation in the world, but by special means not generally known or accepted in the world, he calls 'manipulationist' (e.g., Christian Science). Groups geared to the relief of present individual physical and mental ills 'by special, almost magical dispensation . . . from the normal laws of causality' he calls 'thaumaturgical' (e.g., spiritualism). Sects which believe that some evil of the world might be overcome through reform, in line with the dictates of a divinely inspired conscience, he terms 'reformist' (e.g., Quakers). And finally, groups that wish to reconstruct society 'by returning to the basic principles by which the creator intended [us] to live,' he calls 'utopian' (e.g., the Oneida and Bruderhof communities). As Wilson demonstrates, in accordance with the logic of their response to the problem of salvation, each of these groups uses different elements of the Christian tradition and adopts a distinctive mode of social organization.

For our purposes, the merits of Wilson's specific typology are not important; nor is an understanding of his distinctions or knowledge of the groups he discusses. Rather, our immediate goal is more limited. As the brief description of Wilson's typology graphically illustrates, if sects are subject to such subdivision, so are cults. In fact, cults have been classified in a great number of ways. Bruce Campbell (1978), for example, suggests that cults are marked primarily by their orientation to the 'divine within'. Thus, he argues, they can be differentiated according to their response to the tension between the sacred ideal of individual potential and the profane world in which the empirical personality is rooted. With this in mind, he divides cults into two main groups, with a rather amorphous third possibility. The two main categories are the 'illumination' cult, 'which emphasizes detachment from the personality and the search for direct inner personal experience of the divine' (for example, Theosophy and Spiritualism), and the 'instrumental' cult, in which 'inner experience is sought for its effects, its ability to transform the everyday personality so that it can better meet the demands made upon it' (for example, Scientology and Soka Gakkai). The third possibility is groups like either of the first two, but with a less individualistic orientation. These he calls 'service-oriented' cults. No illustration of the latter, however, is provided.

Thomas Robbins and Dick Anthony (e.g., 1979a, 1987) endeavour to differentiate cults according to the metaphysics inherent in their teachings and the ramifications of the metaphysical positions adopted in responding to the 'moral indeterminacy' of modern mass societies. Groups are divided into 'dualistic' movements, which promote an absolute dichotomy of good and evil forces in the world, and 'monistic' movements, which teach the ultimate unity of all things and a mode of moral relativism. This distinction is then cross-correlated with a distinction between 'unilevel' and 'multilevel' religion. Unilevel groups tend to be literal in their approach to language and texts. Multilevel groups display a higher appreciation of the symbolic and metaphorical aspects of language and regard spiritual teachings as encompassing various levels of meaning. When this is combined with a further distinction between subtypes of monism, 'technical' movements that offer procedures for manipulating consciousness and 'charismatic' movements that stress the emulation of a spiritual leader, an elaborate array of classificatory possibilities unfolds.

Much more simply, Roy Wallis proposes a tripartite typology of cults using a modified form of Max Weber's (1963) well-known differentiation between types of religious systems: he distinguishes between cults according to their attitude to the social world in which they emerge. 'A new movement may embrace the world, *affirming* its normatively approved goals and values; it may *reject* that world, denigrating those things held dear within it; or it may remain as far as possible indifferent to the world in terms of its religious practice, *accommodating* to it otherwise, and exhibiting only mild acquiescence to, or disapprobation of, the ways of the world' (Wallis, 1984: 4; emphasis added). Again, each orientation gives rise to a distinctive social structure for the groups.

Many other typologies of cults could be reviewed (such as Bird, 1979; Beckford, 1985; Gussner and Berkowitz, 1988), but the examples described above serve to indicate the riches born of the typological art in the sociology of religion. Of course, they also highlight the confusion that may result from seeking analytical guidance for the study of cults from a random selection of these typologies. For most purposes, and certainly for this introduction to the subject, typologies like Robbins and Anthony's (see Stark and Bainbridge, 1979, and Beckford, 1985: 69–93 as well) are too complex, whereas typologies like those of Wallis (and Gussner and Berkowitz, 1988) are too beguilingly simple, at least at face value. Before saying more, however, and before I can specify the analytical framework used in this book, two additional basic features of all church-sect-cult typologies must be taken into consideration: (1) the developmental and (2) the relative character of these typological distinctions.

Almost all church-sect-cult typologies are conditioned by the developmental observations of H. Richard Niebuhr. In *The Social Sources of Denominationalism*, Niebuhr (1929) argued that with time sects tend to become more like churches. As new generations are born and socialized into the sects and their ways become set, the original impetus to reject the norms and activities of the dominant society wanes. Likewise, if a cult is fortunate enough to survive and grow it will tend to take on the features and the increased stability of a sect. As sects become churches, and sometimes as cults become more sect-like as well, a new sect or cult may be spawned out of discontent or loss of interest. We are faced, Stark and Bainbridge (1979: 123) observe, with 'an endless cycle of birth, transformation, schism, and rebirth of religious movements'. Certainly much of the growth of new religions in North America stems from this tendency for established groups to splinter. The legacy of Theosophy in particular is germane, since it has been the source of so many other contemporary new religions in America.

Building on Stark and Bainbridge's theoretical perspective, Finke and Stark (1992) argue forcefully in *The Churching of America, 1776–1990* that this pattern actually accounts for much of the more conventional religious history of the United States as well. In the nineteenth century long-established religions, such as Congregationalists and Presbyterians, lost their dominance to younger, more sectarian creeds, such as Methodism, which in turn became too church-like, that is, too worldly, and have been surpassed in this century by other even more sectarian developments, like Southern Baptists.

Church-sect-cult distinctions are also relative in nature, a point often forgotten. In most of North America, the Mormons (the Church of Jesus Christ of Latter-day Saints) operate as a sect. At the same time, however, they should probably be considered a church or ecclesia in the state of Utah, where most of the population is Mormon, and a denomination in southern Alberta, where about a third of the population is Mormon. In other words, the classification of any group depends on the time and place in question. By way of further illustration, let us consider the Roman Catholic Church. In medieval France it was an ecclesia, but in eighteenth-century America, which was dominated by Protestant denominations, it was almost a sect or cult. By the late twentieth century, in both France and the United States, it is probably best deemed a denomination. In Quebec the Roman Catholic Church was essentially an ecclesia until the 1960s but is now a denomination.

So, keeping the developmental and relative character of all church-sect-cult typologizing in mind, what typology should we use to make sense of the diversity of cults in our midst? For theoretical and methodological reasons that need not be fully elaborated here (see Dawson, 1997), I favour a typology based on a one-dimensional formulation of types. In other words, the most useful typology is one in which different cults, and cults, sects, and churches can be arranged along a continuum based on changes in one variable. As the criterion that varies, I favour Weber's original choice for distinguishing churches and sects: the mode of membership of different groups and the consequent form of their social organization.

Amongst other things, a one-dimensional approach has the theoretical advantage of simplicity. Multidimensional types tend to produce a confusing array of mixed types resulting in an infinite regress of type formulation. This state of affairs impairs real comparative analysis, and hence explanation. The one-dimensional approach better accommodates the developmental aspect of all church-sect-cult typologizing as well. As Stark and Bainbridge (1985: 23) stress in their discussion of these matters, to theorize effectively about the movement from sect to church, or cult to church, we need a common measure. Clusters of different attributes associated with each type of religious organization will only breed confusion. The single Weberian criterion of mode of membership and consequent form of social organization is the most empirically accessible and reliable variable for making comparisons between all these different kinds of groups, and between different manifestations of each kind (for example, between different cults) as well.

In line with Weber's stress on the mode of membership and consequent organization, Stark and Bainbridge differentiate between 'audience cults', 'client cults', and 'cult movements'. This simple descriptive typology has gained popularity amongst scholars of NRMs. It is a typology that keeps the developmental and relative nature of the analytical distinctions being made to the fore. Each of these types of cults may exist in perpetuity, but as cults gain in size and social stature they will tend to change from audience cults to client cults and eventually to cult movements. And in different places, such as different regions of a country, the same NRM may exist simultaneously in two or more of these forms. It may be a movement in California, but only a client cult in Connecticut or France. Moreover, with changes in time and location, groups may fluctuate from being client cults to cult movements and then back again to being essentially client cults, and so on. But what do these distinctions entail?

'Audience cults' are the least organized, yet perhaps most pervasive expression of cult activity in North America. The label refers to the loosely structured events at which individuals lecture and distribute literature about a variety of esoteric, mystical, eccentric, and occult topics. At various conferences and meetings certain sets of ideas and certain lecturers may attract a consistent following. But no formal and persistent organization results. The audience for the ideas in question remain mere consumers of cultic goods. This level of cult activity is characteristic of much of the interest displayed in UFO-related material and much so-called neo-pagan and New Age spirituality. In some respects, however, it also holds true for the early years of even such established sects as the Jehovah's Witnesses (see Penton, 1985: 13–33), an organization that began as a loose network of Bible study groups reading the same new literature about biblical prophecies. Similarly, the Church of Scientology began as a series of spontaneously arising study groups applying the method of psychological therapy developed by L. Ron Hubbard in his best-selling book *Dianetics: The Modern Science of Mental Health* (1975; originally published in 1950).

At a more organized level, these situations may develop into 'client cults', or such arrangements may arise independently. Here, 'the relationship between those promulgating cult doctrines and those partaking of it most closely resembles the relationship between therapist and patient or between consultant and client', Stark and Bainbridge suggest (1985: 26). The services of the cult leader or leaders may become quite highly organized, but little effort is made to 'weld the clients into a social movement. Indeed, client involvement is so partial that clients often retain an active commitment to another religious movement or institution.' In many respects, Theosophy began this way, while Scientology and numerous other popular recent groups like est (Erhard Seminar Training) seem to have purposefully sought in many respects to remain at this organizational level. 'In the past, the primary services sold were medical miracles, forecasts of the future, or contact with the dead' (Stark and Bainbridge, 1985: 28). To this list can be added meditation, induced memories of past lives, astral projections to other times and places, and general experiences and knowledge of an expanded universe or levels of reality.

Finally, with success, an audience cult may become a 'cult movement'. Using the spiritualist movement of the late nineteenth and early twentieth centuries as an illustration, Stark and Bainbridge (1985: 29) argue as follows:

> When the spiritualist medium is able to get his or her clients to attend regularly on Sunday morning, and thus, in a Christian context, to sever ties with other religious organizations, we observe the birth of a *cult movement*. Cult movements are full-fledged religious organizations that attempt to satisfy all the religious needs of converts. . . . Attempts to cause social change, by converting others, become central to the group agenda.

Examples of cult movements are Theosophy in its maturity, Krishna Consciousness, and the Unification Church.

Those cult movements are the subject of this book because they are the groups that have achieved some measure of success and hence recognition and significance as religions in North America. Accordingly, they have been the primary focus of sociological research. But the history of each of these groups reveals, of course, aspects of the path of development suggested by Stark and Bainbridge's typology. Each does so, however, in different configurations and to different degrees. In fact, the cult movements in question have displayed the kind of developmental fluctuation mentioned as a possibility above. Each movement grew from humble beginnings, somewhat like client cults, and some, such as Theosophy, have had a reversal of fortunes that has moved them back again into something like the client cult status, at least in parts of the world. Stark and Bainbridge's set of distinctions is most helpful for keeping in mind the developmental aspect of cultic religious phenomena. Two anomalous features of cult movements, though, point to the need to extend and modify Stark and Bainbridge's typology in ways they have not foreseen.

In the first place, as Stark and Bainbridge recognized, there is much variation in degree of commitment and organization, even within the single category of cult movements. These groups entail everything from situations demanding mere assent to the beliefs of a group, regular attendance, and some financial support, to situations of total involvement, where every aspect of an individual's life is given over to the group's maintenance and advancement. It is this kind of variation in form that actually led other sociologists to develop their various typologies of cults. Clearly, then, within the category of cult movements itself, there is a range of groups that replicates, to some degree, the larger contrast of churches and sects, at least with regard to the Weberian criterion of mode of membership and consequent forms of social organization. Stark and Bainbridge, however, have not followed through on this observation.[9] I believe it would be useful, then, to subdivide 'cult movements' along the Weberian lines Stark and Bainbridge themselves indicate for cults as a whole, that is, with regard to mode of membership and consequent forms of organization. This suggestion is supported by the second anomalous feature of the kinds of NRMs that Stark and Bainbridge call cult movements.

As some keen observers of contemporary religion (e.g., Westley, 1978, 1983; C. Campbell, 1978; Bibby, 1987; Bromley and Shupe, 1993; Greil, 1993; Roof and Walsh, 1993: 166–8; Wilson, 1993) have suggested, NRMs that have either stayed in forms reminiscent of audience or client cults or have returned to these forms may be experiencing neither a failure to develop properly nor a regression to some more primitive form. On the contrary, religion in the guise of audience or client cults may actually be a sign of things to come. The appearance of these groups may presage a more pervasive religio-cultural transformation, and they may be the religious success stories of tomorrow. Whether this is indeed the case hinges, of course, on whether one favours Berger's or Stark and Bainbridge's reading of the overall condition of religion in contemporary society. Is the 'commercialization' of religion evidence of its near-demise or just of its transformation? Whatever conclusion one draws, repeated observations of this kind suggest that cult movements themselves tend to cluster around two poles of a continuum with regard to essentially membership and organizational variables, as expressed most clearly in the variant norms of commitment in these groups. Some cult movements tend to resemble audience or client cults in that they are non-communal and more tolerant of multiple commitments. As cults, that is, they display many of the features, with regard to mode of membership and organization, associated with churches. Scientology is a good example. Other cult movements are more communal, and exclusive in their commitment demands. In other words, they are more sect-like; a good example is Krishna Consciousness.

Recognition of this internal subdivision of cult movements itself can be brought into even greater explicit conformity with Stark and Bainbridge's theory of cults, and implicitly with Weber's theory of churches and sects, by incorporating insights into the developmental logic of cult movements provided by Wallis (1984). He proposes that new religious movements will display a tendency to move towards a more exclusive organizational type to the extent that their message and practices are thought to be (1) salient for a broad range of the concerns of individuals or aspects of their lives, and (2) to be unavailable elsewhere. 'That is, a movement is more likely to be exclusive if it is of wide *salvational scope*, or lays claim to a *broad salvational effi-*

cacy, showing the path of truth, salvation or the good life, over a wide range of human preoccupations; and if it lays claim to *unique legitimacy* as the path to these ends' (Wallis, 1984: 125–6). The intent to be comprehensive and the belief in uniqueness lead to greater exclusivity in commitment demands, a pattern that characterizes the general developmental movement from audience cults through to cult movements, and then is replicated again, like a set of identical wooden Ukrainian dolls nested one inside the other, as a gradient amongst cult movements themselves.

In fact, as Wallis (1984: 123–5) persuasively argues, a developmental pattern of variation, ranging from an inclusive to a more exclusive membership commitment, and guided by these two criteria, is typical of all individual involvement in any type of new religious movement, whether audience cult, client cult, or cult movement. The more convinced the participants are of the comprehensiveness and uniqueness of the religious message, the greater their involvement with the group. Of course, the conviction itself grows, in most instances, out of greater involvement, in a kind of feedback loop. Consequently, in most groups, no matter what their outward profile, there is an internal division between a core of devotees engaged in a highly exclusive organizational commitment and a larger group of less exclusively engaged followers or clients. Amongst cult movements, for example, Scientology certainly appears to be one of the most inclusive in its organizational commitments, allowing its members to freely retain and practice other faiths. But at the heart of Scientology is the 'Sea Org' (Sea Organization), an élite body that originally accompanied the reclusive L. Ron Hubbard aboard a fleet of ships. Members of the paramilitary Sea Org sign billion-year contracts of absolute loyalty and service to the highest leadership of the Church of Scientology. Thus all groups will internally replicate the broad differences between more inclusive and more exclusive membership and organizational orientations in a differentiation between an inner cadre and the rest of the membership. But this structural constant will itself vary in form, intensity, and developmental significance from group to group, according to the influence of many other factors that are both internal and external to the group. For example, if a group is prosecuted, the whole group may implode into the cadre and its more exclusive style; this may have either beneficial or disastrous results for the survival and growth of the new religion. See, for example, Bainbridge's (1978) account of the Process, Carter's (1990) study of Rajneeshpuram, and Palmer's (1996) analysis of the Solar Temple. It is conceivable that the same thing may happen because of the unanticipated and sudden success of a group. Lucas's (1995) account of The Holy Order of MANS comes close to this pattern. These dynamics are very complicated and difficult to predict.

Chapter Two

Why Did New Religious Movements Emerge?

Asking the Right Question First

For most people, the first and most important question asked about NRMs is why someone would join one of these cults. Not surprisingly, this is probably also the pivotal question underlying most studies of NRMs by social scientists. These professional students of NRMs are more likely, though, to approach the question indirectly by means of cautious studies about more empirically accessible questions like who joins these groups, how they come to join them, and what the organizational structures, procedures, and ideologies of these groups are. In pursuit of these basic questions, the sociology of NRMs has concentrated on the micro-level analysis of the activities of a myriad of cults. Consequently, we now know quite a bit about who joins, how they join, and what they are joining (see Chapter 3). The 'why' question remains more enigmatic.

An answer to any of these questions, however, hinges on, and in turn contributes to, a more macro-level question: 'Why have so many NRMs recently emerged in North America in the first place?' Obviously, the seemingly sudden upsurge of new religious groups since the 1960s is indicative of social and cultural changes in North American society. To understand why anyone chooses to join a cult, we need to know something about the conditions giving rise to the very possibility of making such a choice. We need to understand, then, the changes in society that have facilitated the growth of cults and that are expressed by the growth of the cults. As Marx (1972: 38) said of religion in general, 'religious distress is at the same time the expression of real distress and the protest against real distress.' Have NRMs arisen in response to some experience of distress? If so, what kind?

As might be expected, there are no straightforward answers. Specula-tion abounds, and we are faced with fragmentary and conflicting concep-tions of the origins of NRMs. It is possible, nevertheless, to discern some dominant themes in the investigative efforts made to date. These themes can set the stage for a more satisfactory understanding of why people may choose to join NRMs. It is probably not possible to arrive at completely sat-isfying explanations for conversion to an NRM, even from the perspective of the individual who has converted. An element of mystery seems to remain intact in these matters, impervious to our probing, no matter how intense or cunning. Of course, this is part of the inherent fascination of religious phenomena. All the same, in this chapter and the next, I will try to describe some of the fundamental aspects of the 'structural availability' of individu-als for joining NRMs, all of which influence the 'biographical availability' of specific individuals for such conversions.[1]

At the risk of oversimplifying, I will argue that the ample literature on the conditions that make part of the population structurally available to new religious activity fall into two broad categories: that which deals with the 'macro-environment' and that which deals with the 'micro-environ-ment'. In this chapter I will discuss the macro-environment under two headings: NRMs as a response to cultural change, and NRMs as an expression of cultural continuity. These two points of view encompass the interpretive tendencies in the literature on the social conditions giving rise to cult activity.

New Religious Movements as a Response to Cultural Change

The views grouped under this heading all 'tend to pinpoint some acute and distinctively modern dislocation which is said to be producing some mode of alienation, anomie or deprivation to which [North] Americans are responding by searching for new structures of meaning and community' (Robbins, 1980: 60). There are many and various opinions on the kind of dislocation afflicting North Americans, but they tend to converge on a few common themes. For convenience I have reduced these themes even fur-ther to three interrelated sets of cultural and social changes that have been affecting the daily lives of North Americans since at least the 1960s: (1) changes in values, (2) changes in social structure, and (3) changes in the role and character of religious institutions.

Approached in this order, our discussion will take on an ever larger social and historical frame of reference, moving us, in the first instance, from the personal and ideological effects of the counter-culture of the 1960s to the processes of social change associated with 'modernization' that most sociologists think have been at work throughout the twentieth century (if not longer). When we turn to a consideration of the views grouped under our second heading, 'NRMs as an expression of cultural continuity', the social and historical frame of reference will become even larger, carrying us back into the history of Western civilization.

A pattern of argument and findings also emerges from consideration of the themes grouped under the heading 'NRMs as a response to cultural change'. Different kinds of 'dislocations' in modern North American culture are identified and given different emphases. But in each instance the rise of NRMs is seen, to some degree, as an attempt to compensate individuals for the consequences of the dislocation in question. In most cases it is further argued that the nature of the response provided by NRMs is more complicated than first appears. These groups do not simply offer individuals a direct compensation or alternative to the troubles of modern North American culture, as Stark and Bainbridge's theory of religion suggests. Rather, NRMs effect, in somewhat different ways, ingenious compromises between the status quo and some alternative state of affairs. If we can discern the nature of the compromises struck by the groups, consciously and otherwise, we will have an important interpretive key for gaining insight into at least three related issues: (1) why some groups have succeeded better than others, (2) how certain internal weaknesses may account for the failure of so many groups, and (3) why NRMs seem to be subject to the polarization, noted in the Introduction, into groups that are more traditional, communal, and exclusive in their commitments, and ones that are oriented more to the modern world, geared to the satisfaction of individual needs, and less exclusive in their commitments. All of these insights are pertinent to gauging the future of NRMs and religious life in general in North America.[2]

Changes in Values

Beginning in the mid-1970s, a number of observers of NRMs formulated different yet convergent explanations for the sudden increase in new religious groups in North America. It was suggested that these groups were responding to a pervasive crisis in moral certainty amongst North Americans (e.g., Robbins and Anthony, 1972; Anthony and Robbins, 1975; Robbins, Anthony, and Curtis, 1975; Bird, 1979; Tipton, 1982a, 1982b; Anthony and Robbins, 1982a; Robbins and Anthony, 1982a; and to some extent Foss and Larkin, 1978; Wilson, 1982b; Levine, 1984; Wallis, 1984; Kent, 1987, 1988; Wuthnow, 1988; Palmer, 1994; Roof, 1993). First broached in Robbins and Anthony's (1972; Anthony and Robbins, 1975) excellent early studies of the American followers of Meher Baba (an Indian Sufi mystic), most variants of this explanation have actually taken their lead from the seminal analysis by their colleague, the eminent sociologist of religion Robert Bellah (1976).

NRMS, Bellah proposed, are best conceived as 'successor movements' to the movements of political protest and cultural experimentation that flourished briefly but powerfully amongst the youth of the sixties. To understand NRMS, today's generation must grasp the fervour, the enthusiastic spirit of reform, and the sweeping social disruption that marked the 1960s. This was the decade of the counter-culture, in which the established order of life and power in society was fundamentally challenged in two ways: by relatively organized movements struggling for political change, and by more amorphous movements of lifestyle experimentation. Both developments, which tended to go hand in hand, deeply eroded the legitimacy of established institutions of business, government, education, religion, and the family. Both developments grew out of a unique combination of three interrelated aspects of life in North America in the time following the Second World War: (1) an unprecedented growth and spread of affluence, (2) an unprecedented rise in birth rates, and (3) a resultant expansion and increase in educational attainment.

In the United States the generation of the sixties experienced the civil rights movement, the student power movement, the feminist movement, the war against poverty, the ecological movement, and most important, the often violent protest against the war in Vietnam, and the military draft. They participated, if only vicariously in many cases, in a decade of civil disobedience, riots, and student strikes (see, e.g., Gitlin, 1987). All of those events were captured with new thoroughness and urgency by an emerging system of truly mass communication. In 1968, for example, in the face of the brutal attack by the Chicago police outside the Democratic Presidential Convention, young, largely middle-class, protesters chanted, 'The whole world is watching.' And indeed, through their televisions, they were. In late 1969, they were watching again when President Nixon ordered US forces to carry the war across the Vietnamese border into Cambodia, escalating the war rather than bringing 'our boys' home. This led to protests and disturbances (often violent) at over half of all American universities and colleges, 51 of which were closed for the rest of the term (Zaroulis and Sullivan, 1984: 318–21; cited in Kent, 1987: 20). These were stirring times. In the late sixties, much of the largest and most privileged generation of youth the world had known, the so-called baby boomers, vented their discontent and pressed for change, while much of the rest of the United States, Canada, and the world watched in shock and dismay.

This was also the era of more pervasive though less shocking cultural change. It was a time of extensive experimentation with drugs, liberal sexual mores, alternative living arrangements (such as cohabitation and communes), and new forms of popular music, dress, hair styles, and psychological therapies. The hippies, with their long hair, beads, beards, peasant clothing, drugs, psychedelic rock, free love, transient lifestyle, organic food, meditation, and incense, were emblematic of the era. American popular life was dominated by the distinct youth culture and the resultant conflict of the 'generation gap'. In its more extreme elements, it was a time to 'turn on, tune out, and drop out' of 'the system'. And as Bellah argues, the two pillars of American ideological self-understanding, of the values people had lived by for decades, came under attack: biblical religion and utilitarian individualism.

In the 1950s, after fifteen years of depression and war, the traditional Christian denominations of North America experienced a rapid and unanticipated growth. More people were attending services than ever before, and there was a boom in church construction as North Americans had babies and moved to the suburbs (see Wuthnow, 1988: Chaps 2–4). Yet by the sixties these same mainstream denominations (e.g., Congregationalists, Presbyterians, Methodists, Episcopalians and Anglicans, Catholics, and Jews) were experiencing a dramatic loss in numbers as many of the baby boomers, as they came of age, ceased to emulate their parents and stopped attending church. Some turned East (Cox, 1977) or elsewhere, to other decidedly unorthodox or un-American forms of religious life. But most simply turned away from organized religion altogether, preferring to guide their lives solely by the principles of utilitarian individualism, the other system of values the young had inherited from their parents (Roof and McKinney, 1988; Wuthnow, 1988; Roof, 1993).

Life from this perspective is primarily a matter of pursuing one's 'interests' by the best means available. The watchwords of the utilitarian ethos are effective organization and freedom from constraint. In this approach to life, rational behaviour is of paramount importance. Yet as commentators on modernity (such as the founding figure of sociology Max Weber, 1958b: 181–3) have observed since at least the turn of the century, the rationality in question seems to be purely formal and devoid of intrinsic ends (see, e.g., Wilson, 1982a: 167). In the absence of a clear sense of a larger purpose and meaning to life, the utilitarian preoccupation with means and efficiency has become an end in itself. This, too, was part of the legacy of the newly prosperous postwar society of North America. The parents of the baby boomers had managed to unite the two aspects of American ideology: they pursued their interests, with a passion for efficiency, but within the confines of a traditional Christian conscience, a sensibility still imbued with a more absolute sense of purpose, and of good and evil. But the rapid rise in educational levels attained in North America, the very success, in other words, of the utilitarian ethos, spelled the end of this cultural compromise (see Wuthnow, 1988: Chap. 7; Roof, 1993). Many of the baby boomers, with their unprecedented exposure to university and college education, turned their backs on religion, but only to find eventually that the utilitarian individualism with which they were left was equally unsatisfying. There was ample evidence of the failure of a culture guided by the standards of utilitarian individualism. The United States seemed trapped in an escalating and pointless war in Vietnam, the popular charismatic liberal leaders of the era, President John F. Kennedy, his brother and presidential candidate Senator Robert Kennedy, and Martin Luther King, the great civil rights leader, were all assassinated. On and off throughout the decade race riots raged out of control in the heart of many American cities, notably, Los Angeles, Newark, and Detroit, and in May 1970 several student protesters were gunned down by the National Guard at Kent State University. Then, in 1973, when Americans were beginning to believe in a return to the status quo, the Watergate scandal broke, forcing President Richard Nixon, the standard-bearer of 'law and order' and 'the silent majority', to resign in disgrace. These public disappointments, combined with the personal struggles many were having with the rising rates of divorce, crime, and drug abuse, and ecological and economic crises, such as the energy crisis and recession set off by the OPEC oil embargo of 1973, fostered a new consciousness among many of the need to seriously reconsider the proper ends of their actions (see Bellah, 1976: 338).

For those engaged in political protest and lifestyle experimentation, these times of trouble gave birth to a new set of 'expressive ideals' with which to guide their lives:

> The counterculture challenged utilitarian culture at the most fundamental level. It asked what in life possessed intrinsic value, and to what ends ought we to act. It rejected money, power, and technical knowledge, mainstays of 'the good life' of middle-class society, as ends good in themselves. Instead, it identified them as means that did not, after all, enable one to experience what is intrinsically valuable—love, self-awareness, intimacy with others and nature. (Tipton, 1982b: 84)

In general, the clamour for change, the experience of disruption, the rising educational levels, and the emergence of new ideals of personal authenticity in the sixties opened the door to a much greater interest in alternative world-views and ways of living. Other readings of 'the good life', like those provided by such NRMs as Scientology, Krishna Consciousness, the Unification Church, Divine Light Mission, Transcendental Meditation, Children of God, Nichiren Shoshu, Vajradhatu, Wicca, and even Satanism, were entertained as serious possibilities. But, as Bellah, Tipton, and other scholars (e.g., Adams and Fox, 1972; Kent, 1987, 1988) insist, the full picture is more complicated. NRMs are not so much the direct products of the ferment of the sixties. Rather, they are better conceived as 'successors' to the movements of political protest and cultural innovation of this period. People turned from 'slogan chanting to *mantra* chanting' (Kent, 1988), because of both the success and the failure of these movements.

The revolutionary impulse of the sixties did change the world of Americans and Canadians in many ways. The United States grudgingly accepted defeat in Vietnam, withdrew its troops, and acknowledged that it might be guilty of imperialism. Repressive attitudes towards blacks, women, and the poor were displaced by more egalitarian views, while social norms with regard to sex, appearance, language, music, marriage, and religious beliefs were liberalized. However, at the end of the decade and the end of their youth the baby boomers were faced with a more sombre set of challenges. They had to get on with life, and all its adult responsibilities, in a world still fundamentally unchanged. The structural realities of modernity, 'technological production, bureaucratic organization, and empirical science' (Tipton, 1982b: 84) had been left intact by the cultural turmoil of the time, and they continued to necessitate a utilitarian orientation to life. As educations ended and jobs loomed, it was difficult to sustain the 'expressive ideals' of the counter-culture, founded on unregulated feeling and pop philosophy. These sentiments were no match for the deeply ingrained demands and aspirations of American utilitarianism. Moreover, the very success of the sixties had, ironically, helped to usher in a more permissive and hedonistic milieu, one that is well suited to the ethic of mass consumption promoted by advanced industrial societies. Accordingly, the sixties gave way to the 'me generation' and the general cynicism of the seventies and early eighties. In American pop culture, disco displaced psychedelic rock, being radical gave way to being a yuppie (young urban professional), and self-help and encounter therapies were substituted for the revolution.

Amidst this 'ideological wreckage', to use Tipton's (1982b: 84) evocative phrase, many of the most committed, who were often the most disillusioned as well, were gripped with anomie—a sense of normlessness, of having lost their way. But some, Tipton and others argue, 'found a way both to cope with the instrumental demands of adulthood in conventional society *and* to sustain the counterculture's expressive ideals by reinforcing them with moralities of authority, rules, and utility.' Calling on the beliefs and practices of various NRMs, which blossomed in the seventies and early eighties, different yet fundamentally similar ways were found to 'mediate and resolve' the clash of moral sensibilities afflicting many young people (Tipton, 1982b: 81). These Americans returned, in new ways, to a characteristically American orientation, one rooted in the early Protestant heritage of North America and the experience of conquering the frontier: the path to social revolution must be through the conversion and transformation of the consciousness and conscience of individuals, beginning with oneself. With variations on the theme, such was the path of development detailed by Lucas (1995), for example, in his account of how some hippies from the failed Haight-Ashbury enclave of San Francisco flocked to the New Age teachings of a peculiar engineer from Cincinnati and helped him found the Holy Order of MANS, which they eventually transformed into an order of the Russian Orthodox Church.

Proposing a threefold typology, Tipton (1982b: 98) suggests one widely accepted way of explaining the appeal of various kinds of new religions to people who need to resolve their sense of moral ambiguity:

> The human potential movement [as reflected in groups like est, Silva Mind Control, and Scientology] recombines the expressive ethic of hip culture with the consequential ethic of utilitarian individualism, with particular plausibility for the middle middle class. Conservative Christian groups recombine the expressive ethic with the authoritative ethic of revealed biblical religion, with particular plausibility for the lower middle class. Neo-Oriental groups recombine the expressive ethic with the regular ethic of rationalized religion and humanism, with particular plausibility for the upper middle class.

In each of these different ways, Tipton (1982b: 98–100) proposes, disoriented elements of the baby boom generation found the rules to live by and an authority they could respect that brought a necessary measure of practical order and peace to their lives, without fully betraying their counter-cultural commitment to the high ideals of self-expression and 'love over money'. NRMs like est or Scientology allowed people to return to conventional careers, families, and activities. They conformed to the utilitarian theory of right behaviour, with its emphasis on doing that which yields the most good consequences for oneself (that is, a consequentialist ethic). But these groups invoked elaborate alternative readings of human nature and the real character of the world that radically shifted the definition of good consequences from material acquisition and improved social status to heightened self-awareness, self-expression, and the experience of various supposed spiritual dimensions of existence.

Conservative Christian NRMs, like the Unification Church and the dozens of Jesus Movement groups born of the sixties, resolved the unhappiness of moral ambiguity by replacing the consequentialist ethic characteristic of utilitarian individualism, whereby anything goes if it produces the desired result, with one of biblical authority. Sin is the root of unhappiness, and happiness follows from doing the right thing, from avoiding sin. Our actions should be guided by our principles, and not just by their consequences. Yet the knowledge of the right things to do stems from the development of a deeply emotional and loving relationship to God and the community of fellow believers. An emphasis is placed, over against more conventional expressions of Christianity, on the development and reality of a very personal and often ecstatic relationship with Jesus. Being 'born again in Christ' is the key.

Neo-oriental groups, like Zen Buddhism, Divine Light Mission, Krishna Consciousness, and Vajradhatu, replace the utilitarian consequentialist theory of right behaviour with one that stresses the prior need to act in accord with rules that conform to the 'real' nature of reality. Right knowledge of human existence will lead to the abandonment of insatiable desires for some unattainable material happiness. This will result in an abiding sense of peace with oneself and the world. Instrumental to this end is the practice of various highly subjective and affectively moving disciplinary activities (that is, rituals and forms of meditation) and the careful cultivation of a deeply devotional relationship with a guru or some other spiritual master.

Whatever the merits of Tipton's particular formulation of these relationships, and there are others that differ somewhat (e.g., Foss and Larkin, 1978; Bird, 1979; Robbins, Anthony, and Curtis, 1975; Anthony and Robbins, 1982a; Wilson, 1982a; Wallis, 1984; Kent, 1988; Palmer, 1994), it is fair to say that there is substantial agreement among the scholars studying NRMs that this approach is possible. Clearly many of the NRMs that suddenly surged into public awareness in the sixties and seventies were responding to a moral malaise felt by the young adults and adolescents of North America. In varying degrees these new religions were also involved, like other puritanical or fanatical religious groups throughout the ages, in reintegrating these estranged young people back into society, or at least redirecting their protest from the realm of overt political confrontation to the less threatening realm of socio-religious experimentation. Robbins, Anthony, and Curtis (1975) specify four ways in which this social reintegration of religious converts is facilitated: (1) adjustive socialization, (2) combination, (3) compensation, and (4) redirection. Any particular religion may be exercising a latent integrative influence on its followers by means of any combination of these processes, and there is some analytical value in calling on this more generic sociological formulation of possibilities to avoid the type-casting of groups that may result from the use of Tipton's tripartite classification of NRMs.

As sociologists of religion have long noted, in connection with primarily traditional Christian sects, some marginal religious groups tend to resocialize individuals to the dominant values and norms of society (Niebuhr, 1929; Holt, 1940; Johnson, 1961). They do so through their emphasis on the strict moral standards required to win salvation. The traditional prohibitions against drinking, gambling, fighting, and laziness have been complemented in many of the new Jesus groups and Eastern religions with admonitions against, and programs to correct, drug abuse, sexual promiscuity, and selfishness. Devotees are encouraged to do everything for the glory of Krishna, God, or their true inner nature in ways that place a high value on hard work and service to others. This is 'adjustive socialization'. 'Combination' is the term used by Robbins, Anthony, and Curtis, independently of Tipton, for the fusion of expressive and utilitarian orientations discussed above. In the Divine Light Mission of Guru Maharaj-ji, for example, the return to 'straight' morality and work habits in the everyday world and a rather uncritical acceptance of modern technology were blended with a self-styled 'revolutionary' ethic of universal love and the daily inducement of ecstasy through meditation (Downton, 1979; Galanter and Buckley, 1983). 'Compensation' and 'redirection', Robbins, Anthony, and Curtis specify (1975: 52),

> do not require the presence of explicit norms either proscribing deviant involvements (e.g., drugs) or legitimating non-deviant commitments (e.g., to conventional 'careers'). Compensation refers to the renewal of commitment to conventional vocational routines, that derives from having the expressive needs that these routines cannot gratify, gratified elsewhere (i.e., in religious groups). Redirection is more exclusively negative and refers to the substitution of socially legitimate religious activities and satisfactions for stigmatized activities and satisfactions (e.g., spiritual 'highs' for drug induced 'highs'), from which the convert is thusly 'redirected'.

In discussing these kinds of reasons for the appeal of NRMs Robbins, Anthony, and Curtis (1975: 56) made a very interesting macro-sociological speculation (building on aspects of Talcott Parsons' structural-functional theory of the social system—see, e.g., Parsons, 1963; also Block and Hirschhorn, 1979). All of these reintegrative processes, operating in various combinations in diverse groups, may serve the larger latent function of managing tension in advanced industrial societies. Modern affluent and increasingly automated societies, it is argued, need an even smaller portion of their populations in the labour force. By inducing a segment of their population to adopt various forms of traditional religious resistance to the quest for material success and social prestige, NRMs are helping to stabilize the social systems of these advanced capitalist societies by alleviating the unrest that arises when too many qualified people wish to participate meaningfully in the workforce and in political and economic decision-making. The monastic orders of the Catholic Church, for somewhat different reasons, are said to have served a similar function during the Middle Ages.

The empirical merits of this theory are difficult to assess but it has the benefit of drawing our attention away from the kinds of micro-analyses that tend to predominate in the study of these small and idiosyncratic groups. Clearly, some more macro-speculations are needed if, by the early 1970s, as Wuthnow (1988: 152) observes, 'the various new religions may have resulted in the organization of more than 3,000 local groups of one kind or another, with perhaps as many as a tenth of the entire population [of the United States] having participated in at least one.' But such speculations are best approached with great caution. In the late 1980s the activity of NRMs tapered off, and membership in the relatively well-established groups like Scientology, Krishna Consciousness, and the Unification Church has stabilized at levels well below those achieved in the early to mid-seventies. Fewer new religions are being formed now, and they are attracting fewer followers. And yet we have little reason to believe that there have been any significant changes to the basic conditions of advanced industrial society, conditions that are thought to have precipitated either a state of moral ambiguity or a systemic need for tension management. From another angle, though, the drop in support for NRMs could be interpreted as evidence for the 'moral crisis' thesis. As times have changed and the baby boom generation has grown older, leaving the counter-culture behind it, the need for NRMs has seemingly become more peripheral.

All the same, the reason why some young people continue to seek out such organizations is still probably related to an element of moral ambiguity (in some unspecified form) in our rapidly changing society. Moreover, while direct experience of the turmoil characteristic of the sixties is no longer pertinent, North Americans continue to struggle with the cultural legacy of those years. In his extensive interviews of members of the baby boom generation, Wade Clark Roof (1993) found that people who actually took part in some of the protests, drugs, and rock festivals of the sixties are far more inclined, even now, to practise or at least accept alternative religions. Within the confines of their otherwise relatively conventional lives, these people have continued to carry the more liberal and expressive values of the sixties, and they have tried to pass them on to their children. But only about half of the baby boomers ever actually 'experienced' the sixties. Many others, Roof reminds us, lived through the sixties in harmony with mainstream society, largely unaffected by the changes that wrought the generation gap. In fact, for a sizable portion of this 'straight' group, the little exposure they had to the counter-culture helped to turn them to the more conservative forms of Christianity that culminated in the cultural and political activism of the New Christian Right that emerged in the late 1970s and continues to the present. Of course, an even larger share of the baby boomers simply abandoned any participation in organized religion altogether.

In the end, it is probably safe to say, in agreement with Tipton (1982b: 105), that many converts to alternative religions, in the past and the present, 'are people who experience ethical contradictions of unusual intensity and as a result look for unusually coherent solutions to them.' Historically, it is a matter of chance that the crisis of meaning experienced by so many baby boomers struck at a time when North America was opening up to an unprecedented measure of cultural and religious pluralism. The gurus happened to be in place, in search of new ideological markets, when the need for their spiritual goods arose. The unexpected explosion of non-traditional religions ensued.[3]

Before we consider how the rise of new religious groups may also have been affected by changes in the social structure of modern societies, it is useful to reiterate the warning against falling into overly reductive lines of analysis. To argue that part of the appeal of NRMs is the latent integrative consequences of participation does not mean we can assume that this function is essential to the existence of these groups. People may join these groups for any number of other reasons, and the groups conceive themselves to be serving decidedly other purposes. Even though integration may often be a valued by-product of involvement, but we must guard against what Bellah (1970: 246–56) calls 'consequential reductionism'. There is no definitive empirical or logical reason to treat the spiritual and other accounts that believers give for their involvement as secondary in explanatory significance to the apparent social or psychological benefits of participation.[4]

Changes in Social Structure

Discussions of the role of moral ambiguity in the emergence of NRMs are often accompanied by a complementary but essentially different explanation of cult activity in North America, one that focuses on changes in the social structure of the modern world (Robbins and Anthony, 1972; Marx and Ellison, 1975; Anthony and Robbins, 1981; Doress and Porter, 1981;

Hunter, 1981; Robbins and Anthony, 1982a; Kilbourne and Richardson, 1982; Levine, 1984; Parsons, 1986, 1989; Robbins, 1988; Cartwright and Kent, 1992; Wright and D'Antonio, 1993; Palmer, 1994). There are two varieties of this social-structural type of explanation. In its most immediate and simple form it links the rise of NRMs to a search by young adults for 'surrogate' families in the face of the demise of what sociologists call 'mediating structures' in society. Drawing on the views of prominent sociological observers of modernity, like Talcott Parsons (1951), S.N. Eisenstadt (1956), and Peter Berger (Berger and Neuhaus, 1970; Berger et al., 1974), the scholars who advance this explanation point to the widening gap thought to exist between our childhood experience of family life and the ever more compelling demands of the educational and occupational institutions of our societies. In its less apparent and more abstract form, this type of explanation calls on the same analyses of modernity to link the rise of NRMs to a more diffuse spectre of cognitive and affective disorientation stemming from the de-institutionalization of many aspects of 'private' life in advanced industrial societies. The argument advanced is essentially the same in each instance. The social structural problem delineated, however, is given a greater breadth of scope in the latter case. The issues are confined less to the experience of adolescents and young adults, and consequently are seemingly less susceptible to any obvious kind of ameliorative action. This is a larger structural dilemma, which shapes the social environment in which all religions, new or old, must operate for the foreseeable future.

THE SEARCH FOR SURROGATE FAMILIES

We are being raised, sociologists and historians argue, in more humane and personalistic families than in the past. Present-day families cater more to the individual material and emotional needs of their children and try to promote a more independent identity in children. This greater personal attention is the result of the decreasing likelihood of death during childhood, smaller families, increasing affluence, higher levels of education, and, until the last twenty years, more leisure time. It is also the result, however, of the increasing isolation of the nuclear family in an urbanized, suburbanized, and geographically and socially mobile North America. The family is becoming the sole, or at least the primary, provider of the kind of everyday psychological and social support that once came from homogeneous and stable neighbourhoods, extended families, churches, voluntary associations, social clubs, and more personal workplaces. These traditional extra-familial sources of support are what sociologists call 'mediating structures'. The term refers to the functioning of such structures in the social system. These groups stand between the world of the nuclear family and the world of large corporate and government bureaucracies. On the one hand, these mediating structures help to buffer the family from the dictates of the mega-structures of modern life. On the other hand, they ease the socialization of the young away from the personal world of the family and into the more impersonal adult world. They perpetuate many of the kinds of face-to-face contact and personal bonds typical of childhood and family life, while simultaneously introducing the young to the more detached and utilitarian procedures of larger organizations. The trouble is, in the face of the continuous expansion of the responsibilities of large corporations and government bureaucracies, there are fewer mediating groups and fewer kinds of such groups. Moreover, the expanding functions of such larger social institutions as schools, social welfare agencies, social-control agencies, and the medical profession, have undermined the traditional legitimacy and integrity of the family. These bodies now perform many of the functions once preserved for the family.

In the last several decades many sociologists have argued that the resultant polarization of social life between the extremes of public and private life has set the stage for a new, intense, and relatively pervasive identity crisis amongst adolescents and young adults (e.g., Erikson, 1968; Wilson, 1982a: 177). The crisis in question is rooted in the jarring transition now experienced by young people between the 'expressive' values, roles, and relationships of the familial milieu and the 'instrumental' values, roles, and relationships of the adult milieu. These terms of reference derive from Talcott Parsons's enormously influential sociological analyses of the institutional transformations that mark the emergence of 'modern' societies (e.g., Parsons, 1951, 1971). By expressive relationships, Parsons (1951: 58–67; cited in Robbins and Anthony, 1972: 123) and others are referring to relations that tend to be (1) ends in themselves and are (2) diffuse, (3) idiosyncratic, (4) particularistic, and (5) affective in nature. Instrumental relationships are (1) means to ends, (2) functionally specific, (3) performance- or achievement-oriented, (4) universalistic, and (5) affectively neutral. For many young people, long immersed in the expressive atmosphere of the isolated suburban family, the struggle to adapt suddenly to the instrumental demands of university or the work world is disconcerting. For those who are particularly sensitive to the disjuncture in orientations, joining an NRM may offer a way to stave off, circumvent, or ameliorate the conflict in values, roles, and relationships. As with the closely related experience of moral ambiguity, NRMs may appear to offer some individuals a compromise between the expressive affectivity of childhood and the instrumental orientation of adulthood.

Most NRMs, especially those of a more communal type, stress the affectionate, loving, family-like character of their internal bonds—for example the Children of God (Richardson and Davis, 1983; Van Zandt, 1991); Hare Krishna (Rochford, 1985; Palmer, 1994); the Unification Church (Fichter, 1983, Parsons, 1989, Palmer, 1994); the Holy Order of MANS (Lucas, 1995); even the Catholic Charismatic Renewal (Neitz, 1987). They are 'spiritual families', held together by ties of brotherly and sisterly love. Charismatic religious leaders present themselves as parental figures, or they are treated as such by their followers. Many members of the Catholic Charismatic Renewal speak of 'daddy God' and 'brother Jesus', Moonies literally see Reverend Moon and his wife as their new parents, while the use of family symbolism is self-evident in the Children of God, now called the Family, and founded and led by Father David (David Berg, known also as Moses David—after another great father-figure). In these groups, diffusely affective and expressive relationships, like those of a true extended family, are reiterated in dozens of ways but in a wider context geared to the service of some greater cause. Through dedication to the cause, the real family of the convert is transcended and, hence, left behind. Yet symbolically and experientially, a highly personal and integrated way of life is sustained. In some cases, independence, with its fearful burden of responsibility and detachment, is held off or sacrificed in favour of continued child-like obedience to a presumably benevolent authority. Arthur Parsons (1986) points out that such child-like filial respect for superiors is central to the Confucian-like patterns of order and emotional intimacy expected in the Unification Church. Jacobs (1989: 5) goes so far as to suggest that the 'rise of charismatic religious movements . . . can be understood as the desire to experience both the ideal family and the fathering of a protective and loving male authority figure. As such, . . . conversion . . . reflects the failure of the middle class family to meet the needs of contemporary society . . . and the attending disillusionment with the nature of fathering in American culture.'[5]

In broader and less contentious terms, the eminent British sociologist of religion Bryan Wilson (1982a: 134) effectively captures the appeal of NRMs by speaking of a return to a greater sense of 'community'.

> In the modern world, natural community has largely disappeared: [people] no longer live, learn, work, play, marry, and die in the same community. Yet there is no doubt that [people] hanker after the benefits of community, seek contexts in which they are personally known, and in which they share responsibilities with others. New religious movements can supply precisely this context in a way that no other social agency can do. Other activities—politics, economics, even recreation—are dominated by specific interests and exchange relationships—only the family shares with religion the idea

of community as an end in itself, and the modern family, now nucleated, is too small to fulfil the functions of a community. Because religious activity is predicated on transcendental concepts, because sharing and caring are the core of its operation, because the celebration of the transcendent truth is also a celebration of the community in which the truth is cherished—for all of these reasons, religious groups provide the intrinsic, as well as the symbolic, benefits of community.

As Robbins and Anthony (1972: 132) also point out, the professed transcendental values and objectives of the NRMs legitimate a post-adolescent return to expressive roles by universalizing their nature and significance. On the one hand, the universalization of expressive roles intellectually marginalizes the dominant instrumental demands of the secular culture, in relation to something more important (i.e., a divine purpose or greater cosmic plan). This opens the door to continued or renewed expressivity in daily life. On the other hand, the universalization of expressive roles actually borrows its aura of legitimacy from the 'universalism' associated with the instrumental roles pursued in the modern secular adult world. In this way, NRMs combine and transform two negatives, childish expressivity and impersonal universalism, into a single positive. Functionally, the NRMs through which this transformation is accomplished are acting as substitutes, for a time, for the traditional mediating structures that have been driven from advanced industrial societies. They maintain some of the personalism of the family in structures dedicated to larger, more impersonal goals. They provide a way to reintegrate the expressive and the instrumental in a single cohesive social unit and, hence, provide a stable identity for their young members. The Canadian psychiatrist Saul Levine (1984) has advanced a similar, though of course more psychological, explanation of cult conversions. His views are summarized in Chapter 3.

COPING WITH DEINSTITUTIONALIZATION

In slightly different yet parallel ways, James Davison Hunter (1981) and Benton Johnson (1981) recast, expand, and add important nuances to this tale of modern youthful fear and alienation. The tension felt by the young, in transition into adulthood, is in fact structurally endemic to life in advanced industrial societies. Building on Berger's basic understanding of the human condition and the social construction of reality (Berger, 1967; Berger et al., 1974; see Chapter 1), Hunter concentrates on a crisis of meaning and personal security stemming from the 'deinstitutionalization' of the modern world. As Berger stipulates, humans are born biologically incomplete. As a species we have sought to fashion a stable cultural order to compensate for our lack of instinctual programming. Ideally this culturally fabricated order will come to be taken for granted and will hold the ever-present threat of anomie at bay. The aspects of human life that become so routinized and so habitual as to be beyond ready questioning are said to be institutionalized. Most of life in traditional societies is institutionalized in this sense. 'Modernity', Hunter (1981: 4) proposes, 'is characterized by an unprecedented degree of de-institutionalization.' This is a problem, which, moreover, is exacerbated by the uneven distribution of the deinstitutionalization process in modern society.

On the one hand, modern individuals live in an environment where more and more aspects of their so-called 'private' lives are being converted from the realm of taken-for-granted experience to that of choice. Courtship, marriage, child rearing, sexuality, gender relations, consumption, vocation, and spirituality are being de-institutionalized. In the private realm, there are no set and secure behaviours. In these spheres of activity traditional institutions have, as Hunter says (1981: 5), 'lost their grip on the individual', and struggles with anomie are common.

On the other hand, in the 'public' sphere of activity, dominated by massive bureaucracies that organize and operate our governments, the law, business and commerce, labour, health care, communications, the military, and even religion, the processes of institutionalization are continuing unabated. The institutionalization in question, however, is distinctive. In the modern world, as Weber stressed (e.g., 1958b: Chaps 4, 5, and 8; 1964: 35–55), institutions are guided increasingly by a strictly 'formal rationality', which is geared to the satisfaction of the functional requirements of social systems, with little or no regard for the desires, needs, or even character of the individual members of the institutions. The effective performance of 'roles' in the service of the institution matters more than any personal features of the incumbents of the roles or the quality of relationships experienced in the institutional environment. One's integrity or simple contentment is secondary to one's accomplishments for the organization (see Wilson, 1982a: 159–68). Consequently, as Hunter comments (1981: 4), there is a profound disjuncture between people's private and public experiences and neither is very satisfying.

In the private sphere everything is seemingly a matter of choice; yet many people yearn for more guidance. In the public sphere, on the other hand, one is compelled to conform. Guidance is manifest, but in ways that belie the meaningfulness of participation for the individual. In this situation, personal identity, promoted as all-important at the private level and as the natural end-product of making the right choices, is frustrated by a structurally diverse public realm that demands an elaborate differentiation of social roles and restricts real choices. It is hard to know who we are when the social system requires us to be many different people in many different functional circumstances, but none with any depth. We are expected to be one person at home, another at school, another at work, and yet another in the store or on the street. In the modern world, so the argument runs, identity is fragmented or at least pluralized. Either way, for many, having a meaningful identity at all has become problematic (see, e.g., Erikson, 1968; Baumeister, 1986). In the face of this, so the argument runs, the proliferating new religions provide a holistic sense of self, in theory and in practice, that transcends the constellation of limited instrumental roles recognized by modern mass society (see also Campbell, 1978; Westley, 1978, 1983; Beckford, 1984).

> The dilemma of modernity, in which all individuals are variously caught, is an oppressively formidable public sphere, which is structurally incapable of providing individuals with concrete and meaningful social confirmation of their sense of reality (including their understanding of social processes, subjective meaning and personal identity), and an enfeebled private sphere, which is distressingly under-institutionalized, and which is structurally unable to provide reliable social parameters for the more mundane activity of everyday life and a plausible, well-integrated system of meaning which gives location and purpose to the individual's total life experience. (Hunter, 1981: 5)

I think Benton Johnson (1981) does an even better job of capturing the structural dilemma of modernity. The contours of his argument are pretty much the same. But he brings the point home with greater force and subtlety by speaking more concretely of the worlds of 'work' and of 'love'. Johnson (1981: 54) traces the rise of NRMs and related new forms of psychotherapy as a response to 'a widespread distress that is produced by an inability to achieve and sustain heightened demands for satisfactions in the areas of work and intimate relations.' The acuity of his analysis is such that it warrants being quoted at length. His descriptions, written more than fifteen years ago, still ring true. Here is the enervating quandary in which modern North Americans are caught every day, and which some people intuitively seek to flee by turning to NRMs.

With regard to the world of work, the node of most people's involvement is the public sector, Johnson says (1981: 54–5):

> The development of modern economies has opened up a great many new opportunities and has encouraged people to expect increasing levels of

material and psychological rewards for occupational achievement. Success in the workplace for many people has become the single most important test of personal worth. But the proliferation of new opportunities for occupational achievement is largely the result of the growth of large-scale organizations. Self-employment has declined steadily for over a century, with the result being that most of us today are dependent on the wages and salaries paid to us by employers. The character of our jobs, including our prospects for success, is increasingly governed by considerations that are systemic in character and therefore beyond our personal control. Work takes place in formal organizations that are hierarchical in structure and are primarily responsive, through their top-level control centers, to the requirements of the market and government. Work relations are therefore highly inegalitarian. Workers tend to be evaluated individually and competitively on the basis of their contribution to the goals of the enterprise. In the world of work there are winners and losers, and those who are winning today may be losing tomorrow. The sense of achievement, and hence the feeling of self-worth, is placed in constant jeopardy because of the uncertainty of the outcome of our efforts. The search for a secure sense of self-worth based on work is made difficult by the structure of work itself—a structure that Americans by and large do not understand and that they do not control.

Faced with what Marxists would call the alienating nature of work in the modern world, Johnson proposes that people tend to increase their demands for satisfaction in their private lives. In their personal relations they demand more emotional support, love, and sexual gratification. But this compensatory move is to no avail, for the private sector is drawn into the same vortex.

The insistence on higher levels of gratification has brought with it a higher potential for dissatisfaction with one's personal relationships. Whereas our ability to control the conditions of work has progressively shrunk, our ability to control the conditions of love has expanded. It is now possible to abandon intimate relationships that are not satisfactory. But this freedom has its costs. It is exhilarating to find fulfilment in a new love, but it is not exhilarating to be abandoned by an old love. To the risks of work are now added the risks of love. Moreover, the risks of the latter are exacerbated by the increasing economic independence of women. For years men have intuitively understood that it is safer to act-out the frustrations of work at home than it is to act-out the frustrations of home life at work. Women's participation in work has not changed the structures of work. It is still risky to act-out home-life frustrations at work, and it now becomes unsafe for either sex to do much acting-out at home. Finally the perils of love are also made more difficult by the competitive character of the workplace and by the tendency to make invidious comparisons in an effort to assess personal worth. Just as the success of competitors can make people envious, the success of loved ones can make people question their own worth. The anarchy of work is reflected in intimate relationships.

For theorists like Hunter and Johnson, the new religious consciousness that emerged in the sixties is quite simply a sociocultural protest against these anomic and alienating conditions. In Hunter's view (1981: 7–9), NRMs represent a 'demodernizing impulse': an attempt to reconstruct the world socially by 'reimposing institutionally reliable meanings upon existence.' The protest of the NRMs tends to concentrate, however, on treating the symptoms of this 'disjuncture of modernity'. The cause is addressed only indirectly, by one of three means: (1) by removing people from the existing social system (that is, from the conventional pursuit of careers and romantic relationships) into alternative communal arrangements and livelihoods, (2) by giving people alternative life goals that take priority over work and love (for example, achieving various spiritual skills and states of being), (3) by encouraging people to abandon their traditional quest for security and instead to seek growth and self-actualization in the flexible acceptance of change and the cultivation of spontaneity. In different groups these strategies appear in various combinations and in a myriad of specific forms.

Changes in the Role and Character of Religious Institutions

The third related theme of cultural change commonly reiterated in the literature that tries to explain why NRMs emerged returns us to the issue of secularization. Having broached this subject in some detail when discussing the clash of paradigms between Berger and Stark and Bainbridge (see Chapter 1), I intend here only to re-canvass the argument for secularization, stipulating how the decay of traditional religion is thought to have created the conditions for new religious activity. If we understand the fate of the established churches, we will have a better grasp of the challenges facing the new religions. To that end, Bryan Wilson's influential theorizing about secularization will be used to supplement the views of Berger and of Stark and Bainbridge.

Like Berger, and like Stark and Bainbridge, Wilson's understanding of the increasingly secular nature of our society is based on Max Weber's conception of global social development in terms of the progressive 'rationalization' of systems of knowledge and information, values and norms, and means of motivating desirable behaviour (Weber, 1958a, 1964). This process of rationalization works against the interests and power of traditional religions in society, in both direct and indirect ways. Historically, an essential manifestation of the rationalization of the social system is what sociologists call 'institutional differentiation' (e.g., Parsons, 1963, 1971). Where once almost all aspects of social life fell under the influence, if not direct rule, of religion, over the last several centuries ever larger segments of daily life have been segregated from religious authority and relegated to other institutions. Such a transfer of authority accompanied the sequential development of independent economic, political, medical, educational, recreational, and even family institutions. This process not only stripped religious institutions of their manifest power in social affairs, but also subverted the latent social functions that religions have long performed as well. Although offering assurance of ultimate salvation has always been the primary function of religion, before the Industrial Revolution religion was also the primary agency of social cohesion and social control in society, the chief source of knowledge about the world, the foundation of personal and group identity, and a major force for the cultivation, expression, and regulation of emotions. These functions are now the prerogative of national governments, legal systems, science, public education and health systems, professional sports, and the mass media and entertainment industry (see Wilson, 1982a: 32–46). Following in the footsteps of Ferdinand Toennies, Emile Durkheim, Weber, and many other sociologists of note, Wilson characterizes the overall change as a shift from community to societal system (1982a: 125 ff., 153 ff.). As life became less religious, it also became markedly less local and personal and more national (even international) and impersonal. In the long term, it is this comprehensive shift in the basic configuration of social life that lies behind the more specific changes in values and social structures associated with the rise of NRMs from the 1960s onwards. It is this shift that is thought to account ultimately for the experiences of moral ambiguity and anomie that made North Americans receptive to the NRMs. The difficulties of the baby boom generation were only a recent phase of a much larger and longer process.

Much like Stark and Bainbridge, then, and Berger in some measure, Wilson suggests that the decline in the social prominence of conventional religions was a necessary precondition for the rise of nationally significant and relatively exotic NRMs. This is true in at least two senses. First, the religious tolerance that came with religious pluralism and the increasing privatization and institutional segregation of religion is a *sine qua non* of cult growth (Wilson, 1982b: 26). Second, the incongruity sensed between systems of religious beliefs and practices born of an earlier, different, and simpler age and the new horizons opening to the educated members of advanced industrial societies undermined the credibility of traditional religious ideas. Unlike Stark and Bainbridge, and more like Berger, however, Wilson thinks that the macro-social changes associated with secularization have intrinsically limited the capacity of NRMs to reverse significantly the privatization of religion in Western culture. Why? Because in the last analysis he believes that most of these movements are largely the products of the modern social system, rather than its opponents.

> New religious movements, whether in the Christian, Buddhist, or any other tradition, are not in the strict sense revivals of a tradition: they are more accurately regarded as adaptations of religion to new social circumstances. None of them is capable, given the radical nature of social change, of recreating the dying religions of the past. In their style and in their specific appeal they represent an accommodation to new conditions, and they incorporate many of the assumptions and facilities encouraged in the increasingly rationalised secular sphere. Thus it is that many new movements are themselves testimonies to secularization: they often utilise highly secular methods of evangelism, financing, publicity and mobilisation of adherents. Very commonly, the traditional symbolism, liturgy and aesthetic concern of traditional religion are abandoned for much more pragmatic attitudes and for systems of control, accountancy, propaganda and even doctrinal content which are closer to the styles of secular enterprise than to traditional religious concerns. The new religions do evidently indicate a continuing interest in, perhaps need for, spiritual solace and reassurance on the part of many individuals, but, in the West at least, they are also very much the creations of a secularized society. (Wilson, 1988: 965)

Who is right, Berger and Wilson or Stark and Bainbridge? Do NRMs represent the remnant of religion as it once was, adapted to a reduced existence in a secular context, or are NRMs simply new religions, with the potential in some cases to be the precursors of a true revival of religion? The issue is too complex to resolve here, or even by the end of this book. Much more information is needed about the specific groups and their circumstances. However, since the question frames the overall analysis of the nature and significance of NRMs, it will be explored further in Chapter 6.

New Religious Movements as an Expression of Cultural Continuity

Under this heading are grouped several different and perhaps even conflicting interpretations of the nature and emergence of NRMs. But the views are united by the claim that NRMs are not as new or different as most scholars and the public think. For convenience I will once again divide the material into two categories: 'NRMs and American religious history', and 'NRMs and the history of religion'. With each category the scope of the analysis is being expanded, across time and geography. In the first instance, links are established between the emergence of the new religions in the sixties and seventies and the history of American religious dissent, sectarianism, and persecution. NRMs are placed in the context of the history of the Great Awakenings, the history of alternative religious traditions in America, and the treatment of Catholics, Mormons, and others in the United States during the nineteenth century. In the second instance, NRMs are placed in the context of the long tradition of religious heresy and occultism in the Christian West and the very origins of Christianity itself as a cult. In fact much that contemporary secular and conventional religious culture finds objectionable in NRMs has its roots in the Christian tradition itself (and the other so-called world religions).

New Religious Movements and American Religious History
The history of religion in North America is marked by periods of sweeping change and fervour that have come to be known as the Great Awakenings. Historians widely agree that many aspects of fundamental cultural identity of Americans were forged during two times of intense religious revivalism, the First Great Awakening, which spread throughout the American colonies from 1730 to 1760, and the Second Great Awakening, which gripped the new nation from 1800 to 1830. To these, some other historians, most notably William McLoughlin (1978), have added a Third Great Awakening, from 1890 to 1920, coinciding with the birth and popularity of modern urban revivalism, and, even more speculatively, a Fourth Great Awakening, coinciding with the rise of NRMs and of the New Christian Right, from the 1960s to the present (see also Lucas, 1992). In other words, McLoughlin and others (e.g., Pritchard, 1976; Moore, 1985) are suggesting that the recent rise of NRMs may be only the latest manifestation of the cyclical pattern of cultural development that has characterized America religion from the beginning. The United States has always been a land of 'new lights', as opposed to the 'old lights' of the established churches, and hence in broad perspective the new religions of today are not so new.

However one chooses to date, number, categorize, or explain these periods of religious tumult in American history, and this is a matter far too complicated to be discussed here, it is clear that social change and religious change have gone hand in hand in the New World and that the pattern of change has tended to be episodic.

The . . . great awakenings [mark] periods of fundamental ideological transformation necessary to the dynamic growth of the nation in adapting to
basic social, ecological, psychological, and economic changes. The conversion of great numbers of people from an old to a new world view . . . is a
natural and necessary aspect of social change. It constitutes the awakening
of a people caught in an outmoded, dysfunctional world view to the necessity of converting their mindset, their behavior, and their institutions to
more relevant or more fundamentally useful ways of understanding and
coping with the changes in the world they live in. (McLoughlin, 1978: 8)

In the first three awakenings, the focus and vehicle of change was evangelical Protestantism. The first awakening broke the hold of the 'old light'
Puritan ethos and institutional order of New England, ushering in a 'new
light' religious pluralism of other forms of Protestantism marked by the positive valuation of individual piety and personal conversions over denominational loyalty and doctrinal formalism. Socially, the experience of revival
helped to weld the people of the American colonies together in a spirit of
independence from the old order that resulted in the American Revolution.
The second awakening furthered these same processes and gave birth to the
Methodists, Baptists, and many other evangelical sects (such as the Disci-
ples of Christ). Over the course of the rest of the nineteenth century and the
early twentieth century, these new evangelical forms of Christianity set in
motion the true 'churching' of America, rendering it the most religious of
nations in the modern West (Finke and Stark, 1992). The Third Great
Awakening was designed to save this largely Protestant America from the
cultural contamination thought to stem from the massive influx of Catholic
and Jewish immigrants into the cities of the United States and Canada in the
late nineteenth and early twentieth centuries. From this third awakening
emerged the modern style of mass evangelism now so familiar to most
North Americans through the contemporary crusades of Billy Graham, Oral
Roberts, Jimmy Swaggart, Pat Robertson, and many other televangelists
(see, e.g., Frankl, 1987; Schultze, 1991). But with time, there also arose out
of this awakening the recognition of America as a land of Judeo-Christian
pluralism. As the sociologist Will Herberg (1955) documented, by the early
1950s being Protestant, Catholic, or Jewish was simply seen as different
ways of being American. For most Americans, to be 'American' required at
least a belief in God and the Bible, and some fairly regular participation in
the services of a church or synagogue.

From the beginning, each of the first three awakenings helped to define,
reinforce, adjust, and extend the collective sense of America as a nation destined to serve some special and probably divine purpose. By doing so, these

revivals worked to bring the nation together and fashion what McLoughlin calls 'a constant cultural core' (1978: 10). Yet the intensity of religious feeling and conviction stimulated by the spirit of revival also gave rise to a plethora of new Christian sects and even cults. With each awakening, old denominations were subject to repeated schisms, and some altogether new revelations came into being (for example, Mormonism, Spiritualism, Christian Science, and Pentecostalism). In effect, through recurrent religious change, necessary ideological adjustments were made to the collective self-conception of Americans, resolving the distortions that periodically emerged between the values and social conditions of daily life in North America. The overriding effect has been to generate a new unity out of diversity. One is reminded of the old adage: 'Plus ça change, plus c'est la même chose' (Karr, 1849).

But what of the Fourth Great Awakening? Are the NRMS that have emerged since the 1960s characteristic of this pattern? Or are they antithetical and evidence of the end of this kind of American religious history? The marked increase in Americans drawn to evangelical Christianity, Pentecostalism, and Catholic Charismatic Renewal conforms to this pattern. But what of the turn East, to use Cox's adroit phrase? How does the spread of Krishna Consciousness or Zen Buddhism reflect an ideological adjustment to the collective self-conception of Americans? What are we to make of the creation and popularity of Scientology or diverse forms of neo-paganism? Noting the obvious parallel in the pattern of concomitant social and ideological change, McLoughlin says they do point to a shift in the self-conception of Americans, and many others are sympathetic to his reasoning. Writing in 1978, however, he lacked sufficient historical perspective, and in truth he does more to declare and describe the elements of this Fourth Great Awakening than to demonstrate convincingly the commonalities linking the present to the past.

Expressing a view of the ferment of the sixties much like that already discussed, McLoughlin argues that the post-sixties period was marked by a self-doubt and pessimism about the American way that was different from the previous awakenings only in the depth of its assault on the core culture: 'When men become self-conscious and analytical about their most cherished cultural myths, they have ceased to believe in them.' The sharp turn of the counter-culture away from continued faith in 'the self-reliant, morally free, and responsible individual (acting in a special covenant with God), . . . signalled that . . . [a]nother era of cultural distortion had begun' (McLoughlin, 1978: 185). The 'new lights' of this new awakening were more truly 'new', though, starting with the Beat poets and writers of the fifties (Allen Ginsberg, Lawrence Ferlinghetti, Alan Watts, Gary Snyder, and Jack Kerouac), moving through the hippies of the sixties, and on into the oriental philosophies and practices of the seventies. Casting his analytical net widely, McLoughlin sees a common spirit of social reform linking the aspirations of contemporary hippies and Jesus freaks to those of Ralph Waldo Emerson in the Second Great Awakening or the exponents of a Christian socialism in the Third Great Awakening. He argues that in different yet consistent ways, each generation of an awakening simply seeks new ways 'to express the transcendent spirit of the cultural core, to find the universal fraternalism of the primitive Christian church before it became bogged down with doctrines, dogmas, rituals, and institutional restrictions upon the Spirit that moves the world' (McLoughlin, 1978: 211). The religio-cultural legacy of counter-culture is a subtle yet pervasive turn to a new yet somehow age-old vision of a more humane Godhead, greater human possibilities, and more social harmony. But it will take a generation or more for this Fourth Awakening to work itself out, since it must grow with the young (McLoughlin, 1978: 214–16).

In one of several typical passages, McLoughlin (1978: 216) evokes a sense of the anticipated change:

> The beginning of a new belief-value system springing from [a] new respect for life and its mysterious source and continuity is found not only in the current distaste for defoliation weapons, carbon monoxide, insecticides, preservatives, fluorocarbons, detergents, nuclear fission, and toxic dyes but in the concern to preserve whales, dolphins, and other endangered species. It is found in the greater respect for the helpless aged and the battered wife, the oppressed races and the incarcerated prisoner, in respect for the materials of craftsmanship and the patient skill with which the craftsman works. Today's countercultural behavior strives for relationships that are tolerant, soft-spoken, respectful of the feelings and opinions of others; it frowns on the aggressive, defensive, hostile, and possessive attitudes of the cultural past; it likes what men and women have in common as individuals and as groups and finds no 'specially chosen people.' It does not measure success in terms of money, status, or power but in terms of friendship, generosity, and the ability to empathize and give. It is concerned preeminently with the quality of life, not its quantity. In that direction the awakening is moving and changing American life.

There are clearly elements of truth in this vision of cultural change. But from the perspective of the late nineties the picture is more ambiguous. In the first place, it is no longer as clear that these features are truly so new to the culture of North America. Nor, secondly, is it clear that these changes have happened, or to what extent and effect. All we can safely say is that a new air of legitimation arose for religious innovation and lifestyle experimentation, and in that respect the recent rise in new religious activity is in continuity with other times in the American past.[6]

More straightforwardly, J. Gordon Melton (1987) and others (such as Raschke, 1980; Werblowsky, 1982; Ellwood and Partin, 1988), have simply argued that 'the blossoming of the alternative religions in the 1970s is not so much a new event in Western culture as the continuation of the flowering of occult mysticism and Eastern thought that began in the nineteenth century' (Melton, 1987: 47–8). With specific reference to the United States, Melton, Raschke, Ellwood and Partin, and others[7] document the founding and significant spread of Eastern religious groups, for example, the Vedanta Society of Swami Vivekananda amongst native Westerners, since at least the 1890s. By 1900 the Theosophical Society was well established and was educating many Americans about Eastern philosophies and religious principles. The many groups that have splintered off from Theosophy in the twentieth century constitute a vast network of occult bodies heavily influenced by Eastern religions. To these Eastern elements of the not so new 'new religious consciousness' can be added a welter of Spiritualist, New Thought, Swedenborgian, occult, and other psychical research groups that were thriving in North America by the turn of the nineteenth century (Stillson, 1967; Campbell, 1980). And as Melton (1987: 49) comments in passing, 'lest we come away with the notion that this alternative religious community grew among people alienated from the mainstream of American culture, let us take note of the center of the alternative religious community in the 1880s: Boston and its environs.'

Similarly, and somewhat ironically, the virulent attack of the anti-cult movement against the NRMs of today, viewed in historical perspective, indirectly provides further telling evidence that the 'newness' of the NRMs is open to question. In their innovative and playful study 'The Tnevnoc Cult', Bromley and Shupe (1979a: 365) conclude:

> . . . As even a cursory review of American history reveals, virtually every major denomination and religious body was met initially with some degree of skepticism, ostracism or persecution. Indeed, the parallels with contemporary religious groups are striking. Much as the Unification Church, Hare Krishna, Children of God, and People's Temple are currently labelled 'cults,' the Tnevnocs once were pejoratively lumped together with groups such as the Mormons and Masons despite their enormous doctrinal and organizational diversity. The stereotypes and litany of charges levelled against contemporary 'new religions' also are remarkably reminiscent of allegations

against the earlier 'new religions': political subversion, unconditional loyalty of members to authoritarian leaders, brutalizing of members, sexual indiscretions, and possession of mysterious, extraordinary powers. . . . And the atrocity stories told by apostates from earlier groups . . . read much like the lurid tales told by former members of contemporary 'new religions'.

What is the Tnevnoc cult? As some may have guessed, Tnevnoc is 'convent' spelt backwards, and Bromley and Shupe demonstrate that the beliefs and practices of Catholic monasticism were the object of suspicion and persecution by the Protestant majority of nineteenth-century America. Other studies of even greater historical detail have developed similar comparisons with regard, for example, to the treatment of Quakers, Mormons, and other new religions of the past (Swatsky, 1978; Robbins and Anthony, 1979b; Miller, 1979; Kent, 1987; Lewis, 1988).[8]

More recently, however, Melton (1987, 1995), and Stark and Finke (1993), have radically called into question the entire presumption that there has even been an upsurge of new religious activity, rooted in the social discontents of the sixties. Contrary to prevailing opinion, Stark and Finke (1993: 114) declare that 'whether or not there have been cultural crises in recent times, they did not prompt significant religious reactions because the alleged eruptions of cult and sect activity never took place.' Citing some rather limited statistics that Melton has compiled on the number of cult movements founded for each decade between 1950 and 1990, these students of NRMs point to what Melton calls the 'steady pace of the founding of new religions' (Melton, 1995: 270). In other words, they argue for a pattern of 'continuity' and 'stability' (Stark and Finke, 1993) and not sudden change. There is no significant increase in the number of new religions founded in the sixties or seventies over the fifties. Reinforcing this interpretation, Stark and Finke call attention to the evidence available (limited again) that indicates the consistently small size of the new religions in question, whether founded in the fifties, sixties, or seventies.

But if such is the case, how did the misconception of a sudden increase in cult activity arise? Stark and Finke (1993) simply claim that such mistakes are far from uncommon in the history of American religion and then go on to note that the prominence of today's cults on university campuses in combination with the disproportionate cultural impact of the baby-boomer generation may well account for the exaggerated significance attributed to recent groups by scholars. Furthermore, with Melton they stress that the sudden yet quiet repeal of restrictive US immigration policies against Asians in 1965 removed a barrier to the natural development of the various long-established Eastern religious traditions in the West. The influx of gurus in the 1960s and 1970s, that is, did not so much set off a dramatic 'turn East' as simply facilitate the 'normalization' of existing and growing Hindu and Buddhist orientations and organizations. Whether indeed this was the case is difficult to say. For the present we lack reliable data, and the arguments of Melton, Stark, and Finke remain controversial.

New Religious Movements and the History of Religions

In their well-known and popular book *Religious and Spiritual Groups in Modern America*, Ellwood and Partin (1988) try to advance our understanding of contemporary NRMs by placing them in the context of the same esoteric religious traditions discussed by Melton, Werblowsky, and others. They quite justifiably expand the context, however, beyond America to the full history of Western civilization. Somewhat crudely, yet not incorrectly, they point to a long lineage of alternative religious and philosophic groups in the West—such as Pythagoreanism, Neoplatonism, Hermeticism, Gnosticism, Kabbalah, witchcraft, and alchemy—of significant size, diversity, and sometimes considerable social influence, that have persisted in whole or in various partial forms since pre-Christian times. These groups have drawn their beliefs from a variety of ancient and invented Greek, Egyptian, and other Middle Eastern religions and European traditions like the Celts. These 'perennial philosophies' (Huxley, 1970) tend to emphasize the continuity between humanity and the divine or supernatural, as opposed to the strict Christian dualism of God and humanity. In each of us, they believe, there is a 'spark of divinity'. Thus true knowledge of the world comes as much from intuitive or mystical insight into our inner self or consciousness as from conformity to the doctrines or the methods of science. The pursuit of this inner awareness reveals little-known and unexpected human capacities. Contrary to the dominant traditions of Christianity and science, with their stress on the rule of reason over feeling and the methodical discovery of the impersonal and law-like character of the physical universe, these more esoteric traditions envisage a world that is as much a mental as a physical place. It is a world that humanity shares with many other, largely spiritual, forms of intelligent life. In this alternative world-view, the boundary between the realms of spirit and matter are much more porous or blurred. Over the centuries the 'truths' of these other worlds and beings and their relevance to the well-being of humanity and of specific individuals has been revealed by a long lineage of esoteric masters, seers, and prophets whose writings provide the key to self-fulfilment and life beyond death: in modern times Emmanuel Swedenborg, Comte de Saint Germain, Helena Blavatsky, Annie Besant, Georges Ivanovitch Gurdjieff, L. Ron Hubbard, and Elizabeth Clare Prophet, amongst others, come to mind. Many of the ideas attributed to the most ancient of these mystical figures can still be readily found, in whole or in part, in the plethora of 'metaphysical' or 'New Age' NRMs in our midst, such as Rosicrucianism, Eckankar, Scientology, and the Church Universal and Triumphant.[9]

In fact, many of the supposedly Christian new religions (such as the Unification Church, the Church Universal and Triumphant, and the Holy Order of MANS) participate in this alternative tradition by incorporating similar esoteric teachings about Jesus into their doctrines. In this sense the truly 'cult-like' nature of the origins of the Christian church is preserved. But it is also useful to remember that the Christian community was indeed originally a cult, in relation to the dominant Greco-Roman world of the time. To most of his contemporaries, Jesus must have seemed but an uncouth and lowly peasant from a backward and distant part of the Roman Empire (that is, the civilized world), who was bizarrely presumed to be the son of God and future king of the world. His early followers were few in number and socially inconsequential. Some of his teachings, such as the Sermon on the Mount, must have seemed simplistic, and others, such as the doctrines of the incarnation and of the resurrection, dangerously fantastic. It was said that he had risen from the grave and could and would eventually raise others, and his devotees regularly met to eat his 'blood' and 'flesh' in mysterious rituals. For these and other presumed practices, and out of sheer fear of the unknown and different, the early Christians were severely persecuted. But with a moment's true reflection the parallels with the plight of many contemporary cults should be clear (see Atwood and Flowers, 1983).

Finally, it must be duly recognized that the history of Christianity itself is littered with the corpses of thousands of 'new religions'—supposedly heretical variants of the Christian message and community of the most diverse type, longevity, and significance (see, for example, Cohen, 1961). As the American theologian and historian H. Richard Niebuhr (1951) so masterfully shows in *Christ and Culture*, there is no definitive way to discern the truth of, or defend, any one of the many possible alternative readings of the cultural consequences of Christian belief. Each has been supported by different eminent leaders of the church through the centuries, such as Tertullian, Abelard, St Aquinas, St Augustine, and Martin Luther. Christianity can exist, normatively and factually, in all manner and degrees of tension with the rest of society. The differences in people's experiences and interpretations have fuelled endless disputes, schisms, and wars in the past, and continue to do so today. The emergence of new religions, as sects or cults, would appear to be the norm of the human condition and not an oddity.

Concluding Remarks

The social and historical forces influencing what seemed to be a sudden flowering of new religious activity in North America in the closing decades of the millennium are exceedingly complex. The reasons for the emergence of contemporary new religious movements are many—no one factor appears to be crucial. As is now also apparent, the claims of change and of continuity are not essentially incompatible. The new religions of today both continue and change ancient, and not so ancient, traditions of esoteric beliefs, and in response to both the novel circumstances of modern society and the perennial questions about the meaning of life. If space permitted, our scrutiny of the sources of recent religious innovation could be carried further to encompass global patterns of disturbance and transformation (see Wuthnow, 1982, 1985; Robertson, 1985; Beyer, 1994; Dawson, 1998b). Enough has been said, however, to establish a more sociologically informed context for understanding new religious movements and their potential importance as barometers of social change. We will return to these issues in Chapter 6 when we discuss the possible cultural significance of NRMs. First, however, we must get to know more about who does join these new religions.

Chapter Three

Who Joins New Religious Movements and Why?

The Stereotypes

The popular conception of who joins NRMs and why is riddled with stereotypes. Sometimes those who join are thought to be young, idealistic, and gullible people duped by cunning cult recruiters. Sometimes they are maladjusted and marginal losers who have found a safe haven in the controlled life of a cult. Simultaneously it is also often asserted 'that everyone is susceptible to the lure of these master manipulators' (Singer, 1995: 17).[1] In the popular press and the anti-cult literature the three positions are combined in ways that manage to cover all eventualities. The question at hand is, What do we really know about who joins NRMs and why? What is revealed by systematic studies, as opposed to the anecdotal evidence on which the media and anti-cultists rely? Over the last twenty years a fairly reliable body of data has accumulated. This chapter draws together and organizes this material to clarify the micro-structural availability of people to cult involvement. What do we know about how people become *interested* in new religious movements and the *social attributes* of those who choose to join?

The larger question of the macro-structural availability of people to cult involvement (that is, the broad social conditions thought to set the stage for the emergence of NRMs) has already been addressed in the previous chapter. In this chapter no attempt will be made to address directly the specific features of the biographic availability of individuals to conversion.[2] The charge that cults secure and maintain their followers through brainwashing or mind control, along with assessments of the mental health of those involved with NRMs, will be discussed in the next chapter. Indirectly, of course, in examining the micro-structural availability of people to joining NRMs, much will be said that is relevant to a determination of these issues as well, but answering the question at hand is a necessary preliminary step to debating the merits of the charges of brainwashing and exploitation of the weak.

Getting Involved with New Religious Movements

Much that we now know about who joins NRMs, and how and why, stems from attempts to apply and criticize two theories that have exerted a pronounced influence on sociological investigations of NRMs: relative-deprivation theory (Glock, 1964) and the Lofland-Stark model of conversion (Lofland and Stark, 1965). Some knowledge of each theory is essential to an understanding of the social-scientific study of new religions. But more important, if the results of the studies prompted by these theories are analysed, a fairly reliable set of empirical generalizations can be made about how people do tend to become involved with NRMs.

Relative-Deprivation Theory

In line with a broader range of popular conservatism and prejudice about movements of social change, like the civil rights movement or women's liberation movement of the 1960s, early sociological studies of social movements and collective behaviour, such as riots, demonstrations, panics, and so on, often assumed or implied that participants were irrational. Those who joined social movements, particularly radical religious movements, were deemed to be deviant. They were presumed to have been recruited from marginal segments of society or at least from groups experiencing bad times or a decline in their fortunes. Their involvement in acts of collective protest or their choice of unconventional lifestyles was often thought to be the result of some irrational process or even a pathological personality (e.g., Freud, 1921; Adorno et al., 1950; Blumer, 1951; Toch, 1965).

With the sweeping social disruptions of the 1960s, particularly the student-led anti-war movement, these attitudes and interpretations began to change. The university students who marched in the streets, fought with the police, and shut down campuses across the United States did not seem to fit the image that the social scientists had fashioned. Unlike the Communists, Jehovah's Witnesses, or other groups associated with social protests just before and after the Second World War, these proponents of change could not be readily dismissed as mentally disturbed or deficient, nor could it be readily said that they had been deprived of the benefits of American life (Skolnik, 1969). Rather they were the 'children of privilege' (Levitt, 1984). In the end, moreover, the wisdom of many of the changes for which these students and others fought, such as an end to the war in Vietnam, greater civil rights, female equality, sexual liberation, and ecological awareness, was accepted by the majority of Americans. In the face of these developments many sociologists turned away from 'irrationalist' theories of the origins of social movements and collective behaviour to theories of 'relative deprivation' (e.g., Aberle, 1962; Glock, 1964; Gurr, 1970). This theoretical framework largely set the interpretive agenda of the sociology of NRMs from the 1960s well into the 1980s. Since the 1980s, relative-deprivation theory itself has been harshly criticized (see Gurney and Tierney, 1982) and largely displaced by resource-mobilization theory (e.g., McCarthy and Zald, 1977), new-social-movements theory (e.g., Hannigan, 1991; Mauss, 1993), and rational-choice theory, (e.g., Stark and Iannaccone, 1993). But its influence shaped much of the literature on NRMs, and it continues to exert a powerful influence on most popular conceptions of why people join cults (see, for example, Pfeifer, 1992) and on some academic conceptions (e.g., Levine, 1984; Kent, 1987; Deikman, 1990; Stark and Bainbridge, 1987). So let us briefly look at the relative-deprivation approach as developed by Charles Glock (1964), probably the most prominent exponent of the theory in the sociology of religion. Then, after also examining the Lofland-Stark model of conversion, we can specify some of the key empirical generalizations about how people become acquainted and involved with NRMs, generalizations that tend to discount the adequacy of the relative-deprivation explanation of conversion to NRMs.

In addressing the question of why people join various religions in general, sociologists and others have traditionally thought in terms of some complementary set of 'pushes' and 'pulls'. Certain forces or characteristics are commonly thought to push people in certain directions, predisposing them to certain interests or actions. Other forces, such as the beliefs or ideology of a group, are thought to attract people, pulling those with the right predispositions into group membership. In studies of why people joined new religions of a predominantly Christian sectarian type in the nineteenth century and the first half of the twentieth century (for example, Seventh Day Adventists, Jehovah's Witnesses, Pentecostalism), sociologists and historians argued that the primary push was simply economic deprivation. The pull was thought to be the promise of reward in the next life for proper Christian humility (that is, acceptance of one's lowly lot in life), in combination with both the compensatory spiritual legitimation that results from faith in this promise (the belief that 'while we may be poor, we are virtuous') and the more immediate psychic compensation of ecstatic and highly emotional religious experiences. People were seeking an escape from the hardships and humiliations of life. Sociologists and historians reached this conclusion in large measure because the members of these organizations came disproportionately from the lower socio-economic strata of society.

Since the 1960s, however, these views have begun to change with the grow-ing evidence that the socio-economic status of sectarians is rising (e.g., Wil-son, 1961; Calley, 1965) together with the emergence of the new cults of the 1960s, whose participants seem to be drawn from university and col-lege campuses of North America, and not from the poor and abused. As we will see, the successful cults of today seem to 'skim more of the cream of society than the dregs' (Stark and Bainbridge, 1985: 395).

Glock (and others) tried to account for some of these developments by distinguishing between 'absolute' (or real) deprivation and 'relative' depri-vation. Whether people really are deprived or not, it is argued, may not be very important in determining who joins either social or religious move-ments. If people think there is a discrepancy between the social rewards they feel entitled to and the rewards they think they are getting or they believe others are getting, and if they do not accept some rational explanation for their deprivation, then there will be an incentive to launch or join a move-ment that promises change or compensation. The deprivation in question is subjective (though it may also be real), and Glock greatly expands the scope of analysis by proposing that there may be several different forms of this subjective sense of being deprived (1964: 27–8): (1) it may be 'economic deprivation', related to the unequal distribution of income; (2) it may be 'social deprivation', related to the unequal distribution of social status, pres-tige, and the markers of power; (3) it may be 'organismic deprivation', related to the unequal distribution of mental and physical health; (4) it may be 'psychic deprivation', relating to unequal distribution of various kinds of psychic rewards, like love and affection; (5) it may even be 'ethical depriva-tion', related to an individual's feeling that the dominant values of society no longer provide a sufficiently meaningful way to live.[3]

Glock argues that relative deprivation in some form is a 'necessary' con-dition for the rise of NRMs. It explains why even relatively privileged individ-uals would be willing to make sacrifices to join a movement and change their lives. It is not, however, a 'sufficient' condition—it is not enough, by itself, to explain the emergence of an NRM. To bring an NRM into being it is also nec-essary 'that the deprivation be shared, that no alternative institutional arrangements for [the] resolution [of the relative deprivation] are perceived, and that a leadership emerge with an innovating idea for building a move-ment out of the existing deprivation' (Glock, 1964: 29). Nevertheless, a study of the beliefs, practices, and organization of particular groups, Glock implies, should tell us quite a bit about what kinds of deprivations probably motivated people to join the groups in question (Glock, 1964: 33).

There is a common-sense appeal to the relative-deprivation thesis: 'The view that movements of all types arise out of deprivation, however it is defined, is almost universal' (Hine, 1974: 651). Clearly, elements of this view can be detected in Berger's theory of religion and even more explicitly in Stark and Bainbridge's theory. But regrettably, decades of research using this approach have generated a host of theoretical and empirical criticisms, more criticisms than we need to concern ourselves with here. Suffice it to say, scholars have been unable to establish the causal links claimed with sufficient consistency or exactitude. In an excellent review of the literature, Gurney and Tierney (1982: 40) conclude that most applications of the theory 'take as given the very link which must be empirically established to render [relative-deprivation] theory plausible. Their failure to link convincingly psychological states with antecedent societal conditions on the one hand and with subsequent movement participation on the other hand is the Achilles heel of [relative-deprivation] research.' Even if the necessary causal links were isolated, however, a more fundamental theoretical objection remains: we can never be certain whether there are not just as many non-participants as participants in social and religious movements that are experiencing some kind of relative deprivation (see Gurney and Tierney, 1982: 38; Stark and Bainbridge, 1985: 308). In fact, there is the possibility of 'greater variation in [relative-deprivation] levels among participants than between participants and nonparticipants.' So the evidence that many converts to NRMs may have experienced some type of relative deprivation does not give us any very specific information about why these particular movements arose. It does not allow us to discriminate effectively between joiners and non-joiners, and hence the concept of relative deprivation loses its explanatory value. Contrary to Glock's assertion, in other words, it cannot even be said with confidence that the experience of relative deprivation is a 'necessary' condition for joining an NRM.

Wilson (1990: 195) drives the point home with a few adroit questions: 'Why . . . do some people not feel deprived when by all objective criteria, they are deprived, and why, even of those who feel deprived, do only a proportion become absorbed by religious groups? Do none of the undeprived become religious?' Picking up on the last point, Hine (1974: 654) observes scathingly, 'In refining the concept of deprivation, [researchers] seem at times to be going out of their way to avoid the possibility of positive motivation!' Theoretically, that is, the search for some explanatory form of relative deprivation to account for every unconventional religious choice smacks of reductionism, and the approach comes dangerously close to being self-fulfilling and irrefutable (that is, non-scientific).[4]

Even our peripheral examination of the many different typologies of cults revealed the variety of NRMs in existence. There are pronounced differences in their beliefs, practices, organizations, and patterns of commitment. As cautioned, it is folly to try to account for the many different motivations that may exist for joining different kinds of groups on the basis of one highly generalized theory like the theory of relative deprivation. Matters are more complex, and the diverse claims of the religious themselves warrant more consideration.

Faced with these and other problems, many students of social and religious movements shifted their focus to the more empirically manageable question of how such movements operate, succeed, and fail. From such a vantage 'resource-mobilization theory' (e.g., McCarthy and Zald, 1977) displaced relative-deprivation theory as the primary focus of research. Assuming that some discontent is a constant of everyone's lives, the question became what organizational factors were associated with the expression of certain discontents as social movements of some significance. The answer to this question hinged on how effective leadership, money, public support, political influence, and media relations were acquired, mobilized, and controlled by a group (e.g., Richardson, Stewart, and Simmonds, 1979). But here our focus is on what we know about who joins NRMs and why. To that end it is time to turn to a consideration of the Lofland-Stark model of conversion. Derived independently of relative-deprivation theory, this model nevertheless has a similar orientation in some of its elements. It adopts a more multi-factorial and processual approach, however, and has played a crucial role in generating additional and more reliable insights into the factors influencing the choice to join an NRM.

The Lofland-Stark Model of Conversion

This model of religious conversion grew out of field research into what was then a small and obscure deviant religion, newly imported to the United States from Korea. Dubbed the 'Divine Precepts' by Lofland and Stark, the group in question was in fact the early Unification Church (that is, the Moonies) in the United States. Gathering the accounts of converts to this cult and observing the many other attempts made to recruit others, Lofland and Stark formulated a seven-step model of the process of conversion to this group. More specifically, they charted the seven factors they thought must come into play in order to transform a potential recruit into a 'verbal convert' first and then eventually a 'total convert'. Verbal converts are 'followers who [profess] belief and [are] accepted by core members [of the group] as sincere, but [who take] no active role in the [movement].' Total converts are those 'who [exhibit] their commitment through deeds as well as words.' It is only with the onset of the last stage of the seven-step conversion process, Lofland and Stark assert, that a verbal convert becomes a total or true convert (1965: 864).

Briefly, the Lofland and Stark model stipulates that for persons to convert to a cult they must (1) experience enduring, acutely felt tensions in their lives, (2) within a religious problem-solving perspective (as opposed to a psychiatric or political problem-solving perspective), (3) which leads them to think of themselves as a religious seeker. With these three 'predisposing conditions' in place, the individuals must then (4) encounter the cult to which they convert at a turning point in their lives, (5) form an affective bond with one or more members of the cult, (6) reduce or eliminate extra-cult attachments, and (7) be exposed to intensive interaction with other converts. With the completion of the latter four 'situational contingencies', the new convert can become a 'deployable agent' of the cult. It is the cumulative effect of all of these experiences, Lofland and Stark believed, that produces a true conversion. Each step is necessary, but only the whole process is sufficient to produce a true conversion.

Over the years this model has been tested repeatedly, in different contexts, with mixed results (e.g., Seggar and Kunz, 1972; Austin, 1977; Heirich, 1977; Richardson and Stewart, 1977; Snow and Phillips, 1980; Bankston et al., 1981; Greil and Rudy, 1984; Singer, 1988; Knox et al., 1991). In the study of a quite large NRM imported to America from Japan, Nichiren Shoshu (also known by the name of its lay organization, Sōka Gakkai), Snow and Phillips (1980) found reason to be conceptually and empirically suspicious of the applicability of all but two of the seven steps of the Lofland-Stark model of conversion. Greil and Rudy (1984), to cite another example, arrived at a similar conclusion after scrutinizing the data on conversion available from ten case studies of widely divergent NRMs. On the other hand, Merrill Singer (1988) and to some extent Knox et al. (1991) found almost all aspects of the model to be relevant to the study of the Black Hebrew Nation and of Dutch adolescents who had converted to either the Unification Church or the Pentecostal Church. The debate over the merits of the theory has become complex. For instance, as a result of their research into Nichiren Shoshu in America, Snow and Phillips (1980) are quite dismissive of two aspects of Lofland and Stark's model. They reject the claims that potential converts must experience enduring and acutely felt tensions and some turning point in their lives (such as failing at school, experiencing a divorce, taking a long trip). In a study of the same NRM in Britain, however, Wilson and Dobbelaere (1994) found that many members at least say that they experienced chronic or acute crises in their lives and a turning point. This disparity in findings can be explained in many ways. But these kinds of divergent results suggest, as Knox et al. (1991) propose, that the steps outlined by Lofland and Stark do not represent so much an integrated and cumulative model of the actual process of conversion as a fairly adequate statement of some of the crucial 'conditions' of conversion (with the understanding that these conditions may vary independently and that their significance may vary for different religions and in different circumstances).

Although many scholars have clearly overgeneralized the relevance of the Lofland and Stark model, the research inspired by their model has consistently confirmed some of these 'conditions' and led to the formulation of some systematic reasons for why they may vary. Those empirical and theoretical insights constitute the body of what we can say confidently about why people become involved with NRMs.

Seven Empirical Insights

In order, roughly, of the degree of empirical support (that is, research consensus) that exists for them, the micro-structural availability of people to cult involvements is conditioned by the following seven generalizations.

In the first place, studies of conversion and case studies of specific groups have found that recruitment to NRMs happens primarily through pre-existing social networks and interpersonal bonds. Friends recruit friends, family members each other, and neighbours recruit neighbours. Contrary to public belief and the assertions of many proponents of the 'brainwashing' theory of cult conversion, the figures available support neither the proposition that everyone is equally susceptible to recruitment nor that most converts are recruited through individual and single contacts in public places. Groups like the Unification Church, Krishna Consciousness, and Children of God (to name but a few) have been condemned for their aggressive and persistent forays into public places to proselytize and disseminate literature. Yet the evidence strongly indicates that these recruitment drives are not very successful, that in fact in some regards they are dismal failures in relation to the effort invested in them (with regard to the Moonies, see the figures in Barker, 1984: 141–8, and Galanter, 1989: 140–1). Rather, the majority of recruits to the majority of NRMs come into contact with the groups they join because they know one or more members of the movement (e.g., Harrison, 1974; Beckford, 1975; Lofland, 1977; Bainbridge, 1978; Snow et al., 1980; Stark and Bainbridge, 1985; Rochford, 1985; Latkin et al., 1987; Palmer, 1994; Lucas, 1995).

The results of a recent and quite comprehensive study of Nichiren Shoshu (Sōka Gakkai) in Great Britain are characteristic:

> Only 6 per cent of those in our sample had encountered [the Nichiren Shoshu] through the impersonal agencies of the media—through exhibitions, concerts, the movement's own publicity, or the various media

accounts of the organization which had appeared in Britain. Ninety-four per cent met the movement through social interaction. Friends represented the largest category of people who introduced members, amounting to some 42 per cent; 23 per cent were brought into contact with it through their partners or family members. The remainder were first presented with information by acquaintances, work or student colleagues most particularly, but 14 per cent owed the encounter to casual acquaintances. (Wilson and Dobbelaere, 1994: 50)

Even the anti-cultist Margaret Singer supports the proposition that most converts are recruited through social networks (Singer, 1995: 105). She cites a figure of 66 per cent, but like much of the anti-cult literature, she does not give any reliable information about her sources. Nor does she seem to detect any inconsistency between this claim and another made on the same page, namely, that 'all of us are vulnerable to cult recruitment.'

In the study of NRMs, however, as stressed in the Introduction, there are exceptions to every rule. Barker (1984: 95–100) denies that existing personal networks account for the majority of converts to the Moonies in Britain. But her claim is somewhat ambiguous since she notes that networks do account for over a quarter of the British membership and for a third of the membership in the rest of Europe. Moreover, she does not clearly explain how the majority of members *are* recruited. By implication it would appear that she has in mind chance encounters between recruiters and individuals in the streets. Some efforts that have been made to account for these kinds of discrepancies will be discussed.

Second, as some of even the harshest critics of the Lofland-Stark model reaffirm, Lofland and Stark were correct in specifying the importance of affective ties with members of an NRM in the recruitment of new members (e.g., Snow and Phillips, 1980; Greil and Rudy, 1984; Stark and Bainbridge, 1985; Knox et al., 1991). Again, Wilson and Dobbelaere's findings with regard to the Nichiren Shoshu in Britain are typical: over a third of the respondents in their study stressed 'the quality of the membership' as the primary reason for their initial attraction to the group. Wilson and Dobbelaere provide numerous quotations from their questionnaires and interviews full of praise for the vibrancy, warmth, openness, joy, and positive outlook of the members first encountered by the respondent. In general, case studies of people who joined NRMs or of the groups themselves commonly reveal the crucial role of affective bonds with specific members in leading recruits into deeper involvement (e.g., Harrison, 1974; Enroth, 1977; Lofland, 1977; Bainbridge, 1978; Galanter et al., 1979; Richardson,

Stewart, and Simmonds, 1979; Levine, 1984; Barker, 1984; Rochford, 1985; Van Zandt, 1991; Palmer, 1994).

Third, and equally strongly, from the same studies it is clear that the intensive interaction of recruits with the other members of the group is pivotal to the successful conversion and maintenance of new members. A good example is found in 'Waiting for the Ships', Robert Balch's (1995a) last academic paper on the Bo and Peep UFO cult before it was catapulted from obscurity into the international spotlight under its new name, Heaven's Gate. In this paper Balch describes how the leaders systematically reversed the rapid disintegration of their fledgling group, some twenty years earlier, by introducing an elaborate schedule of daily routines designed, in part, to promote the regular and intensive interaction of all members of the group. Conversely, the apparent loss of such intensive interaction is often decisive in the deconversion or apostasy of members of NRMs (Jacobs, 1989). On these three points there is little disagreement in the literature. Other findings, however, are subject to greater variation and dispute, even though they are often applicable to specific groups and situations.

Fourth, cult involvement seems to be strongly correlated with having fewer and weaker extra-cult social ties (e.g., Lofland, 1977; Downton, 1979; Stark and Bainbridge, 1985, 1987; Balch, 1995a; Bader and Demaris, 1969). Part of the reason for the disproportionate representation of adolescents and young adults in NRMs is simply that this segment of the population is relatively free of other social and economic commitments. They have the time and the opportunity to indulge their spiritual appetites and to experiment with alternative ways of living. The more freedom one has in that regard, the more likely one is to accept the 'invitation' of a cult recruiter to dinner, a lecture, or a meditation session (see Snow et al., 1980). This also helps to explain the popular image of cults preying on the lonely. Students who are away from home to attend university or are 'on the road' are more susceptible to cult recruitment. But the condition of being temporarily unattached is not the cause of being recruited. Although the experience of intense loneliness is pervasive amongst self-conscious young adults, most individuals who join an NRM do not do so simply out of loneliness (a most direct form of relative deprivation). Their being alone—that is, their lack of social attachments—is due largely to the transitional and unencumbered status that our society tends to accord to its youth, and as such it is merely an aspect of the increased structural availability of this segment of the population. In their more elaborate deductive systematization of their theory of religion, Stark and Bainbridge (1987) develop this point, arguing in general that people with relatively 'low stakes in conformity' (that is, attachments, investments, involvements, and beliefs) are more likely to join NRMs that are in high tension with society. This is quite simply because these people are likely 'to incur minimal costs by deviating, and may, in turn, have much to gain from it' (1987: 190–1). Bader and Demaris (1996) have independently confirmed this claim, demonstrating statistically that low stakes in conformity increase the likelihood of membership in cults and sects.

Evidence from Barker's analysis of a large sample of participants in Unification Church recruitment workshops suggests that 'non-joiners' are actually more likely than 'joiners' to be in a transitional state in life (for example, unemployed, travelling) (1984: 199). This is a point to which we will return in Chapter 4. But this information only appears to be in conflict with the reasoning of Stark and Bainbridge. With regard to the growth and success of NRMs, everything is a matter of degree and balance. As Stark and Bainbridge (1987: 225–8) further specify, empirical studies suggest that too low an investment in conformity can lead to a condition of 'chronic seekership' that prevents certain people from forming lasting bonds with any religious group. Structurally, those most likely to convert to an NRM will have relatively few extra-cult social ties, but they will not be complete loners. Otherwise, it would also be difficult to explain why empirical studies of recruitment to NRMs have shown so strongly that cults secure most of their new members through pre-existing social networks. As we will see in Chapter 5, if for various reasons an NRM becomes almost totally isolated from outside social networks, like the Peoples Temple at Jonestown, Guyana, it is likely to become too extreme in form and be in danger of becoming violent or of failing.

Fifth and similarly, then, cult involvement seems to be strongly correlated with having fewer and weaker ideological alignments. Most researchers now discount Lofland and Stark's suggestion that converts to NRMs were probably pre-socialized to adopt a religious problem-solving perspective. In fact, the data actually suggest that the 'unchurched', as Stark and Bainbridge (1985) call them, are more likely to join. In many cases, lack of prior religious education and family life seems to leave young people more open to alternative spiritual explanations of the world and its hardships (Snow and Phillips, 1980; Stark and Bainbridge, 1985). More will be said about this in the discussion of the social attributes of converts to NRMs in the next section of this chapter.

Again, however, there are clear exceptions to this generalization. As Richardson and Stewart (1977) suggest, for instance, in the case of many neo-Christian movements (such as the Unification Church) and Jesus movements we may be dealing with the phenomenon of 'returning fundamentalists'. Recruits to these groups often do seem to have been raised in strict religious households from which they lapsed or rebelled as adolescents (see also Tipton, 1982a). Similarly, it would seem that recruits to the Catholic Charismatic Renewal and its offshoots are overwhelmingly from Catholic backgrounds (Neitz, 1987).

Sixth, while 'seekership'—the active search for religious answers to one's problems—does not seem to be as necessary to all conversions to NRMs as Lofland and Stark thought, it does precede many such conversions (e.g., Straus, 1976; Balch, 1980, 1995a; Bromley and Shupe, 1986; Poling and Kenny, 1986; Kilbourne and Richardson, 1989; Puttick, 1997). People inclined to be interested in even the possibility of joining an NRM have been reading related religious and philosophical literature and giving some serious thought to the 'big questions' in life (What is the meaning of life? Is there a God? Is there life after death?). This does not necessarily mean that the converts in question have fully adopted a 'religious problem-solving perspective'. But similar findings are reported in Rochford's study of Krishna Consciousness (1985: 54), Wilson and Dobbelaere's study of Sōka Gakkai (1994: 88), Jones's study of the Church Universal and Triumphant (1994: 49–50), and Balch's study of the early followers of Bo and Peep, or Heaven's Gate (1995a: 147–8): at the time of their conversion to the NRM a little fewer than half of the members were either actively practising a religion other than that in which they were raised or had previously been members of another non-traditional religious group. Here again, though, Barker found aspects of seekership to be far more prevalent amongst the 'non-joiners' in her sample of people participating in Unification Church workshops than amongst 'joiners' (Barker, 1984: 199), and in their detailed survey of the members of ten Eastern meditational groups in North America, Gussner and Berkowitz (1988) found little evidence of any notable period of seekership.

Seventh and lastly, as Stark and Bainbridge (1985, 1987) stress in their theory of religion, we should be careful when trying to account for the conditions of conversion not to neglect the obvious. Whether one wishes to postulate a degree or kind of relative deprivation to explain why any individual joins an NRM, it should be recognized that such groups provide many kinds of direct rewards or 'specific compensators' to their members. They commonly offer such positive inducements as affection and heightened self-esteem, esoteric and exoteric knowledge that provides a sense of power and control over one's life, as well as simple material and social aid, security, new career opportunities, and prestige. Sometimes, in fact, the rewards of participating in the new reality constructed by the group may become more important than satisfying 'the ends such participation was originally intended to procure' (Wallis, 1984: 122).

The degree to which any or all of these factors are involved in recruitment to any particular NRM can vary. As Snow and Phillips (1980), Snow et al. (1980), and Stark and Bainbridge (1987) have demonstrated, the degree to which successful recruitment requires that potential converts have weak extra-cult ties or ideological alignments depends on how deviant and particularistic the group is and the extent of the commitment demanded by the group. If joining an NRM does not entail a dramatic transformation of one's values and lifestyle, as in the case of Scientology, there is less need to sever extra-cult bonds to effect a conversion. On the other hand, if there is a pronounced difference between the orientation and activities of the new religion and the family and friends of the recruit, as is usually the case with Krishna Consciousness, then the weakening of prior ties is more crucial to the conversion process. Similarly, for groups stigmatized by the dominant society because of the peculiar or revolutionary character of their worldview, a strategy of isolation may be used to neutralize that stigma. The use of this strategy may also depend on the extent to which a group insists that it has the exclusive path to truth and salvation. The more particularistic a religion is, the more it will demand a sharp separation from the world and from the convert's past social and ideological attachments. Finally, the more complete the commitment demanded by a group, the more likely it is that new members will be recruited through contact in public places rather than through interpersonal bonds and social networks. This latter linkage may explain Barker's findings for recruitment to the Unification Church in Britain, findings that seem to be at odds with the strong role of social networks in recruitment detected in most other studies of NRMs.

A similar correlation has been found between seekership and the degree to which an NRM is stigmatized by society (Greil and Rudy, 1984). Seekership is far more likely to be relevant in conversion to seemingly 'deviant' religious groups than to others. For groups like the Moonies and Krishna Consciousness, personal ties with the 'outside world' are minimized, hence it is less likely that individuals will find and join these groups 'unless they have defined themselves as being "in the market" for conversion' (1984: 317).

Various combinations of these factors limit who is structurally available to join NRMs. But, judging from the small number of people who do join such groups, those factors are not sufficient in themselves to predict who will join an NRM. It is therefore necessary to see these social factors against a backdrop of yet more contingent and situational factors. For example, recruitment can be influenced by the degree and type of hostility to NRMs in the dominant culture, the presence or absence of missionaries, and the presence of competitor groups (Stark and Bainbridge, 1985, 1987). It

makes a world of difference whether an NRM arises in the relaxed and experimental atmosphere of modern California or the highly conformist social
and religious environment of Ireland or Iran. Contrasting Japan and the
United States, Wilson (1982b: 24) points out that we must be careful not
to assume even that new religions fulfil the same functions in different cultural and historical circumstances (see also Werblowsky, 1982). To the convert it often seems miraculous that a representative of a particular new religion happens to be at hand at the crucial moment of doubt or decision in
their lives. If other similar kinds of groups, competitor religions, or functional equivalents to religion (such as a cathartic encounter therapy group,
a revolutionary political movement, or an idealistic social service organization) were present instead, the conversion in question might never happen
(see Levine, 1984).

A further possibility is that 'in some measure, movements may *awaken*
needs in particular individuals, giving them increased specificity in the
terms of the movement's own ideology, and so defining the situation for
prospective adherents, supplying both the sense of needs and the means of
its fulfilment' (Wilson, 1982b: 25). New religions, like many new commercial enterprises, are in the business of 'consciousness raising' about needs
and how they can be satisfied. But in any event, this still means we 'need to
know why people should accept the proposed definition of their situation
and the proffered solutions' (Wilson, 1982b: 25). In other words, this valuable insight merely reconfigures the problem of explaining conversions.[5]

Of course, in the attempt to explain any and all conversions much also
hinges on factors of biographic availability, that is, individual psychology
and personal circumstances. To speculate about the states of mind of other
people, however, is to enter treacherous territory (Dawson, 1994b), and we
simply lack sufficient insight and generalizable data about the personal lives
of enough converts to NRMs.[6] In Chapter 4 I will summarize what little we
do reliably know about the psychological condition of converts to NRMs.
Here we can still say more, however, about the social attributes of those
who join; the picture that emerges is contrary indeed to the popular stereotypes.

The Social Attributes of Those Who Join

It is difficult to specify a reliable social profile of typical converts to cults.
Two things are clear from the numerous studies: (1) because of the different
recruitment methods of different cults, each new religion tends to attract a
rather homogeneous group of followers; (2) the *overall* membership of NRMs
is much more heterogeneous than commonly expected, since each group

tends to attract somewhat different kinds of followers (e.g., Latkin, 1987; Poling and Kenny, 1986; Palmer, 1994). Nevertheless, it is still possible to make some broad generalizations.

First, the members of most NRMs are disproportionately young. Barker (1984: 206) found that 50 per cent of the members of the Unification Church in Britain were between 21 and 26 years of age. The average age at which people joined the movement was 23 (pp. 199, 206). Rochford (1985: 47) reported that 56 per cent of the members of Krishna Consciousness were between 20 and 25 and that more than half had joined before their twenty-first birthday (see also Judah, 1974). More recently, Wilson and Dobbelaere (1994) found that while the members of Nichiren Shoshu in Britain were also young, they were not as young as those who join the Unification Church or Krishna Consciousness. Their extensive survey revealed that 68.2 per cent of the members were under the age of 34 and that 88.4 per cent were under 44. With rare exceptions, the new religions of today are a game for young people and, in relation to the population, middle-aged and old people are markedly under-represented.

As some of the NRMs of the 1960s have aged, of course, these figures have changed (e.g., Palmer, 1994: 39; Barker, 1995b: 168–9). For example, the first generation of converts to Krishna Consciousness, the Unification Church, and the Family (formerly the Children of God) are now in their late thirties and early forties. But many people drop out of these organizations when they reach middle age or before, since they often cannot meet their more mature needs. This is especially true of NRMs that are more communal and more exclusive in their commitments, for the demands and desires that accompany family life and the raising of children are often in conflict with the continuing obligations of membership in these groups. There is some reason to believe that the new religions that are less exclusive and extreme in their commitment expectations, like Scientology, Eckankar, Nichiren Shoshu, and so on, will maintain a better spread in the age distribution of their members as the groups grow older. For example, on the basis of an admittedly small sample, Wallis (1977) found that the average age of recruitment to Scientology in Britain was about 32; similarly, Wilson and Dobbelaere (1994) report a mean age for starting the practice of Nichiren Shoshu of 31, and Latkin et al. (1987), Carter (1990), and Palmer (1994) place the average age of followers of Bhagwan Shree Rajneesh in the mid-thirties. In another instance, the Church Universal and Triumphant seems to be aging along with its leaders: approximately 53 per cent of the members are between 40 and 60 (Jones, 1994: 42). In the popular press there was some surprise expressed at the more mature age of the membership of the Solar Temple and Heaven's Gate groups. Palmer (1996: 305) says that the Solar Temple 'seemed to attract a clientele of predominantly middle-aged, prosperous and highly cultured professionals'. In line with popular expectations, the first news reports of the Heaven's Gate tragedy stated that thirty-nine identically dressed young men had taken their lives. Yet soon it became clear that twenty of the thirty-nine were actually women, and the ages of the dead ranged from 24 to 72. The majority were certainly middle-aged, and many had been with this new religion for over a decade. Similar observations about older ages than expected have also been made with regard to the Church of Satan (Alfred, 1976), est (Babbie and Stone, 1977), and many Eastern meditational groups (Gussner and Berkowitz, 1988: 154).

Second, with few exceptions studies have found that recruits to NRMs are on average markedly better educated than the general public. Wallis (1977: 163) reports that in his admittedly rather small sample, 56.7 per cent of the Scientologists had either professional training or college or university degrees (29.7 per cent were university graduates). Likewise, Wilson and Dobbelaere (1994: 121–4) found that 24 per cent of their large sample of the membership of Sōka Gakkai in Britain had attended university, whereas in 1990 only 8 per cent of the population had a university education. In the United States, Jones (1994: 43–4) actually found that one-quarter of her respondents from the Church Universal and Triumphant had an advanced technical or professional degree, for example, M.B.A., M.S.W., M.D., or Ph.D. Latkin et al. (1987) report that 64 per cent of the members of Rajneeshpuram in Oregon had at least a college degree, and a further random sample of 100 members uncovered 24 per cent with a master's degree and 12 per cent with a doctorate. In surveying the membership of ten American religious meditational groups, Gussner and Berkowitz (1988: 154) found that a striking 79 per cent had completed four or more years of college, 28.6 per cent had master's degrees, 10.3 per cent professional degrees, and 8.0 per cent Ph.Ds. Even Rochford (1985: 48–50) discovered that 65 per cent of his sample of very young American devotees of Krishna had at least one year of college. Barker (1984: 197–8) cites comparable findings for the Moonies in Britain, as Stark and Bainbridge (1985: 406–10) do for other American groups. In fact, in their study of over 12,000 subjects, Bader and Demaris (1996) discovered that each year of educational attainment increased the likelihood of cult membership and decreased the likelihood of sect and church membership.

Why do NRMs tend to attract the well-educated? Wilson and Dobbelaere (1994) and others (e.g., Stark and Bainbridge, 1985) suggest the answer is fairly obvious: 'To be properly understood, the teachings [of most NRMs] demand literate intelligence, a willingness to study, and lack of fear in the face of unfamiliar concepts and language' (Wilson and Dobbelaere, 1994: 123).

Third, and not surprising given the educational levels, recruits to NRMs are also disproportionately from middle- to upper-middle-class households, the advantaged segments of the population. The findings are similar for Scientology (Wallis, 1977), the Unification Church (Barker, 1984: 198, 206–8), the International Society for Krishna Consciousness (Judah, 1974; Rochford, 1985; Poling and Kenny, 1986; Palmer, 1994), Rajneesh (Latkin et al., 1987; Carter, 1990; Palmer, 1994), other Asian-based meditational groups (Gussner and Berkowitz, 1988), and the Church Universal and Triumphant (Jones, 1994). The fathers of converts come primarily from the professional, business-executive, or administrative segments of the occupational world; skilled or unskilled manual labourers are clearly under-represented.

Fourth, on questions of sex there seems to be some dispute. Machalek and Snow (1993) suggest there is an over-representation of women in NRMs. At some points, Stark and Bainbridge (1985: 413–17) do as well. But the evidence, as Stark and Bainbridge themselves admit, is highly variable. In the past, women were disproportionately present in fringe religions: for example, Christian Science in the 1920s was 75 per cent female (Stark and Bainbridge, 1985: 413), and Wilson and Dobbelaere (1994: 42–3) found about 59 per cent of the Sōka Gakkai movement in Britain to be female. Latkin et al. (1987) and Palmer (1994) also report a disproportionate number of women in the Rajneesh movement. Barker (1984: 206), however, reports a two-to-one ratio in favour of men for the Moonies in Britain, and Wallis's (1977: 165) sample of Scientologists is 59 per cent male. Rochford (1985), Lucas (1995), and others imply that there is little substantial discrepancy between the sexes in the groups they studied. On the whole, it would seem that while some cults may attract more of one sex than the other, there is no strong evidence that women are any more susceptible to joining NRMs than men (see Palmer, 1994).

It does appear, though, that many groups undergo a kind of developmental shift in their sex ratios as they mature. Krishna Consciousness began life in America as a largely male phenomenon, but this imbalance in sexual representation has been corrected as the movement has aged and become an order of 'householders' and not strictly priestly ascetics (Palmer, 1994: 32). In Korea and Japan, before its emergence in America, the Unification Church actually appealed more to women, as did the Rajneesh movement in its beginnings in India (Palmer, 1994: 62, 90). These imbalances also adjusted with time. Reliable membership figures, though, especially ones that differentiate between the sexes, are hard to come by.

Fifth and last, what about the religious background of recruits to NRMs? Here there is ambiguity as well. On the one hand, with the limited evidence available, Stark and Bainbridge (1985: 400) conclude: 'Church membership and membership in a conservative denomination are preventives against cultism. The unchurched and those affiliated with the more secularized denominations are more open to cult involvement.' The level of participation in NRMs of American Protestants, Catholics, and Jews varies from group to group. On the whole, though, Stark and Bainbridge think that Protestants are under-represented, reflecting the strength of right-wing evangelicalism in the United States, whereas the participation of Catholics is roughly proportionate to their numbers in the population. Jews are another matter. They are extraordinarily over-represented. Latkin et al. (1987), for example, found the following distribution in religious backgrounds for members of Rajneeshpuram: 30 per cent Protestant, 27 per cent Catholic, 20 per cent Jewish, 14 per cent 'none', 4 per cent Hindu or Buddhist, and 4 per cent 'other'. Even more startling was Tipton's (1982a) finding that 50 per cent of the members of the San Francisco Zen Center were Jewish. Why the over-representation? Stark and Bainbridge (1985: 402–3) point to the many indicators of the heightened secularization of the American Jewish community, compared to other religious groups. Support for this stress on the relatively 'unchurched' character of converts to NRMs comes from the British followers of Nichiren Shoshu Buddhism: 'Fully 76 per cent of the respondents said that they had not belonged to any religious organization before they joined' (Wilson and Dobbelaere, 1994: 79). In fact, 47 per cent declared that previously they had not been religious at all, leading Wilson and Dobbelaere to call into question the contention that religious 'seekership' is a necessary precondition for conversion to NRMs (p. 88). Latkin et al. (1987) report that only 40 per cent of the members of Rajneeshpuram saw themselves as religious before joining, and a survey of the Church Universal and Triumphant revealed a slight over-representation of religious 'nones' (13.67 per cent). But in the latter instance, seekership would seem to be a significant factor since 49 per cent of the sample reported one or more previous associations with other non-traditional religions after childhood, such as Rosicrucians, Theosophy, and various Hindu and Buddhist groups (Jones, 1994: 49–50). Of course, to interpret the real meaning of these data, we would need more information about the kinds of associations to which the respondents had belonged.

On the other hand, Rochford (1985: 51–7) found that the American followers of Krishna came from fairly religious households. More than 50 per cent of his sample said religion was stressed in their childhood homes, 77 per cent had received formal religious education as children, about 50 per cent had attended religious services regularly, and another 30 per cent had attended irregularly. Likewise, Barker detected a strong correlation between high levels of church attendance and a general emphasis upon religious beliefs and values in childhood and joining the Unification Church (Barker, 1984: 212–13). Like the British members of Nichiren Shoshu, at the time of conversion most of Rochford's and Barker's respondents had lapsed in the practice of their childhood faith (Barker, 1984: 217) and only 25 per cent of Rochford's sample were practising some other religion. But the contrast with Stark and Bainbridge's conclusion remains pronounced.

Some Reasons for Joining

We cannot claim to know definitely why people join these organizations. But in *The Making of a Moonie,* Eileen Barker suggests a profile of the typical convert to the Unification Church in Britain (Barker, 1984: 210–16, 221). She states that Moonies she came to know often seemed idealistic people from fairly happy, conventional, and highly 'respectable' families that placed a higher value on public service and duty than on simply making money. They had grown up in sheltered environments, in which they were encouraged and rewarded for being over-achievers at school and in other activities, but seem to have had their emotional development retarded so that they failed to experience the usual crises of adolescence until later in life than most of their peers. Consequently, it seems that many of them experienced 'disappointments, hurt and disillusionment' when they 'first ventured out into the world'. They may have found the transition to life at university or on the job and away from home more difficult than expected. The implication is that they may have joined the Unification Church to re-establish themselves at least temporarily in more satisfying circumstances (that is, in a more structured and idealistic environment).[7] Her comments call to mind the speculations discussed in Chapter 2 about the search for surrogate families and ways of coping with the loss of mediating structures in society.

The psychiatrist Saul Levine (1984), who interviewed and observed hundreds of young members of various NRMs, presents a similar profile. He insists that he found 'no more sign of pathology among [the members and ex-members of NRMs that he studied] than . . . in any youthful population.' He also notes that the joiners he met were largely children of privilege; they were 'good kids from good backgrounds' (1984: 4). Yet they engaged in the kind of 'radical departures', as he calls them, that are highly disturbing to their families and friends. These radical departures are extraordinary, but seen from the right perspective, he argues, they make sense. 'They are desperate attempts to grow up in a society that places obstacles in the way of the normal yearnings of youth' (1984: 11). The young people who join NRMs, he believes, are distinguished by their curious inability to effect the kind of separation from their families consonant with passage into young adulthood (see 1984: 31–8, 46–7, 61). They are psychological 'children' trapped in a predicament that our fragmented and indulgent society may have induced. They wish to sever the parental bond and achieve independence, but they lack a sufficient sense of self to do so. On the one hand, the prospect of relinquishing the overly close tie they do have, in 'reality or fantasy', with their mothers and fathers is terrifying; it instils a great fear of personal 'depletion'. On the other hand, the self they display, whether seemingly normal or rebellious, feels 'fraudulent'. Such young people feel trapped: they can live neither with nor without their parents. All the while, though, as the children mature, their parents' foibles are becoming apparent, turning them into 'fallen idols'.

It is symptomatic, Levine says, that joiners have usually not experienced any mature romantic relationships and that they lack the kind of intimate peer relationships in which teenagers 'probe, analyze, confess, explore, and lay bare their very souls to one another' (1984: 35). But the social supports their parents had been able to call upon on in their youth for guidance—churches, ethnic communities, patriotic activities, and a liberal arts education—have either disappeared or now appear 'plastic' and unreal. Enduring this kind of acutely felt tension, these young people yearn for a quick cure for their sense of isolation and confusion (Lofland and Stark, 1965). They seek a sense of full belonging and purpose in life, independent of their families, but without engaging in the struggle to achieve true 'mutual understanding' between individuals or the serious 'analysis' of their situation required to find and shape their own identity. With so little real self-esteem, they are seeking to avoid, for a time at least, the responsibility of making choices. Then at a moment of crisis, a 'turning point', in Lofland and Stark's terminology (1965), they encounter the missionaries of one or another NRM offering just such an alternative path to (or temporary detour from) maturity.

If there is some plausibility to Levine's theory, then in the end, the radical departure in question is in some respects not a departure at all (Barker, 1984: 210–11). Moonies, for instance, 'do not appear to be rejecting the values that were instilled into them during their childhood; they appear, on the contrary, to have imbibed these so successfully that they are prepared to respond to the opportunity (which society does not seem to be offering them) to live according to those very standards.' Similar conclusions have been drawn concerning the Moonies (Parsons, 1986; Palmer, 1994: 92,

100). The pattern may well vary for other NRMs, but Palmer found elements of it in each of the seven NRMs she studied, and her findings are reminiscent of the views Tipton expresses in *Getting Saved from the Sixties* (1982: Chap. 2). This perspective certainly accords with the consistent finding that most of the people who join NRMs leave voluntarily within about two years (Barker, 1984; Levine, 1984; Stark and Bainbridge, 1985; Wright, 1987; Jacobs, 1989; Galanter, 1989; Palmer, 1994). It is less helpful for understanding those groups that attract older followers to begin with and are less exclusive in their demands for commitment and less communal in organization, such as Scientology, Nichiren Shoshu, and Eckankar.

For example, on the basis of their extensive survey of 327 members of ten Asian-based meditational groups in North America, Gussner and Berkowitz (1988: 164–5) conclude:

> There is little evidence from our data that [respondents] were needier than others with comparable background characteristics. [Respondents] were generally integrated into a secular world, well-educated, and successful in primarily professional careers. While [respondents] were more closely identified with religious denominations while growing up than the U.S. population, generally, there is little evidence in their backgrounds of chronic religious seekership. The majority had simply switched from their original religion to the present group. . . . Although a larger proportion of [respondents] had been divorced than in the population, there is little evidence that this played a role in the decision to affiliate with Asian-based groups. . . . While many have argued that persons who become affiliated with NRMs did so out of immaturity during their high school or college years, out of failure to make important life-transitions, or to pursue real world careers, our data clearly indicates that those who affiliate with these groups tend to do so later in life and have been successful in most maturational tasks. . . . There is strong evidence, moreover, that affiliation constitutes a longterm commitment for most respondents.

Tipton (1982a), Robbins and Bromley (1992), and Palmer (1994), however, have developed various theories that encompass these kinds of NRMs as well, theories that are similar in crucial respects and compatible with the speculations of Levine and Barker. Palmer's theory, which invokes elements of gender as well, will be examined below. In all cases, however, there is little evidence that the decision to join an NRM differs significantly from other kinds of decisions in life, such as what university to attend or what occupation to pursue. As Stark and Bainbridge (1985, 1987) insist, given enough information on the background of converts and the social circumstances of their conversion, we can go a long way towards formulating a plausible explanation of their conversion in terms of their relatively rational calculation of their best interests at the time. Neitz (1987) certainly found this to be the case, quite independently, in her exacting and empathetic ethnography of a Catholic Charismatic community. External observers, with hindsight or broader knowledge, may wish to question the decisions of converts on one ground or another. But this possibility does not discount the relatively rational character of the converting process as converts try to assess their needs and determine the balance of rewards and costs associated with accepting a particular religious package of specific and general compensators. We all have occasion to think that we may have behaved irrationally or less rationally than we could have at various points in our past. But that does not mean we did not act rationally, with the information available under the circumstances, in making these past choices. All judgements of the rationality of all acts are ultimately contingent on our present state of affairs and frame of mind. We are trapped in an infinite process of re-evaluating our decisions in the light of new information. What sociologists (and others) need to agree on are some more independent criteria for determining if an act, like a conversion, was more or less rational given the circumstances at the time. But scholars have only begun to think about the complicated things that must be taken into consideration in assessing the relative rationality of conversions (e.g., Dawson, 1990, 1994b; Neitz, 1987; Stark and Bainbridge, 1987; Sherkat, 1997).

Meanwhile, these speculations are just that, speculations. In the end it is difficult to assess the generality of the insights of Levine and others. The empirical data provided above, although more prosaic, are more reliable. We must remember, however, that while this information helps us to define who is more likely to join an NRM, the delimitation is still insufficient, given the small numbers of actual converts. Certainly the data, as the next chapter establishes further, run counter to many of the assertions and stereotypes of the public and the anti-cult movement. But from a social-scientific perspective, there is still a crucial and easily overlooked element of mystery about why people choose to be religious, especially in so radical a manner. So a full explanation of why people choose to convert still eludes our grasp. In these circumstances we must duly appreciate that people may well convert for precisely the reasons the religions themselves say they do: because they have achieved some form of enlightenment or insight into their salvation. At the very least they have had a very positive experience (mystical or otherwise) that they wish to pursue further through membership in a group. This conclusion may seem sophomoric to some, but in the face of such relatively reductionistic theories as that proposed by Levine, I think this point must be explicitly made to help ensure that we continue to respect the religious choices people make, no matter how foreign they may be to our sensibilities.

Gender Roles: A Special Consideration

Gender, the socially constructed identity (masculine or feminine) ascribed to us by virtue of our sex (male or female), is what sociologists call a 'master status'. That is, it is one of the crucial determinants of our sense of self and of how others will interact with us. Not surprisingly, then, many sociologists of religion have begun to investigate the role, if any, of this great differentiating factor in explaining the emergence of NRMs and why people join them. Do men and women join NRMs for different reasons? The differences found in the initial sex ratios of many NRMs, such as the Unification Church, Krishna Consciousness, and the Rajneesh movement, suggest that the gender question may be important. Moreover, to the extent that theorists are correct in linking the emergence of NRMs to disruptions and deficiencies in the private sphere of life, it is likely that women, who were traditionally identified with that sphere as lovers, wives, mothers, and housekeepers, should be strongly affected. As Hunter stipulates, the de-institutionalization of the private world (see Chapter 2) has de-stabilized the accepted patterns of courtship, sexuality, marriage, reproduction, and child rearing in our society. The rise of the feminist movement, coinciding with the rise of the NRMs, while liberating and beneficial for many, has also been disruptive (see, for example, Davidman, 1990: 405). By helping to fracture the consensus on traditional gender roles, it has created a heightened sense of anomie for many women. This is especially the case in combination with the added burdens born of the growing economic necessity for families to have two incomes. Women in particular are under stress from the growing fragility of the marriage bond, the weakening of the parent-child bond, and the increased penetration of all aspects of life by the 'contractual' (that is, instrumental) social relations of the contemporary workplace (Palmer, 1994: 5–8). Feeling the weight of their quadruple burden as wives or lovers, housekeepers, workers, and mothers, the absence of an adequate normative order can produce in some women a nostalgia or utopian yearning for a simpler society and more social support for the nuclear family. Under such circumstances, as Berger's theory of religion predicts, it is not surprising that many individuals seek out a new 'sacred canopy' with which to reorder and legitimate their lives. Indeed, in study after study, sociologists have found that the delineation of new and clear guidelines for the nuclear family and corresponding gender and sex roles is pivotal to the construction of reality and the appeal of new religions, sects and cults alike (e.g., Richardson, Stewart, and Simmonds, 1979; Aidala, 1985; Rochford, 1985; Ammerman, 1987; Neitz, 1987; Rose, 1987; Warner, 1988; Davidman, 1990; Palmer, 1994; for a fuller set of references consult Davidman and Jacobs, 1993). Like the Shakers, Mormons, Oneida Society, and others before them in the nineteenth century, 'modern prophets exhibit a profound concern for what they deplore as the increasingly secular and materialistic approach to sex and marriage in American society', and they 'hope to achieve harmonious relations between the sexes based on new models of gender that reflect the divine cosmos' (Palmer, 1994: 4).

In a path-breaking study of religious and non-religious communes founded since the 1960s, Angela Aidala (1985) found a common preoccupation with issues of sexuality and gender. But whereas the non-religious communes adopted an experimental orientation guided by the constant negotiation and renegotiation of gender norms and functions, the religious communes were oriented to the consistent implementation of a particular, well-defined, and usually conservative vision of male-female relations. Investigating the backgrounds of members of the religious communes, Aidala (1985) unearthed evidence of a 'low tolerance for ambiguity'. Palmer (1994: 236) similarly says that the women in NRMs that she interviewed displayed a marked 'intolerance for the perceived chaos in [contemporary] social relations'. Given the crucial role of gender identities in the development of our self-conceptions, it is not surprising then that religious communes should emerge out of the flux of the counter-culture and the contemporary world in general. These groups often seem to reinstate and reinforce the patriarchal patterns of authority and responsibility characteristic of the idealized family life of the baby boomer's youth. Good Christian and Jewish wives or Krishna wives are to be submissive to their husbands and confine their influence and activity to the domestic sphere. Their primary role is to support and nurture their husbands and children, materially, emotionally, and spiritually. Governance of the movements and the responsibilities of public leadership are a male preserve.

Meanwhile, both more and less than the traditional male role is expected of the men in these new religions (Aidala, 1985; Rose, 1987; Stacey, 1990; Palmer, 1994). On the one hand, the men are expected to be more actively and intimately involved in family life and caring for children than their fathers (as a generation) ever were. On the other hand, because of the communal system of mutual support and the ideological clarity of these groups, young men are relieved of some of the anxiety born of being the breadwinner, protector, and primary authority in the family. In theory and in practice, all members of the group care for each other as one family, and within the couples a corresponding pattern of mutual respect, open discussion, and decision-making tends to prevail. It appears that the 'women within these groups negotiated and willingly made compromises in order to "build-up" their men into responsible, and responsive partners who would cooperate in the maintenance of a stable family unit' (Davidman and Jacobs, 1993: 180). The men in question, it must be remembered, were often the rather anarchistic and perhaps disillusioned ex-leaders of the counter-culture and the student protests of the 1960s.

In her more recent and excellent study of women in seven quite diverse NRMs, Palmer (1994) clarifies and adds some interesting twists to this picture. In the first place she discounts the tendency to group NRMs by gender issues into such simple dichotomies as Robbins and Bromley's (1992) differentiation between patriarchal (for example, the Unification Church, Krishna Consciousness, and most Christian-based communes) and feminist-empowerment groups (for example, Rajneesh movement, many forms of neo-pagan Goddess worship, and witchcraft groups) or even Aidala's distinction between religious and secular communes. Instead, as Palmer demonstrates, there is a surprising diversity of complex gender relations available to women in NRMs. For analytical purposes, she, too, sorts the possibilities into a typology, a tripartite typology of sexual ideologies: sex-polarity groups, sex-complementarity groups, and sex-unity groups. As I will illustrate, however, Palmer alone highlights the real diversity of new religious beliefs, practices, and organizational forms through which each of these sexual ideologies may be expressed.

Sex-polarity groups (such as Krishna Consciousness, 3HO, the Rajneesh movement, and many kinds of feminist and lesbian Goddess worship) view 'the sexes as spiritually distinct, separate, and unessential or irrelevant to the other's salvation'. The spiritual superiority of one sex is asserted, and the sexes are usually only 'permitted to engage in limited, highly controlled relationships'. Sex-complementarity groups, like the Unification Church, the Church Universal and Triumphant, and the Mormons, regard 'each sex as endowed with different spiritual qualities and emphasize the importance of marriage for uniting two halves of the same soul to form one, complete androgynous being.' It is often thought that the right marriage and procreation will help 'usher in the millennium' (Palmer, 1994: 10). In the case of sex-unity groups, the body and gender are seen 'as a superficial layer of false identity obscuring the immortal, sexless spirit'. Encouraging an 'inner distance' from gender roles, such groups often believe 'that letting go of sex identification can release the power and infinite potential of the "Being" (the [Institute for the Development of Harmonious Human Potential]) or enable it to assume control of its reincarnation cycle (Scientology's "Thetan")' (1994: 10-11). For some groups falling within this type, such as the Raelians, the followers of Bo and Peep, and Scientologists, one's sex is open to choice and change by various means (such as elective surgery, theories of cloning, or reincarnation).

No matter how the links between gender and salvation are envisioned in each instance, many different paths to enlightenment exist within each type. Contrary perhaps to our presuppositions the sex-polarity category, for example, encompasses such seemingly ideologically antithetical groups as Krishna Consciousness and the Rajneesh movement. The International Society for Krishna Consciousness, in line with traditional Hindu asceticism, is a communal organization that allows the development of families but seeks largely to segregate the sexes, even after marriage. In spiritual matters the male quest for salvation takes priority, and male householders are ultimately expected to abandon their families and return to the celibate life in their quest for spiritual purity. Krishna Consciousness is a puritanical movement geared to the strict differentiation of gender roles and the ritualistic regulation of sexual relations. For women the spiritual ideal is the obedient, devoted, and supportive wife.

The movement founded by Bhagwan Shree Rajneesh, on the other hand, is libertarian in its sexual relations. Following the Tantric tradition in Indian religious philosophy, brief and intense sexual experimentation between the sexes within a communal policy of free love is the primary means of securing the inner knowledge and detachment from conventionality that is essential to psychological well-being and spiritual enlightenment. The inspirational messages and spiritual exercises of Rajneesh place a priority on the superior spiritual energy and wisdom of the feminine. Accordingly, traditional female gender roles are rejected in favour of a spiritualization of the role of 'lover', and the leadership of the group tends to be dominated by women.

As might be expected given these differences, Palmer found that the two NRMs attract markedly different kinds of women. Note the many ways in which her observations resonate with things said in this and the preceding chapter:

> Women joining the Krishna Consciousness movement tend to be young—in their late teens to early twenties—and tend to be from middle to upper-middle-class families. Judging from the interviews, they remember their family life as materially privileged but dysfunctional, and themselves as abused or neglected children. Many of them appear to be exchanging the uncontrolled, arbitrary patriarchy of their fathers' rule for what they consider a benevolent system of male protection based on the authority of an

ancient lineage of guru succession. The ISKCON community, therefore, beckons to these women as a safe haven where masculine tyranny and passion has no place; where they will find protection and will not be sexually exploited (Palmer, 1994: 42).[8]

. . . I would argue that [the Rajneesh] movement attracts a *type* of woman: the middle-aged, upper-middle-class woman who is accustomed to independence and a lucrative employment, and who tends to be childless, unmarried, and highly educated. Moreover, this type of woman chooses to participate in this NRM because it offers an alternative philosophy of sexuality that is consistent with her previous life-style, and that validates her life choices. Finally, it will be argued on the basis of data found in the interviews that the role of 'lover', as defined by Rajneesh, is perceived by these women as offering *religious* solutions to problems of intimacy and family life that they have encountered in their previous life. (Palmer, 1994: 45)

Similar though not quite as stark differences exist between the specific NRMs Palmer examines under the sex-complementarity and sex-unity categories.

In the face of such diversity, Palmer insists nevertheless that, in line with the insights of Aidala, Davidman, and others, the seven NRMs she studied share common features that display an abiding concern with problems of gender ambiguity and sexual abuse experienced by contemporary women (1994: 209–10):

(1) 'Each group rejects the courting phase in favor of arranged marriage or instant intimacy';
(2) 'Each group emphasizes one (or at most two) role(s) for their women,' defining them as sacred and rejecting all others as profane;
(3) 'Each group rejects the model of the child-centered family by providing cooperative day care, and . . . either delaying parenthood, shortening its term (ISKCON), or . . . [abandoning] parenthood altogether.

It is these common features, she suggests, that have led women to join NRMs, in pursuit of a '*safe and sacred environment* where they can explore their sexual identity and pursue their relationships with men' (Palmer, 1994: 232). The women are seeking an environment free of the anxieties stemming from such problems as high divorce rates, the unjust burden of working mothers, the weakening of the bond between parents and their children, child abuse, sexual harassment, homosexuality, AIDS, wife beating, abortion, and last but not least, the heartbreaks of romantic love (Palmer, 1994: 210, 219).

With regard to divorce, for instance, Palmer says (1994: 215): 'It could be argued that new religious women are seeking to avoid accountability in their love life. They are relieved of the anxiety and burden of choosing their mates. In the NRMs that encourage the power of choice (as in the Raelian or Rajneesh movements) women and men do not have to *live* with that choice.' The argument is reminiscent, in form at least, to Levine's theory of why young people join NRMs.[9] Likewise, it calls to mind Davidman's comments on the young women who joined a Lubavitch Chassidim community she had studied, and establishes the connection with Aidala's study. Palmer continues:

> The prominence of [negative sexual experiences] in the accounts of women who come to [the Lubavitch community] indicates that within their own self-understanding these experiences play a major role in their attraction to a religious community that demands they surrender control over their sexuality. *They actually seem relieved to follow the community's norms and to be given external reasons for not being sexually active.* This finding is similar to that of Aidala who reports that recruits to religious communes were attracted by the 'religious ideology [that] promised easy resolution of uncertainties regarding sexuality and patterns of gender relating.' For these young adults who had been troubled by the lack of clarity about these norms in the broader culture, 'in many ways the simplest solution to confused and unanchored sexual feelings is total abstinence.'

In the end, though, Palmer's explanation of why women join NRMs is more nuanced than Levine's or that of Aidala, Davidman, and others. Two differences emerge from her rich interview data and observations. First, women are drawn to various movements, not just because they provide a way to escape gender abuses and ambiguities in society or moral accountability, but also because the 'theologies of love' of the various charismatic leaders and the behaviour of their followers promise a *sacred* as well as a safe haven. 'Rather than insisting that women join NRMs to pursue particular *kinds* of relationships,' she states (Palmer, 1994: 235–6), 'it might be more accurate to suggest that they join to find a hidden, sacred *meaning* or *spiritual dimension* to their interpersonal relationships—a dimension that appears to be lacking in secular, contractual relationships.' In other words, the declarations of the women she met convinced her of the need to be particularly leery of falling too readily into a fully reductive interpretation. These women could have had recourse to other solutions to their problems (for example, through careers, therapy, or various secular movements and

causes), but they preferred to find *spiritual* solutions to the negative consequences of social change. They were after a *spiritualized* sense of their
sexuality (1994: 236–7).

These new devotees are seemingly quite different, then, from the secular women joining a large Orthodox synagogue studied by Davidman
(1990: 389; see also 405):

> Nearly every woman I interviewed specifically mentioned a longing for fam-
> ily and a committed relationship as an important factor in her attraction to
> Orthodox Judaism. The dominant theme that comes through in my inter-
> views is *not* the search for God or metaphysical truth or spiritual experience.
> In fact, half of the women at Metropolitan Synagogue were not even sure
> they believe in God! Yet every woman I spoke with spontaneously high-
> lighted the salience of her desire for a family.

Is the difference between Palmer's and Davidman's findings simply a function of their different samples—true cults versus a more conventional sectarian form of religious expression? Or do the differences strictly lie in the
interpretive proclivities of the two authors? Davidman (1994: 388) notes
that the women in her sample are older (in their thirties) and well educated
and tend to work in well-paid positions in business or the professions.
Could there, in fact, be more similarities between these women and the
kinds of women Palmer found to be attracted to the Rajneesh movement
than the surface clash of the authors' interpretations suggests? There are no
clear and easy answers. The juxtaposition of perspectives points to the need
for more and more detailed and comparative studies.

Second, and contrary once again to the thrust of the argument of
Aidala, Davidman, and others, Palmer concludes (1994: 262):

> Our data suggest that the innovations in sex roles and sexual mores
> presently developing in NRMs, far from representing a conservative reaction
> against mainstream experimentation and feminism, might more accurately
> be characterized as offering even *more* extreme, intensified, and diverse ver-
> sions of the ongoing experimentation already occurring outside these
> utopias. The highly organized and strictly supervised group experiments
> occurring in NRMs appeal to prospective members as safe havens in which
> they might engage in more radical forms of experimentation than are pos-
> sible in the secular sphere. Our informants appear to be responding not so
> much to gender ambiguity per se (Aidala 1985, 287), but to the disorga-
> nized and haphazard ways in which 'sexual experiments' were being con-
> ducted in the larger society.

In conclusion, it is worth noting that Palmer (1994) believes that these findings, in conjunction with the discovery of different sexual ideologies in NRMs, the diversity of types of women attracted to different NRMs, and the different sex ratios of different NRMs, 'challenge prevailing notions that "cult women" are the passive victims of the ineluctable forces of charisma and "brainwashing"' (p. 240). The seasoned exponents of the brainwashing scenario, however, are rarely deterred by such evidence, if they choose to pay attention to it at all.[10]

Chapter Four

Are Converts to New Religious Movements 'Brainwashed'?

The Issue and Its Significance

The followers of NRMs are brainwashed! How else can one account for the seemingly sudden and unexpected conversion of ordinary middle-class young people to such unusual, even outlandish new religions? How else can one account for the apparently sudden and sweeping changes in their beliefs, attitudes, and behaviour? With this oft repeated, yet little understood, accusation we move to the heart of the contemporary controversy about cults. The charge carries us beyond the public lectures, books, and newspaper articles by which the message of the anti-cult movement is spread into the courts of law. An assessment of this claim has been pivotal to the resolution of numerous criminal cases and civil suits. Hoping to override the legal right of their adult children to choose whatever religious practices or world-view they wish, parents have sought to invoke the spectre of brainwashing to convince judges that their children are incompetent and in need of rescue. Deprogrammers,[1] having rescued many of these 'children', by force, have called on theories of brainwashing to defend themselves against charges of kidnapping and assault, arguing that their actions were the lesser of two evils (Bromley, 1988). Meanwhile former members of cults have sued various NRMs for damages, arguing that they have been harmed by their alleged experience of brainwashing while in a cult.

But are the charges of brainwashing true? In some cases, judges and juries have been convinced; in others they have not. (See Anthony, 1990; Anthony and Robbins, 1992, 1995; and Richardson, 1991, 1995d, 1996a, for excellent overviews of the issues and specific legal cases.) If true, even sometimes, then it can be argued that many NRMs do pose a serious public risk. If they are not true, then the primary risk to the public is posed by those who try to use this claim to suppress the civil liberties and religious freedom of others, rights entrenched in the US Constitution and character-istic of most modern democratic societies (Bromley and Robbins, 1993).

It is understandably difficult for the parents of converts to see their dreams of worldly success for their children thwarted by the other-worldly demands of life in some unknown and exotic new religion. Recast as 'brain-washing', the unconventional religious choices of these young people can be seen as a medically definable deviance, subject to the same state scrutiny and intervention as other public health and social problems, such as gang violence, drug abuse, and AIDS (see Singer, 1995: 5, 84; Robbins and Anthony, 1982b). Do NRMs indeed use sophisticated techniques of 'mind-control', 'thought reform', or 'coercive persuasion' to entice and hold their devotees? Or does the brainwashing scenario simply allow parents and other opponents of NRMs to avoid facing other unwelcome possibilities? Per-haps the NRMs are actually offering their children something that they need or desire? Or perhaps the world they have created for their children is unsatisfactory in some crucial regard? The courts, scholars, and the public have not arrived at any definitive answers to these questions. But we can survey and clarify what is meant by these charges and the nature of evi-dence at hand so far.

Most of the scholars associated with the academic study of NRMs are increasingly of the opinion that the charge of mind control has not been substantiated and is theoretically implausible. Most of them tend to dis-count the admissibility of claims of brainwashing in NRMs that have been made by expert witnesses or otherwise in court cases. Rather, the vast majority of the scholars studying NRMs, with a few notable exceptions, are of the opinion that accusations of brainwashing significantly distort the realities of cult life as revealed by years of systematic empirical study (e.g., Robbins and Anthony, 1979b; Robbins and Anthony, 1982b; Bromley and Richardson, 1983; Coleman, 1984; Barker, 1984; Levine, 1984; Robbins, 1984; Richardson, 1985, 1995b, 1995c; Wright, 1987; Society for the Sci-entific Study of Religion, 1988; Rochford et al., 1989; Anthony, 1990; Daw-son, 1990, 1996; Shinn, 1993). Such accusations are considered primarily to be tools of propaganda designed to persuade the public and politicians to act against the interests of NRMs. Nevertheless, despite the recent legal reversals suffered by the anti-cult movement, in part because of this grow-ing scholarly consensus, media reports indicate that there is still a nearly complete faith in the accuracy of the brainwashing supposition (e.g., Langone, 1993; Singer, 1995).[2]

I cannot pretend to be totally impartial in these matters. Long ago I was persuaded to dismiss the brainwashing scenario by my own experience with

NRMs and the cumulative scholarly record. But there are many who still think otherwise, including many judges, lawyers, government officials, psychiatrists, psychologists, and even some sociologists. So let me summarize the arguments for and against the practice of coercive conversion by NRMs, trying as much as possible to let the facts speak for themselves. Since the literature on both sides of the issue is vast, and also highly repetitious, I will first summarize the essential elements of the case made by the anti-cultists, drawing on the views of such writers as the American psychologist Margaret Singer (1995), the American sociologist Ronald Enroth (1977), who writes from an evangelical Christian perspective, and Steven Hassan (1988), an ex-Moonie and exit counsellor for people who have left NRMs. The work of these authors is well known and is representative of the kinds of people interested in campaigning against 'cults' in North America. Their comments also display the remarkable consistency of the argument made against the recruitment activities of NRMs, an argument that has changed little in over twenty years.

I will then present my own critique of this argument, based on the summary critiques already advanced by such other prominent scholars of NRMs as Robbins (1984), Barker (e.g., 1984), Richardson (e.g., 1993b and 1995c), Rochford (Rochford et al., 1989), and many others. This critique will deal with both the sociological and psychological evidence provided by twenty years of academic research into how people both convert to and deconvert from NRMs (e.g., Wright, 1987; Lewis, 1988; Jacobs, 1989). In other words, my critique will highlight the very data that Margaret Singer and other opponents of NRMs seem to have studiously ignored.

The chapter will end with a look at one of the broader benefits of research prompted by the brainwashing debate. Work on the coercive-conversion controversy has resulted in a vastly improved understanding of the processes of religious conversion in general (e.g., Rambo, 1993). Not only is the brainwashing scenario implausible, but it now seems that people are not 'converted' to a new religious movement, as much as they 'convert themselves'.[3] The process of conversion, that is, appears to be much more 'interactive' and 'active' than previously assumed.

The Case against the Cults

Early in the public debate about 'cults', the threat supposedly posed by these new religions was described as a 'very frightening form of thought control or brainwashing', a 'syndrome of seduction and mental subversion' (Enroth, 1977: 156; see, e.g., Patrick and Dulack, 1976; Conway and Siegelman, 1978; and Clark et al., 1981). On the basis of anecdotal accounts of life in the cults, an analogy was drawn with the experience of the political thought reform of some American prisoners of war during the Korean War (1950–3). In that war, for purposes of propaganda, the Communist Chinese had attempted systematically to break the will of some American prisoners in order to make them confess publicly to war crimes or betray their allegiance to the United States.[4] Through repeated reference, the analogy drawn between the fate of these POWs and converts to NRMs soon took on an aura of factuality, and some people, like John Clark (M.D.) of Harvard University, even warned the American people of the extreme 'health hazards' posed by 'destructive cults' (cited by Enroth, 1977: 156). But the early analyses offered by Enroth (1977) and others were clearly speculative and based on a handful of stories of cult participation. The stories in question were presented as 'atrocity tales', designed to galvanize anti-cult sentiment, though many of these stories were in fact ambiguous. Soon the concepts of brainwashing and cults became synonymous in the minds of a naïve and fearful public (see Introduction). In fact anti-cultists, like Singer and Hassan, incorporate the concept of mind control into their very definition of 'cults' (Singer, 1995: 7; Hassan, 1988: 55). By definition all NRMs are destructive of individual integrity and autonomy. It is merely a matter of degree how bad (in this regard) they are. Some cults, the anti-cultists admit, are less harmful than others. But the use of some measure of brainwashing is necessitated in almost every case, they argue, by the hidden and true agenda of these organizations:

> Cults basically have only two purposes: recruiting new members and fund-raising. Established religions and altruistic movements may also recruit and raise funds. Their sole purpose, however, is not simply to grow larger and wealthier; such groups have as goals bettering the lives of their members or humankind in general, either in this world or in a world to come. A cult may claim to make social contributions, but in actuality these remain mere claims or gestures. In the end, all work and all funds, even token gestures of altruism, serve the cult. (Singer, 1995: 11)

Of course, the cults place a near total emphasis on growth, it is asserted, to enhance the wealth, pleasure, and power of the cult leaders. NRMs are essentially exploitive. In Singer's words (1995: 6): 'Cults seem to have no end to their peculiar practices. Cult leaders seem to have no end to their unconscionable behaviours and their capacity to abuse their followers.' The statements of Enroth, Hassan, Singer, and many other anti-cultists (e.g., Conway and Siegelman, 1978; Delgado, 1980) tend to be extreme and absolute on these points. Yet Singer bizarrely insists that her use of the term 'cult' is 'merely descriptive, [and] not pejorative' (Singer, 1995: 11).[5]

Cults, as a class of things, are to be indiscriminately feared and discredited because their recruitment practices run contrary to the primary value that Americans place on individual freedom. The success of the anti-cult movement rests, in other words, on the supposition that all, or at least most, cults employ brainwashing. Let me illustrate this point with a passage from Hassan (1988: 51–2):

> The casualties of mind control include not only the millions of cult members themselves, their children, and their friends and loved ones, but also our society as well. Our nation is being robbed of our greatest resource: bright, idealistic, ambitious people who are capable of making an enormous contribution to mankind. Many of the former members I know have become doctors, teachers, counsellors, inventors, artists. Imagine what cult members could accomplish if they were all set free to develop their God-given talents and abilities! What if they channelled their energies into problem solving, rather than trying to undermine America's freedoms with some warped totalitarian vision?

Here we have the standard objections to the cults: they are redirecting talented people into useless, wrong, or even subversive causes, and these people are not free to return to more useful, right, and properly American ways of life. Whether NRMs are right or wrong in their goals and activities, or whether the pursuit of spiritual, as opposed to more worldly, goals is valuable or not is an ideological issue and not susceptible to any clear empirical determination. The best that social scientists can do is document and clarify the actual doctrines and doings of specific NRMs and let the readers of their studies draw their own conclusions. But whether or not people join or leave NRMs 'freely' is a topic open (with some qualification) to an important measure of empirical investigation.[6]

What do the anti-cultists have in mind when they say NRMs recruit and maintain their members through 'mind control'? Though the details differ, there is a remarkable uniformity to the arguments advanced by writers on this subject. As classically delineated by Edward Hunter (1951), Joost Meerloo (1956), William Sargent (1957), Robert Lifton (1961), Edgar Schein et al. (1961), and many others, processes of 'brainwashing' roughly conform to a three-stage model of radical resocialization by which an old identity is stripped away and a new one is created. At one point both Hassan (1988: 67–72) and Singer (1995: 74–7) use Schein's terminology to characterize these stages as 'unfreezing', 'changing', and 'refreezing'. But other terms have been used for these stages, like 'stimuli control', 'response control', and 'normative control', and other models have been used as well that do not explicitly employ a three-stage scheme (e.g., Singer, 1995: 52–74).

In the first stage or phase, the 'unfreezing', the victims of brainwashing are subjected to various incapacitating physical, psychological, and social conditions designed to induce a nearly complete cognitive, emotional, and social breakdown. The two primary means used are various forms of either sensory deprivation or sensory overload. In the case of prisoners of war or political prisoners in Communist China and elsewhere, this often entails torture. In general, though, solitary confinement, as used regularly in our prisons to punish unruly inmates, is a standard way of causing sensory deprivation. With few exceptions, completely isolating someone from normal social contact, let alone light, sounds, and proper warmth or food, is an extremely effective way of bringing about at least temporary behavioural reform. Sensory overload is just the opposite of sensory deprivation. This technique was used by the FBI against the inhabitants of the Branch Davidian compound in Waco, Texas, during their fifty-one-day siege in 1994. The compound was flooded with bright spotlights, while loud and harsh music and other sounds blared from loudspeakers around the clock. The object of sensory overload is to disrupt and constantly change the daily routines and behavioural expectations of those being brainwashed. Physically weakened and psychologically disoriented by such practices, these people lose their sense of reality and their sense of self—the stable personality characteristics that anchor a person's behaviour. In this confused state the victims of brainwashing are susceptible, it is believed, to suggestions for alternative ways of ordering their lives and re-establishing peace and sanity. With NRMs in mind, Singer expresses this state of affairs as follows (1995: 75):

> Successful behavioral change programs are designed to upset you to the point that your self-confidence is undermined. This makes you more open to suggestion and also more dependent on the environment for cues about 'right thinking' and 'right conduct'. Your resistance to new ideas lessens when you feel yourself teetering on the edge with massive anxiety about the right choices in life on the one side, and the group ideas that offer the way out of this distress on the other side.

In the second stage or phase of brainwashing, the 'changing', this openness to suggestion is used to impose a new identity—a new set of thoughts, feelings, and behaviours. Those being brainwashed are systematically and ever more intensely introduced to new daily routines, expectations, group activities, and rewards and punishments. Carefully monitoring and controlling all activity and social interaction, the brainwashers try to fashion a new environment with which those being brainwashed will identify out of their extreme need for predictable order and meaning in their lives.

The third and final stage or phase, the 'refreezing', attempts to consolidate and reinforce those changes by rapidly and thoroughly immersing the subjects of brainwashing in a new, stable, and supportive social environment, suffused with ritualized activities. Working together and hard on a new set of group tasks will generate new bonds of loyalty, as well as new conceptions of happiness, purpose, and self-worth. It is assumed that by the repeated and relentless control and manipulation of the external behaviour of the subjects of brainwashing (their words and deeds), these people can be conditioned to continue to censor and refashion themselves. Ideally, the change effected should be permanent, short of another round of counter-brainwashing (like the 'deprogramming' attempted by the anti-cultists).

How is this process applied in NRMs? Again, the details discussed by different proponents of the brainwashing scenario differ, as does its presumed manifestation in different NRMs. Nevertheless, in one way or another, most discussions advance the following twelve or so claims (see, e.g., Enroth, 1977: 157-64; Hassan, 1988: 53–67; Singer, 1995: 113–19 and 128–72; Loomis, 1997):

1. It is repeatedly asserted that many of the NRMs, most notably groups like the Moonies, the Church of Scientology, and the Family (previously the Children of God), are very systematic and sophisticated in their recruitment activities. They have researched and applied social-psychological techniques of influence and have planned and rehearsed responses for many eventualities. Recruiters are carefully selected, trained, and supervised.

2. The training that the recruiters receive includes instructions on how to target and approach likely candidates for conversion. Recruiters are to look for evidence that the person is alone, in a period of transition in life, or otherwise 'vulnerable' in some way (for example, young, wearing a backpack, seemingly not in a hurry to get somewhere, or looking distressed in some way).

3. Another part of the training is learning how to be deceptive, at least initially, in approaching potential recruits. New recruits, it is charged, are rarely told about the true or full nature of the group and its objectives. The identity of the group and the demands it places on its members are revealed only gradually as the recruit becomes more interested and involved. By the time of full disclosure, however, the processes of mind-control or brainwashing have taken hold, preventing the informed consent of the convert.

4. After the acceptance of one or more relatively innocuous invitations to dinner, a lecture, workshop, entertainment, or other social event, persons

that have shown some interest in the group are coerced into signing up for a rapidly escalating series of lectures, study groups, retreats, training sessions, and other activities.

5. In these sessions and activities, new recruits are never allowed to be alone or to discuss what they are doing with each other. They are always in the presence of members, and all challenging inquires are directed to senior members of the organizations for a response. On the whole, however, negative comments or questions from the potential recruits are evaded or discounted as much as possible. Troublemakers and sceptics are weeded out of the pool of recruits (Galanter, 1980) or subjected to strong group pressure to stay quiet and wait for answers to their questions once a greater understanding of the beliefs and practices of the group has been achieved. Attention is focused on maintaining an uplifting sense of group harmony and an immediate and rather superficial aura of individual happiness.

6. At retreats and other events, potential recruits are kept abnormally busy. They are cajoled and coerced into participating in a frenzied round of daily activities: lectures, games, plays, sing-alongs, therapy groups, charity work, and so on. The object, it is presumed, is to stop the recruits from having the opportunity to reflect seriously on the new ideas and practices to which they are being exposed.

7. As much as possible these recruitment events take place in isolated environments, in the countryside perhaps, or in special facilities where the group can control the recruits' access to information and other people. The recruits are encouraged to begin the process of cutting themselves off from their aimless or evil past and, hence, from their friends and family.

8. Techniques like 'love-bombing' will be used to ensnare the candidates for conversion and to lessen their natural scepticism. In love-bombing the new recruit is surrounded with praise, compliments, flattery, affection, hugs, and other forms of emotional support, much as parents attempt to reassure and bolster the confidence of a young child trying something new (like skating or swimming). This 'love' is presumed to be insincere.

9. Simultaneously, recruits will be drawn into various types of 'confessional' activities, by which the group can learn something of the past, fears, and self-conceptions of potential converts. This information will be used to play upon their natural feelings of guilt and anxiety about past experiences and future uncertainties. Enroth, Hassan, and Singer all place particular stress on the supposed manipulation of the feelings of inadequacy so common amongst young people.

10. Having thus implemented a kind of sensory overload, the cult leaders mix in a most basic form of sensory deprivation. Recruits are fed inadequately, often on vegetarian diets, and prevented from sleeping enough.

Thus their ability to think clearly or offer emotional resistance is physio-
logically undermined.

11. Even more perniciously, cults, it is charged, use sophisticated yet low-
key methods of hypnosis to induce trance states in recruits so that their psychological defences can be systematically stripped away and suggestions
implanted for a new way of life. The methods vary from lengthy, droning, repetitious, and rhythmical lectures, to guided-imagery sessions and the practice
of meditation. The latter two techniques, in various forms, have an ancient
religious lineage in both the East and the West, and they are commonly used
in psychotherapies of all types. Cult leaders, however, allegedly abuse these
techniques to serve their own selfish ends. Singer (e.g., 1995: 139) in particular argues that these and other means are used to induce altered states of
consciousness and other physiological affects that the group can 'reframe' for
the recruit as experiences of partial enlightenment or spiritual progress or
regression. As the interpretations proffered by the groups are often less than
scientifically accurate, it is assumed that the groups must have some deceptive purpose in mind in religiously 'reframing' the recruits' experiences.

12. Last, but not least, NRMs often seek to effect a complete transformation of identity by giving the converts new names, changing their clothes,
hairstyle, diet, and other personal habits. Often, people are asked to abandon or donate all of their material possessions to the group and to live com-
munally and very simply, forgoing their own needs and aspirations in
favour of those of the group. This is said to create a condition of direct
material dependency that binds the convert to the group and further
inhibits thoughts of leaving.

Each of these claims is supported by Enroth, Hassan, Singer, and others with reports of interviews with ex-members of cults or the written
accounts of ex-members (often those who, like Hassan himself, have been
deprogrammed). Some of these stories stem from the authors' own research,
others come from other sources. One must read the accounts to get an adequate sense of the specifics and to decide if the stories recounted warrant
the generalizations drawn. But the stories cited are usually presented with
little development of the broader context, and traceable references to specific NRMs or incidents are rarely provided. They are 'stories', collected in
different ways by different people for different purposes, but they do not
constitute systematically secured data.

The net result of cult involvement, we are told repeatedly, is that the
recruits experience and display a marked impairment, even a regression, in
their capacity to think logically and independently. In fact, it is often more
or less suggested that converts to NRMs have altogether lost the capacity to
think for themselves in any sustained way. In some cases Enroth (1977:

164) goes so far as to propose that there is evidence (unspecified) of a loss of basic cognitive skills, like the ability to read and write at normal levels. Certainly, the recruits are thought to have mortgaged their futures by interrupting their educations, losing their possessions, and damaging their health, in return for shoddy, if not false, spiritual goods. Converts characteristically display a long-term emotional flatness, we are told, and become deeply alienated from their families and past friends. In some cases, we are warned, the destabilizing recruitment milieu has induced true states of psychopathology, ranging from blackouts and phobias through schizophrenic episodes to severe depression and even suicide. Despite many seeming qualifications, in the literature and the presentations of the anti-cult movement, the bottom line is stereotypically clear: with few exceptions, cult recruiters use deception along with sophisticated and powerful techniques of influence to find and exploit the personal vulnerabilities, deficiencies, or just desires of potential converts, with results that are always socially and psychologically damaging.

The Case against Brainwashing

The reasons for being doubtful of the brainwashing charge made against NRMs are many and cannot all be discussed here (see, e.g., Robbins and Anthony, 1982b; Richardson and Bromley, 1983; Robbins, 1984; Coleman, 1984; Barker, 1984; Anthony, 1990; Richardson, 1993b; Anthony and Robbins, 1994). A persuasive case can be made, however, by formulating a critique based on twelve of the most telling criticisms made by academic students of NRMs.

But first let me reiterate that our concern is with the charge of brainwashing. In defending NRMs against this specific and pivotal accusation we need not conceive of NRMs as somehow free of error. Some NRMs, at some times, have clearly engaged in objectionable or suspect practices. For example, it is well known that for a time the so-called Oakland Family of the Unification Church in California did practise 'heavenly deception' while recruiting. They introduced themselves to prospective recruits under various false guises (for example, as a fairly conventional Christian youth group, or spiritually inclined environmentalist commune) and postponed revealing their true identity and connections with the Reverend Sun Myung Moon for as long as possible (see Barker, 1984: 94–120, especially 100–3, and 176–8). They also used a lot of high-pressure social tactics to persuade recruits to make a commitment. The Unification Church, like many other NRMs, such as Scientology, was also in the habit of issuing wildly exaggerated membership figures (e.g., Galanter, 1989: 110). This was done, quite simply, to put a better face than was the case on the success and significance of their activities, in order to promote recruitment and secure respectability. Likewise, for a time in the mid-1970s the International Society for Krishna Consciousness became preoccupied with securing funds for its activities and employed some deception (for example, by wearing conventional street clothes and even wigs) in their aggressive campaigns to sell literature, flowers, incense, and other items in airports, on the streets, and in other public places (see Rochford, 1985: 171–89; Rochford, 1988). Even more notorious was the practice by the Children of God of encouraging their young female members to use sexual flirtation and favours to attract new male members. This practice of 'flirty-fishing', which lasted from about 1977 to 1987, was eventually repudiated, but the reputation of the group has been permanently damaged (see Richardson and Davis, 1983: 406–20; Van Zandt, 1991: 46–8 and 169–70; Lewis and Melton, 1994). Other errors of judgement brought on by the zeal for new visions of the world could be enumerated. But the history of all religions is littered with such incidents. A century ago, for example, most mainstream North Americans feared and spoke out against the scandalous emotionalism and irrationality, as well as supposed deception, of Methodist camp revival meetings (see McLoughlin, 1978: 122–38; Finke and Stark, 1992: 87–108). Whatever the failings of religions, new and old, this chapter is not intended as an apologia for NRMs. The question at issue is solely whether the highly generalized claim of brainwashing made by the anti-cult movement enhances or inhibits our understanding of NRMs.

Moving roughly from general to specific, twelve criticisms can be made about the adequacy of the brainwashing scenario:

1. With few exceptions (most of them very recent), the literature of the anti-cult movement displays a persistent tendency to lump all NRMs together. By repeated implication, if not stated as fact, accusations made against any one group are generalized to almost all other new religions (and many similar organizations), ignoring their marked differences in origins, doctrines, practices, objectives, and organizational structures. Illustrations, in the form of 'atrocity stories', are opportunistically drawn from an indiscriminate array of NRMs and used to 'prove' the accusations levelled with little regard for the varied nature and circumstances of the groups cited. No systematic means of comparison is even attempted, because it is assumed in advance that all cults are essentially the same. To recognize the inadequacy of this assumption requires some familiarity with the very real differences between NRMs, something most members of the public lack. But with only a passing knowledge of the obvious differences in the origins, doctrines, practices, objectives, and organizational structures of Scientology and

Krishna Consciousness, for instance, it is hard to see how we can assume that these and other groups practise some uniform mode of recruitment.

2. One cannot help but detect a consistent ideological bias in the attempts made to apply brainwashing theories to NRMs. Apart from the obvious and admitted Christian polemic of much of this literature, it is clear that the communal and collectivist sentiments and practices of many NRMs clash with the markedly materialistic and individualistic orientations of contemporary Western, and particularly American, culture. Moreover, elements of ethno-centricism and even racism can be detected: 'The fact that a number of new religions are from outside Western culture and were founded and led by foreigners should not be ignored in understanding the propensity to apply simplistic brainwashing theories to explain participation and justify efforts at social control' (Richardson, 1993b: 79). Remember that the sudden visibility of NRMs in the 1960s stems, in part, from the repeal of the Asian exclusion laws in 1965 (see Chapter 2). These immigration laws had systematically prevented Oriental gurus and their followers from settling in the United States.

3. As Eileen Barker (1984: 126–7) and dozens of other commentators on the cult controversy have observed, there are neither logical nor empirical reasons for the repeated anti-cult assertion that only someone who is brainwashed could believe some of the incredible doctrines of most NRMs. As the historical and anthropological record amply documents, there are few limits to the exotic character of the beliefs different people have held over the years. The strangeness of the beliefs adopted does not, in and of itself, demonstrate or necessarily even imply that the process by which they were adopted was coercive. There are few if any universal criteria of reasonable belief, and all conclusions about the religious beliefs of others are a matter of perspective. As an old adage specifies, 'one man's meat is another man's poison' (cited by Barker, 1984: 158). The same holds true for the common assumption that the seeming suddenness of many conversions to NRMs proves that brainwashing was used. 'Suddenness' is not *proof* of 'brainwashing'. There is considerable reason to believe, in any event, that the supposed 'suddenness' of these conversions is more apparent than real (see the last section of this chapter).

4. A close study of the original theories of brainwashing cited by the anti-cultists as authorities poses problems for their case. The theories of Hunter (1951), Meerloo (1956), Sargent (1957), Lifton (1961), and Schein et al. (1961) are based on contradictory ideas of human nature and psychology. Hunter and Sargent explain brainwashing by means of psycho-physiological stress theory, whereas Meerloo and Lifton employ various combinations of behaviouristic learning theory and psychoanalysis. There

is no one theory of brainwashing. In most instances, the ideas of these supposed authorities are used so superficially by the anti-cult movement that these and other inconsistencies in their explanatory frameworks are barely noted, let alone thought to matter.

There are also problems with the lineage and foundation of these original theories of thought reform and control. The journalist Hunter, who first popularized the term 'brainwashing', was a CIA operative, and his book was written for propagandistic purposes (Richardson and Bromley, 1983; Anthony and Robbins, 1994: 459). Moreover, all of the theories are based on extremely small samples of men subjected to various programs of thought reform, and they rely on largely anecdotal and retrospective accounts. We have little information about the prior lives of these victims of brainwashing or about their lives after these episodes. Of the almost 350 American POWs systematically subjected to brainwashing during the Korean War, only 21 ever chose to betray their country (Anthony and Robbins, 1994: 460).

In 1956, the psychiatrists Lawrence Hinkle and Harold Wolff, of Cornell University, undertook an exhaustive study of brainwashing, with the support of the government and full access to the secret files of the CIA as well as some former Communist interrogators and their prisoners. Their declassified, but conveniently overlooked, report refutes the effectiveness of all efforts to brainwash anyone—especially through inducing altered states of consciousness. Where thought-reform techniques do seem to have produced results, they argue, we are merely witnessing behavioural compliance brought on by threats and the experience of physical abuse (see Anthony and Robbins, 1994: 460–1).

5. Even a slightly sceptical reading of the books of Enroth, Hassan, Singer, and others will quickly reveal the tendency of these authors to make dramatic claims based solely on anecdotal evidence, which is non-falsifiable by empirical test. Members of NRMs constantly reiterate, for example, that they are perfectly free to come and go as they please and that they made a conscious and free choice to join these new religions. Yet the anti-cult movement simply argues that these beliefs are held only because the members have been brainwashed to believe and say they are free (Barker, 1984: 122–3). How is one ever to know this, and how can one ever argue against such a self-validating point of view? No counter-arguments are possible in the face of such a mind-set (Richardson, 1992b).

The practice of 'love-bombing' is another case in point:

The display of affection toward new and potential converts ('love bombing'), which might be interpreted as a kindness or an idealistic manifestation of devotees' belief that their relationship to spiritual truth and divine love enables them to radiate love and win others to truth, is also commonly interpreted as a sinister 'coercive' technique. . . . Yet successfully deprogrammed ex-devotees have enthused over the warmly supportive and 'familial' milieu at post-deprogramming 'rehabilitation' centers such as the Freedom of Thought Foundation (e.g., Underwood and Underwood, 1979). Could this also be 'love bombing'? (Robbins, 1984: 245)

Many of the complaints made by the anti-cult movement are like their misgivings about love-bombing. Without some preconceptions, it is often not immediately apparent that we are dealing with a truly objectionable practice. In fact, Barker notes (1984: 186–7):

Most Moonies would be genuinely shocked at the suggestion that they are being deceptive when they offer their guests affection. They would not only protest that they *ought* to love them as people (and many undoubtedly do develop a genuine affection for some of their guests), they would also be convinced that it is in the guest's own interests (as well as the interests of the world) for him to become a Moonie.

For the impartial observer, there is no independent way to choose between what Robbins calls 'empathetic internal perspectives' of cult activities, like love-bombing, and 'critical external perspectives' (Robbins, 1984: 244).

Contrary to the thinking of the anti-cultists, however, common sense combined with some knowledge of other religious traditions can go a long way towards defusing many of the more naïve yet fervently advocated criticisms of NRMs. Let me illustrate my point with the following passage from Margaret Singer. In discussing how cults induce trance states to seduce their victims, Singer says (1995: 155–6):

Sometimes the induction method is speech filled with paradox and discrepancy—that is, the message is not logical and you are unable to follow it, but it is presented as though it were logical. Trying to follow what is being said can actually detach the listener from reality. A good example of this technique comes from the cult leader Bhagwan Shree Rajneesh's comments at an initiation ceremony in which he gave each disciple a new name along with . . . a necklace with his picture on it. Reading what Rajneesh said can give you a feeling for what words can do to cause a person to enter a light trance, or space out.

'First, the picture is not mine. The picture only appears to be mine. No picture of me is really possible. The moment one knows oneself, one knows

something that cannot be depicted, described, framed. I exist as an empti-
ness that cannot be pictured, that cannot be photographed. That is why I
could put the picture there. . . . The more you know the picture—the more
you concentrate on it, the more you come in tune with it—the more you will
feel what I am saying. The more you concentrate on it, the more there will
not be a picture there.' (Quotation marks added)

Is this nonsense or, even worse, sinister nonsense intended to dangerously
detach the followers of Rajneesh from reality? Viewed without prejudice
and a bit of understanding of traditional Eastern religious philosophy, a
moment of reflection reveals otherwise. In line with a long tradition of mystical thought, present in the West as well, Bhagwan Rajneesh is using paradoxical language and the focal symbol of his picture to serve a number of
ends: (1) to highlight the folly of identifying our true selves with our physical bodies, or, even worse, our physical appearance; (2) to highlight the
spiritual (that is, non-material) character of our true selves; (3) to highlight
the bewitchment of language and the inadequacy of ordinary concepts in
the face of the ineffable character of the truth. Rajneesh may also be allud-
ing to the basic Buddhist doctrine of 'not-self' (*an-attā* in Pali, *an-ātman* in
Sanskrit)—the claim that there is no permanent self or eternal soul. His picture and the words he uses in the initiation ceremony are analogous to a Zen
Buddhist *koan*. Like the well-known puzzle 'What is the sound of one-hand
clapping?', these seemingly nonsensical questions and claims are used as foci
of concentration in meditation to break the hold of conventional patterns of
thought (i.e., Singer's logical thought), opening the consciousness to a
higher sensibility (*satori* in Zen). From a knowledge of these things one may
still ultimately wish to question or even reject these and other teachings, but
to hold them up to ridicule from sheer ignorance, as Singer does, is counter-
productive and morally suspect.

   6. In all the original reports of the brainwashing of prisoners of war and
political prisoners, the victims were forcibly confined and physically tor-
tured. Yet no academic or legal evidence has ever been presented that any
NRM has ever held potential recruits or members against their will, let alone
physically abused them (e.g., Barker, 1984: 141). Cults are what sociologists
call 'voluntary associations', and that is why their opponents have had to go
to such extremes to establish a psychological justification for the intervention of the state and professional deprogrammers. But, as the original studies of thought control suggest, the evidence is weak for assuming that the
full and involuntary transformation of identity signified by 'brainwashing'
can occur in the absence of physical restraint and abuse. The process of
deprogramming, on the other hand, is defined by the fact that people are

kidnapped from the NRMs, physically held against their will, and subjected to a hostile and intimidating interrogation for days or even weeks.

7. The literature of the anti-cult movement is, as already indicated, distorted by sampling bias (Barker, 1984: 128–31). The brainwashing scenario of NRMs relies heavily on the testimony of individuals who have undergone deprogramming or 'exit counselling'. The latter is the non-coercive equivalent of the former. In her initial popular discussion of the brainwashing accusation, for example, Singer (1979) notes that 75 per cent of her subjects had been deprogrammed. These people are under great pressure to account for their aberrant behaviour (that is, joining a cult) and to direct the blame away from themselves, their families, and the community (Richardson, van der Lans, and Derks, 1986). This may be necessary in order to make peace with their families and regain entry into other community groups (for example, when returning to school or a job), or simply to resolve the cognitive dissonance they are experiencing from the contrast of their present and past behaviour. The brainwashing scenario, to which they are 'programmed', provides a non-stigmatizing way to absolve everyone, most importantly themselves, of responsibility and actually secure the sympathy of others. Furthermore, as discussed, the books and articles of the anti-cultists tend to employ small and non-random samples of stories drawn from sources that are identified either inadequately or not at all. Several academic studies, on the other hand, have revealed a marked and consistent discrepancy between the post-involvement attitudes of converts who leave these groups voluntarily and those who are deprogrammed. Only the latter show a strong statistical correlation with negative views of their cult experience (e.g., Solomon, 1981; Wright, 1984; Lewis, 1986; Lewis and Bromley, 1987; Galanter, 1989; Introvigne and Melton, 1997). Most people who leave an NRM voluntarily (and most of those who leave do so voluntarily) continue to express very positive feelings about their involvement. Wright found that 67 per cent of voluntary defectors said they were 'wiser for the experience' of membership, and only 9 per cent invoked the brainwashing explanation for joining in the first place (Wright and Ebaugh, 1993: 127; see also Levine, 1984: 188). From his study of the Unification Church, Galanter (1989: 116) reports 'a striking contrast' in attitudes between voluntary defectors and those who were deprogrammed:

> The first group had mixed feelings about their experience but expressed a relatively benign view of both their own involvement and the ongoing participation of their remaining compatriots. Most (62%) still felt strongly that they 'cared for the ten members they knew best,' and the large majority (89%) believed that they 'got some positive things' out of membership. On

the other hand, those who were deprogrammed had a much more negative attitude toward the sect and . . . eight out of ten deprogrammed ex-members had participated in attempts to coerce other members to leave, whereas none of those who left voluntarily had done so.

In fact, Wright (1984) and Jacobs (1989) found that half to three-quarters of those who deconvert voluntarily from one NRM eventually join another similar group.

8. The issue of sampling bias, however, raises a related and more complicated problem, that of accounts (Turner 1978; Beckford, 1978; Wallis and Bruce, 1983; Dawson, 1994b; Zablocki, 1996). The study of conversions in general is largely dependent on the 'accounts' provided by converts, whether still members of groups or former members. The problem is to what extent we can trust people's descriptions of their own actions, especially their past actions. Everyday life, history, the social sciences, and the law demonstrate that there is much potential for inaccuracy and deception (including self-deception). Studies of the accounts of deviants, such as murderers and child molesters, and of natural scientists—two seeming extremes—reveal similar interpretive problems (Dawson, 1994b). But conversion accounts have proved to be especially problematic because converts often take the opportunity to witness or proselytize for their faith. In fact, some scholars have argued that the best indicator that a religious conversion has occurred is evidence of the rhetorical phenomenon of biographic reconstruction (Snow and Machalek, 1984; Staples and Mauss, 1987). Religions normatively expect converts to reinterpret their pasts in ways commensurate with their new identities. Converts to all religions, new and old, are strongly inclined to exaggerate the sinfulness or distress of their pre-conversion lives and the rewards of their post-conversion lives. The reverse surely holds true for those who have been deprogrammed. In her research on NRMs, Barker (1984: 170–1) found that respondents often change their interpretations of experiences at some later point. Many who have left NRMs

admitted that they had believed at the time that they were having a religious experience, but had subsequently come to the conclusion that it had been their imagination or the result of some mundane trigger. Conversely, those who had since become part of a religious community were more likely to say that they had dismissed the experience at the time, but now realized that God had been talking to them.

So at the very least, we must be very cautious in accepting conversion accounts at face value, far more cautious than the anti-cultists have even

thought to be, but also more cautious than even most other scholars studying NRMs have been. As Richardson, Balch, and Melton (1993: 217) recom-
mend, when studying any NRM every researcher should seek to use 'a number of data sources simultaneously . . . data should be gathered from
members and ex-members, from apologists *and* detractors, from leaders *and*
followers within the group, from parents *and* from sons and daughters who
are members, and so on.' The inevitable clash of claims will have to be
weighed against the presumably more neutral and exacting observations of
the researcher.

9. The entire credibility of the brainwashing explanation of cult conversions is called into question by the information now available to us on
the low rates of recruitment and high rates of defection experienced by
most NRMs. Contrary to the impression created by the anti-cult movement,
only a very small number of the many thousands of people approached by
NRMs ever agree to attend a lecture, dinner, workshop, or other recruitment
event. An even smaller number choose to join, and most of these soon leave
voluntarily. In her detailed study of the Unification Church, one of the
prime targets of the brainwashing rhetoric, Barker (1984: 144–8, 259)
found that only about 10 per cent of the small number of participants in a
workshop chose to join the group. One-third of these left of their own
accord after four months, and few lasted more than two years. In fact Barker
calculates that no more than 0.5 per cent of prospective converts who visit
a Unification Church centre will be associated with the movement two years
later (see Levine, 1984: 65–6 and James Beckford, cited in Wright, 1987: 2,
for similar estimates). Sampling a more diverse array of groups, Bird and
Reimer (1982) found that two-thirds of the most highly involved members
eventually left, while for the twenty or more NRMs he studied, Saul Levine
(1984: 15) concludes, 'Over ninety per cent [of radical departures] end in
a return home within two years.' In the face of these bleak figures does talk
of brainwashing have any credibility? If the cults use sophisticated techniques to turn their followers into psychological captives and slaves, then
why are the results of their recruiting so poor and how is it that so many
defect voluntarily?

10. In her award-winning study of conversion to the Moonies, Barker
(1984: 194) speaks of a 'checklist' she found herself drawing up of the
'characteristics and experiences . . . frequently taken to indicate that [a] person will be particularly vulnerable . . . to the "lure of the cults".' This checklist, she explains,

> included things like the immaturity of youth; a history of mental distur-
> bances, drug abuse and/or alcoholism; poor and/or erratic performances in

school; divorced parents and/or an unhappy childhood; lack of ability to keep friends; being in a transitory state and/or having no clear prospects or direction in life; and a tendency to be indecisive, and/or to drift from one job and/or girl/boyfriend to another.

These are presumably the kind of characteristics and experiences that mark someone as particularly prone to the 'suggestibility' exploited by mind-control techniques. The trouble is, the data she collected did not conform to the checklist:

> The Moonies did score slightly higher than the control group on some of the characteristics on the checklist, but on others they scored slightly lower, and on yet others there were more similarities between the British Moonies and the (British) control group than there were between the British and European or American Moonies. In other words, national or cultural differences were often more obvious than Moonie/non-Moonie differences. (Barker, 1984: 196)

Pressing on, Barker made an even more startling and complex discovery (1984: 198, 203). Only a small portion of the Moonies seem to display the characteristics indicative of being more prone to 'passive suggestibility' than her control group of ordinary people. What is more, it was the people *most* at risk amongst the attenders of Moonie workshops 'who did *not* join, or, if they did, were among those who would leave pretty quickly'. Some of the Moonies had also 'suffered the sort of experiences which might make the "refuge from society"' explanation a plausible account of their membership. But on the whole their experiences were not markedly worse than those of the control group. And again, those with the more traumatic experiences tended either *not* to join the church or to *leave* shortly after joining. So whatever may draw people to the Unification Church, and perhaps to other NRMs as well, it would not appear to be their susceptibility to being brainwashed, at least not as normally understood and argued by the anti-cult movement.

11. There have been a reasonably large number of psychological and psychiatric studies of people who still are or recently have been members of NRMs (see the summary analyses provided by Rochford et al., 1989; Saliba, 1993; and Richardson, 1995c). Using various combinations of clinical interviews and/or standard psychological tests, researchers have examined the psychological well-being of people involved with such diverse groups as the Unification Church, Hare Krishnas, the Children of God/the Family, Scientology, Zen Buddhism, the Divine Light Mission, the followers of Bhagwan Shree Rajneesh, and various Pentecostal and Jesus movements. The

results, which are very diverse and often divergent, do not support the brainwashing scenario. But more systematic research is needed to clarify the issues that have been raised.

Problems stem from the tendency of the studies undertaken so far to divide into two camps: studies of current members of NRMs, and studies of deprogrammed or disgruntled ex-members. 'More than 75 per cent of studies of the former type tend to show that the psychological profiles of individuals tested fall well within "normal" bounds' (Saliba, 1993: 106). In fact, many of these studies suggest there is evidence for the therapeutic effect of cult involvements. As discussed in point (8), though, the testimonials of cult members hardly constitutes a sound source of information on this point. Certainly some people experience a certain 'relief effect' from their cult involvements (e.g., Galanter, 1989: 35; Rochford et al., 1989), but this effect could well be temporary or superficial. 'Studies of the latter type generally conclude that ex-members suffer from serious mental and emotional dysfunctions that have been directly caused by cultic beliefs and practices.' But this is speculation. No logical way exists for causally linking the distress noted and the instructional programs and lifestyles of the new religions (see Rochford et al., 1989: 69–71). 'It is equally plausible and consistent with the data that the impaired mental and psychological condition of these ex-members existed prior to entry into the cult or is the result of the deprogramming methods themselves' (Saliba, 1993: 107). Moreover, as already noted, too many of these studies fail to employ such fundamental methodological safeguards as random samples and control groups. We know little, that is, about how the results obtained by the anti-cultists compare with data for other groups of people, especially young people. The psychiatrist Saul Levine (1984: 4) says that the hundreds of converts and ex-converts he interviewed 'showed no more sign of pathology . . . than is found in any youthful population.' From the discoveries of Barker discussed in point (10) above, the importance of making such comparisons with control groups is readily seen (see also Barker, 1984: 131–4).

In fact, the strong correlation found by sociologists between people with negative views of their cult involvements and the experience of deprogramming or exit counselling (e.g., Solomon, 1981; Wright, 1984; Lewis, 1986; Lewis and Bromley, 1987) supports the counter-charge that the only deleterious brainwashing, and hence psychological impairment, occurs with deprogramming. It is not difficult to understand why deprogrammed ex-members report far more psychological problems adapting to life after their cult experiences than those who have left of their own volition. As both Steven Wright (1987) and Helen Rose Fuchs Ebaugh (1988) have established, the process by which anyone gives up any role in life, whether an occupation, a marriage, or a religious identity, tends to follow a fairly set pattern of stages by which the person psychologically and socially anticipates and prepares for the impending change (see Wright and Ebaugh, 1993: 124–8). That process is short-circuited by deprogramming, which leaves involuntary ex-members ill-prepared to assume a new identity. In place of gradually forging new grounds of self-worth and purpose in life, those who are deprogrammed are assigned, and often assume, the identity of a victim. But this passive identity causes them to feel vulnerable and in need of completing the process of role exiting. The resultant quest for some more secure identity may explain why so many of the deprogrammed have become deprogrammers themselves.

To clarify the psychological picture, we need reliable psychological profiles of converts before they joined NRMs and of the large number of converts who have left voluntarily. For obvious methodological reasons, it is not likely that we will ever obtain the former. But more studies of the latter type could and should be done. Nevertheless, a survey of the existing literature does clarify one thing: 'The brainwashing model begs the questions it purports to ask and has generated little productive research' (Saliba, 1993: 107).

In general, the diagnostic devices of psychology are not well suited to dealing with the complex issues raised by the cult controversy. Saliba (1993) and Richardson (1995c) both stress that such devices display a fairly consistent normative bias in favour of the modern Western pursuit of individual independence and a pronounced measure of cognitive relativism. When applied, then, to members of those NRMs geared to a more collectivist life and absolutist moral agenda, they tend to produce negatively skewed results: 'Individuals, who for ideological reasons and emotional satisfaction prefer an arranged marriage and/or communal style of living in which their individuality is subordinated, are not necessarily suffering from a personality disorder, as the psychiatric diagnostic manuals infer or assert' (Saliba, 1993: 108). Richardson (1993c) has specifically documented and criticized the negative religious stereotyping and ambivalent attitudes towards religion, especially NRMs, found in *The Diagnostic and Statistical Manual of Mental Disorders* (3rd edition), the bible of the American psychiatrists, psychologists, and social counsellors.

In the end, the inconclusive results of the psychological study of members and ex-members of NRMs cannot conceivably be used to support either the case for or against brainwashing. In the face of the quite specific and dramatic claims of psychologists like Singer, however, it seems odd that the reliable psychological data available so far are so inconclusive, if not largely contrary to the expectations of the anti-cult movement.

12. Are the followers of NRMs brainwashed? There is not much reason for believing so. Are many recruits to NRMs subjected to strong social pressures to join and rapidly introduced to systematic programs of indoctrination? Undoubtedly such is sometimes the case. Barker (1984: 174) comments that there 'can be little doubt that the Moonies are successful in controlling the environment of their workshops.' All is carefully planned, activities are not optional, guests are seldom out of the presence of enthusiastic Moonies, there is little opportunity for the recruits to discuss seriously the teachings being presented amongst themselves, and the lectures and other activities are received with so much enthusiasm by the surrounding Moonie 'cheerleaders', as Barker (1984: 174) calls them, that it can be most difficult to resist the urge to conform. But as she also comments, these practices are 'by no means . . . unique'. Religions have been in the business, throughout the ages, of emotionally prompting and physically and socially supporting the abandonment of old habits of thought, word, and deed and inducing new ones. The American psychiatrist Marc Galanter specifically notes the parallels between the practices of some NRMs and the sponsorship system employed by Alcoholics Anonymous, as well as the kind of group-based induction techniques pioneered by earlier Christian sects (Galanter, 1980; cited in Barker, 1984: 286). Conversions, in religions new and old, occur by way of processes of deconditioning and resocialization, processes readily delineated by established theories of social psychology (see, e.g., Kanter, 1972; Preston, 1981; Long and Hadden, 1983; Wilson, 1984; Richardson, 1993b; Rambo, 1993).

In the face of increased and ever more successful opposition to their medicalized brainwashing model of cult conversion to the best known NRMs, the anti-cult movement has increasingly (1) dissociated itself from true deprogramming in favour of less coercive forms of 'exit counselling' and 'strategic intervention therapy'; (2) expanded the types of organizations targeted as 'destructive cults'; and (3) shifted its legal focus to questions of deception (e.g., Shupe and Bromley, 1994; Coates, 1994; Hassan, 1994; Singer, 1995). Formally, most anti-cult organizations deny that they are still in favour of the forcible removal of members of NRMs. In part this is due to the increased professionalization of the movement, as the leadership has acquired more psychological and legal expertise (see Shupe and Bromley, 1994). Nevertheless, the largest such organization, the Cult Awareness Network, was forced into bankruptcy by the courts in June 1996 when its legal liability for facilitating the failed deprogramming of a young Pentecostalist was demonstrated in a civil suit. As this case shows, the category of destructive cults has also been expanded to include such other new threats to public health as 'therapy cults, political cults, or commercial cults' (Coates, 1994: 93), as well as more traditional Christian groups like fundamentalist and Pentecostal or charismatic sects (e.g., Coates, 1994: 97). This larger number of targets, of course, expands the field of opportunities for the more professionalized anti-cult organizations in the face of the shrinking audience for critiques of the Moonies, Hare Krishna, and so on. Finally, it is clear that issues of deception have acquired a new strategic significance in the anti-cult literature. Once again, using a wholly inappropriate and unrealistic medical definition of 'informed consent', Hassan, Singer, and others claim that acceptable religions should fully disclose all information about themselves, their past, and their practices, as well as any possible negative consequences of joining, to all recruits upon first meeting them (e.g., Singer, 1995: 79–80). As Singer herself comments, under such legal restraints it is unlikely that anyone would ever join another cult. Of course, it is equally unlikely that anyone would ever join the vast majority of voluntary associations operating in the United States, including most of the established religions, if they were compelled to operate under the same guidelines. Outside of strictly experimental circumstances (in medical or psychological research), these kinds of ethical dictates for complete disclosure are completely unrealistic, inappropriate, and unenforceable.

The Active versus Passive Convert

It is ironic that in carrying the assumptions of human passivity underlying the dominant social-scientific models of conversion to an extreme (e.g., Lofland and Stark, 1965: Chap. 3), the brainwashing scenario of the anti-cult movement prompted a series of researches into the processes of conversion in NRMs that have fostered a new image of converts, one that is quite antithetical to the anti-cult position (see Richardson, 1985, and Dawson, 1990, for overviews). Roger Straus (1976, 1979), for instance, uses the testimony of converts to various evangelical and charismatic Christian groups, Nichiren Soshu, Divine Light Mission, Transcendental Meditation, Kundalini Yoga, Eckankar, and Scientology to suggest that religious seekers, far from being manipulated by cults, are often creatively exploiting religious collectivities to effect desired self-transformations by instrumentally experimenting with new roles and meanings in their lives. And on the basis of the cumulative empirical record, Bromley and Shupe (1979b, 1986) argue that the processes of affiliation with and disaffiliation from the Unification Church, Hare Krishna, and the Children of God (now the Family), are best thought of as rather ordinary transitions in people's social roles. These affiliations and disaffiliations are the result of various *ad hoc* processes of negotiation between those converting or deconverting and the NRMs, and as such are subject to their mutual influence.

The prototypical conversion experience in Western culture is that of St Paul, the great Christian evangelist and founder of the Church (Acts 9: 1–19). Paul, a Palestinian Jew, we are told, was on the road to Damascus to persecute Christians when he was suddenly smitten blind by a brilliant flash of light from which Jesus spoke to him. Three days later his blindness was healed by a pious Christian from Damascus sent to restore his sight by Jesus. Paul then converted and was baptized into the new faith. This simple story has set in place the almost normative features of Christian conversion experiences. Much like Paul's experience, conversions are traditionally thought (1) to be sudden and often dramatic, (2) to be emotional and even irrational, (3) to be single events, (4) to create total life changes that last a lifetime, (5) to be individual experiences, and not a collective phenomenon, and (6) to be something the convert passively receives as a result of the actions of some seemingly external agency. For centuries, of course, the external agency was thought to be supernatural (for example, God). From the psychological and/or sociological perspectives of today, the external agency is often conceived to be some compelling set of unconscious processes or cultural and social expectations and pressures. The pattern of change in question is usually understood in terms of a sequence of changes in *beliefs*, followed by changes in *attitudes*, that produces congruent changes in the *behaviour* of converts.

The new view emerging from the study of NRMs and from other developments in the social sciences postulates a much more 'active' involvement of converts in the fashioning of their own experiences (see Richardson, 1985; Dawson, 1990). This more active interpretation is based on a number of observations:

1. Sudden conversions are actually rare. More commonly, conversion experiences, even those that seem sudden, are rooted in long-term, though partially cloaked, struggles of conscience and identity. Mounting tension and discontent, combined with anticipatory socialization, may result in a triggered moment of exhaustion and self-surrender that becomes identified as the moment of conversion.

2. Many converts engage in some measure of 'seekership' before converting. They have been actively searching for information and opportunities. Moreover, they often have what has come to be called 'conversion careers' (Richardson, 1980). That is, many have been affiliated with other groups before converting to their current faith.

3. Processes of conversion appear to be largely social (that is, collective). They are the result of definable interactions between specific individ-

uals and groups where an exchange of rewards is negotiated. Contact itself is most commonly the result of social networks, and involvement instrumentally depends on the development of close interpersonal bonds between converts and members of the group to which they convert.

4. In-depth interviews with converts and observation of participants of various NRMS has revealed much more rational calculation and conscious lifestyle experimentation than expected. Converts are more reflexively aware of their situation than social scientists expected—assessing circumstances, weighing the advantages and disadvantages of affiliation. In fact, they often display latent reservations, when pressed, about their actions long after converting. In some instances, they even have begun to plan their post-cult lives while still being actively involved, even as leaders, in their religions (Wright, 1987).

5. Consequently, it appears that many conversions entail more role playing than actual transformation of the personalities or self-conceptions of converts. Converts learn how to pass for a member of the group they have joined. They learn the 'convert role' in order to explore possibilities within the group (Balch, 1980). *Behavioural* changes, that is, precede any real changes in *attitudes* and then finally *beliefs*. In fact, the latter changes may or may not follow at all.

The growing evidence that conversion is a more active than passive process points the way to a rational-choice approach to the study of religion, as discussed in the Introduction. Within the limits of the convert's own definition of the situation, social scientists have no *a priori* reason for assuming that religious activities, like conversions, are any more irrational and hence inexplicable than other kinds of social actions. As Gartrell and Shannon (1985), Stark and Bainbridge (1985, 1987), Neitz (1987), Dawson (1990), Stark and Finke (1993), and Stark and Iannaccone (1993) have argued, principles of exchange apply in this context as well as elsewhere. Individuals and groups satisfy each other's demands and needs in an exchange of goods and services. Dissolution rather logically follows from declining returns and diminished or changed needs. It is often difficult, however, to decipher from the data at hand the real and precise nature of the exchange and the individual and group needs at stake. This requires first-hand familiarity with the individuals and groups in question, something academics rarely have the opportunity to acquire and the anti-cultist rarely even try to acquire.

Concluding Remarks

Given the inherent weaknesses of the case for coercive conversion, and our increased awareness of how converts actively participate in their conversions, why does the talk of 'brainwashing' persist? Thomas Robbins offers the best answer when he asks and answers a very typical sociological question: Who stands to benefit from the perpetuation of the coercive conversion myth?

> The medicalized 'mind-control' claim articulates a critique of deviant new religions which not only obviates civil libertarian objections of social control but also meets the needs of the various groups which are threatened by or antagonistic to cults: *Mental health professionals*, whose role in the rehabilitation of victims of 'destructive cultism' is highlighted; *parents*, whose opposition to cults and willingness to forcibly 'rescue' cultist progeny are legitimated; *ex-converts*, who may find it meaningful and rewarding to reinterpret their prior involvement with stigmatized groups as basically passive and unmotivated; and *clerics*, who are concerned to avoid appearing to persecute religious competitors. An anti-cult coalition of these groups is possible only *if medical and mental health issues are kept in the fore-front* . . . and if the medical model is employed in such a way as to disavow the intent to persecute minority beliefs and to stress the psychiatric healing of involuntary pathology. (Robbins, 1984: 253; see also Richardson, van der Lans, and Derks, 1986)

This state of affairs continues to make it necessary for scholars of NRMs to speak out against the misconceived yet still pervasive public paranoia about NRMs, in spite of the risk of appearing biased.

In the end, though, all parties to this dispute must guard against indulging too readily in reductionistic analyses. We are often quick to question the motives or causes of other people's behaviour, even though we expect others to accept our motives at face value. We may deny others this courtesy just because we dislike or fail to understand their point of view. Yet because everyone's thoughts and actions are socially conditioned, all that we say or do may at times bear the marks of rationalization, self-deception, or simply ignorance. For that reason social scientists are cautious in attributing motives, especially if they are contrary to those given by the persons in question. Such is particularly the case with reasons given for religious beliefs. Special care must be taken in the face of the irresolvable metaphysical questions raised by claims to knowledge of the transcendent, and the exercise of free will (Dawson, 1986, 1988). We cannot simply discount the claims of converts to be acting in accord with some divine plan and to be acting freely. We have no conclusive way either to verify or to refute such claims.

Chapter Five

Why Do Some New Religious Movements Become Violent?

Making Sense of the Seemingly Senseless

I was prompted to write this book by the inadequacy and hostility of the immediate public response to a tragic case of cult violence, the mass murder-suicide of the Solar Temple (l'Order du Temple solaire) in 1994. Like the Jonestown massacre of 1978 and the Waco débâcle of 1993, the unexpected deaths of the Solar Temple galvanized public alarm about NRMs. Such events keep alive the exaggerated fears of the anti-cult movement in the minds of a public that is rarely affected, in any direct way, by the activities of any cults. Since then the curiosity and worries of the public have been heightened by the further death of five more members of the Solar Temple, followed rapidly by the suicide of thirty-nine members of the Heaven's Gate cult, on 22 and 26 March 1997.

For the anti-cult movement these new tragedies are fuel for the fire of cult controversy. They can be used to ensure the continued attention of the public to their cause.[1] Yet, in the end, the anti-cult account of the NRMs, with its programmatic reliance on the brainwashing scenario, does not help us understand the dynamic leading to violence that really does occur in some NRMs. The explanations offered in so many television documentaries and films about cults do no better. Purporting, as they all tend to do, to tell the 'whole' or 'true' story, these journalistic accounts seem content to chart the course of events leading to disaster, while highlighting the material, social, and other benefits enjoyed by the leaders of the groups in question. An accurate description in combination with an imputation of avarice is somehow thought to be sufficient to render these bizarre events self-explanatory. But the images in our memory of the sun-bloated bodies of the men, women, and children of Jonestown, the Davidian compound burning to the ground in Waco, the charred remains of the members of the Solar Temple, and the neatly arranged and cloaked bodies of Heaven's Gate defy such easy treatment. Do the events themselves, along with suppositions about ulterior motives, really explain why so many people were willingly to put their lives in danger or surrender them altogether?

In the media binge that immediately followed each of these tragedies, the spectres of criminality and insanity loomed large. How else could one account for the implausibility of people choosing to die for their religious beliefs in our seemingly secular age? Seeking to capitalize on the lurid appeal of the unexpected carnage, journalistic investigators speculate too readily about the motives of those who died. Rumours and fragments of uncontested testimony circulate in the press as facts. But a real understanding of how or why these extraordinary events happened hinges on more systematic and empathetic study of the groups involved, their beliefs and practices, their histories, and the social and psychological attributes of their members and leaders. As it is, we are just beginning to discern some of the complex conditions that may have led these particular people to collectively sacrifice themselves for their religious visions of the future.

Detailed studies have been undertaken of Jim Jones,[2] the Peoples Temple, and the death of 914 people at Jonestown (e.g., Reiterman and Jacobs, 1982; Hall, 1987; Chidester, 1988; Maaga, 1998); the death of eighty people during the stand-off at the Branch Davidian compound in Waco, Texas (e.g., Wright, 1995b; Tabor and Gallagher, 1995); and the murder-suicide of seventy-four members of the Solar Temple[3] (Introvigne, 1995; Palmer, 1996; Hall and Schuyler, 1997). With these and other studies in mind (e.g., Melton, 1992b; Wessinger, 1998), can we now say something more about the forces that precipitate cult violence? Are there some factors and processes that are trans-situational, factors and processes that might help us to discern if and why we may witness such tragedies again? Others have already reconstructed what happened to the Peoples Temple, the Branch Davidians, and the Solar Temple (see the studies cited above); my focus is on a more generic line of inquiry: let us pry into why such events happen at all.[4]

The answer sketched is restricted to a consideration of some of the social-situational factors noted in the excellent analyses of the specific cases at hand. No attempt will be made to deal with the more speculative and theoretically loaded explanations of these instances of cult violence in terms of various theories of psychopathology or depth psychology (e.g., parts of Robbins and Anthony, 1995, and Anthony and Robbins, 1997; Strozier, 1994, 1997). In my opinion it is far too difficult, and probably unnecessary, to determine if the followers and leaders of the Peoples Temple, Branch

Davidians, Solar Temple, and Heaven's Gate fit the profile of some problematic 'personality type' (narcissistic, authoritarian, or whatever), and then
to stipulate further how this psychological type may be prone to violence
under certain circumstances. In each case we simply do not know enough
about the psychology of the actual members of these groups. However, the
behaviour of these sacrificed souls can be at least partially explained by calling on some simpler, well-known, and more empirically substantiated principles of social psychology—principles that seem to apply to all of us. Of
course, the analysis offered in this regard remains tentative and incomplete.
A more complete understanding of the dynamics of cult-related violence
transcends the scope of this introductory text.

We are always fearful of the strange and unknown, and this is the root
of our attitudes towards NRMs. The popular media are just as prone to this
fear, a fear they often exploit to get headlines, sell papers, or attract viewers. The presence of violence, with the implied threat that it may happen
again, heightens the anxiety that breeds misunderstanding between NRMs
and the public. The anti-cult movement, moreover, does its professional
best to sustain this fear of violence. In an environment fraught with emo-
tion and suspicion, dubious claims are made and accepted, minor wrong-
doings exaggerated, and exonerating reports downplayed or ignored (see
Melton, 1992b). At different times in the early 1990s, for example, the children of the Family (formerly the Children of God) were taken from their
parents in sudden and sweeping midnight police raids in Spain, Australia,
Argentina, and England. The raids followed widely circulated yet often
anonymous reports of child abuse. Each of these cases attracted considerable international publicity—but not so the findings, many months later, of
the courts. In each country the charges were dismissed as unwarranted and
ill-conceived, but one has to search the back pages of the newspapers to
learn this or discover why (see Richardson, 1996: 894–9).

This is not to suggest that there is no violence associated with new or
at least marginal religions. As Melton (1992b) carefully documents, groups
like the Black Muslims, Synanon, Hare Krishna, Scientology, House of
Judah, the Children of God, Church Universal and Triumphant, and various fringe Mormon and Christian groups have been involved in incidents
of assault, the harassment of opponents or defectors, the stockpiling of
weapons, interference with or resistance to civil authorities, abuse of children, death threats, and even, in a few instances, murder. But in fairness,
three points must be kept in mind. First, in all but a few cases the incidents
in question have not been systematically linked to any specific policies of
the religious groups.[5] Rather, in most cases they appear to be the aberrant
acts of overzealous or unstable individuals associated with these groups. In

some cases, of course, the defensive, perhaps even paranoid, attitudes of religious leaders towards outsiders and defectors helped to motivate some members to commit illegal and dangerous acts. But the circumstances differ quite significantly from case to case. Second, when one considers the claims made by the anti-cult movement itself about both the number of NRMs in existence (often stated to be 3,000 or more), and the number of people ever involved with such groups (often stated to be about ten million in the United States alone), then the number of incidents of cult violence is not exceptional, especially in comparison with the remarkably high levels of violent crime in America. Third, and in a similar vein, one need only think of the surprisingly numerous cases of child molestation that have recently scandalized the Catholic Church to appreciate that NRMs have no monopoly on deviant behaviour. Few people, however, would be inclined to condemn the Catholic Church as a whole for the errant ways of some of its members. Placed in proper cultural context, then, the crimes of most NRMs are rather ordinary, though none the less regrettable and truly worthy of condemnation. The tragedies of Jonestown, Waco, the Solar Temple, and Heaven's Gate call out for special attention precisely because they are extraordinary, even within the context of other known incidents of cult violence.

As the historical reconstruction of these events has demonstrated, each tragedy is the result of the confluence of a rather idiosyncratic set of factors, so that it is not easy to draw general conclusions. In fact, as Robbins and Anthony (1995: 237) point out, the eruption of violence stems from the interaction of a diverse array of external circumstances, which they call 'exogenous factors', and internal processes, which they call 'endogenous factors', and 'the relative weight or significance of the contributions of exogenous and endogenous factors may vary from one situated event to another.' Robbins and Anthony (1995: 237–8) use a comparison of Jonestown and Waco to illustrate their point:

> To elicit a fatal violent response from Jim Jones's Peoples Temple required only that a congressman and a press entourage visit Jonestown and attempt to return to the United States with a handful of defectors. In contrast, to set off the immolations in Waco (assuming that the Davidians were responsible for setting the fire), what had to transpire was not only the initial military-style raid on the 'cult compound' by the Bureau of Alcohol, Tobacco, and Firearms (BATF) but also the subsequent breaking down of the walls of the compound by armoured vehicles and the insertion of CS gas. It may therefore be a viable thesis that the role or weight of exogenous factors was smaller at Jonestown compared to Waco. Or to put it another way, the

Branch Davidian community at Waco was less internally volatile or vio-
lence-prone than the Peoples Temple settlement in Guyana.

The exogenous factors that condition cult-related violence (for example, the nature and levels of the hostility, stigmatization, and persecution
experienced by a group) can be highly variable and difficult to assess com-
paratively. A survey of the limited literature available reveals, however,
that analysts have repeatedly linked at least three endogenous features of
NRMs to the outbreak of violence: (1) apocalyptic beliefs or at least world-
rejecting beliefs; (2) heavy investments in charismatic leadership; and
(3) processes of social encapsulation that may lead to problems of symbolic
boundary maintenance (see Hall, 1981; Smith, 1982; Mills, 1982; Wallis
and Bruce, 1986; Galanter, 1989; Robbins and Anthony, 1995; Palmer,
1996). No one of these factors will generate violent behaviour, nor will their
simple combination. These three endogenous factors constitute some of the
prime conditions that seemingly are 'necessary' for the eruption of major
incidents of cult-related violence, but they are not 'sufficient' to predict this
violence.

An interesting analogy can be drawn, for example, with what we know
about a related phenomenon: the response of marginal religions to the failure of their predictions or prophecies (e.g., Festinger et al., 1956; Hardyck
and Braden, 1962; Zygmunt, 1972; Balch et al., 1983; Melton, 1985;
Palmer and Finn, 1992; Dein, 1997). Marginal religions are often apocalyptic, and when the world is not destroyed as they predicted, or the alien
space ships fail to arrive to rescue the chosen from some disaster, what happens? Do the groups in question collapse, as common sense suggests they
would? Or do they seek to compensate for the failure by renewing their
efforts at proselytizing, as hypothesized by Festinger et al. (1956) in their
famous book *When Prophecy Fails*? The response will vary, we now realize,
with the presence or absence of several additional variables of a largely
endogenous kind (for example, the type, quality, and use of the channels of
communication available between members of a group, or the inclination of
the leadership to provide some immediate and plausible explanation for the
failure of their predictions). Can a similar pattern of identifiable determinants be specified for incidents of cult violence? It is beginning to look as if
such may indeed be the case.

Apocalyptic Beliefs

In each of the recent instances of mass religious violence involving NRMs,
apocalyptic beliefs—prophecies about the ultimate end of human history—

have played a crucial role in structuring and motivating the acts of the people who died, either by their own hands or at the hands of others. Belief in such prophecies date back to antiquity and are present in almost all cultures. But they have been particularly strong in the West, and especially in the Christian tradition. Biblical sources have stimulated speculation about and preparation for the time when 'time shall be no more', prompting many violent episodes over the centuries. In 1525, for example, during the Protestant Reformation, visions of a new age and the final triumph of good over evil inspired the radical and charismatic Protestant theologian Thomas Münster to lead a mass revolt, known as the Peasants' War. This ill-conceived venture resulted in his own execution and the death of tens of thousands of his followers (see Lewy, 1974: 110–16; Boyer, 1992: 58). Nine years later, however, the same apocalyptic convictions guided Jan Matthys and his Anabaptist followers (that is, believers in the rebaptism of adults, hence *ana*baptists) when they seized control of the German city of Münster, declaring it to be the New Jerusalem and instituting a new order of Christian communism and free love. Their utopian experiment soon turned into a reign of terror and oppression, and like Thomas Münster and his supporters before them, they too perished, massacred by the forces of the ruling German princes (see Lewy, 1974: 116–29; Boyer, 1992: 59–60).[6]

These well-known incidents from European history are far from unique. The Middle Ages were marked by hundreds of these apocalyptic uprisings, all with equally disastrous results (Cohen, 1961). The apocalyptic beliefs that inspired so much calamity, if not the acts of violence themselves, have persisted in some strength into the modern world. They have played a particularly prominent role in the cultural history of the United States, more prominent than we are now inclined to recall. 'From the early seventeenth century through to the late eighteenth century, the entire span of American colonial history was marked by speculation about America's role in God's plan. That the colonizing venture began at a time of intense apocalyptic awareness in England meant that it, like everything else in these years, took on an aura of eschatological meaning' (Boyer, 1992: 68). Though less prevalent in the nineteenth century, prophecies of the dramatic and imminent end of the world inspired many important and uniquely American religious groups, like the sensationalistic Millerite movement of the 1830s and 1840s, which gave rise to the Seventh Day Adventists; the new apocalyptic vision of Joseph Smith, which laid the foundations of the Church of Latter Day Saints (that is, the Mormons); and the apocalyptic claims of Charles Taze Russell, which undergird the teachings of the Jehovah's Witnesses (see, e.g., Penton, 1985). In fact, talk of the apocalypse permeated the revivalistic culture of the Methodist and Baptist churches throughout the nineteenth century and continues to this day. One need only listen to a Billy Graham crusade or to the programs of a host of other televangelists to hear the familiar apocalyptic refrains and admonitions repeated over and over again.

But what is the basis of this apocalyptic fervour? In brief, God's plan for the end of human history is laid out, in rather cryptic form, in four main texts of the Bible: in the Old Testament the important passages are chapters 37–9 of the Book of Ezekiel and the Book of Daniel; in the New Testament, the relevant sources are the thirteenth chapter of the Gospel of Mark and the Book of Revelation. The latter text, the last book of the Bible, is the best known, most influential, and most extensive account of the apocalypse. The Book of Revelation presents a narrative of the end times of staggering symbolic complexity, ambiguity, and detail. The account takes the form of the prophetic vision of John of Patmos, a Christian being persecuted by the Romans. In nineteen brief chapters the Book of Revelation gives a detailed and truly bizarre description of the miraculous events that will precede and accompany the return of Christ to earth and the beginning of a millennium of peace. The early Christians eagerly awaited the events foretold, for John's vision states that 'the time is at hand' (Revelation 1:3). Throughout the centuries, however, countless people have believed that the events of their own times conformed to the events prophesied by John, and so they have prepared themselves to meet their Maker and to suffer the terrible tribulations that they have been told will first afflict humanity. For the time just before the end, the time of apocalypse, is to be bloody indeed, as numerous wars and natural disasters, such as plagues, earthquakes, and fires from heaven, are destined to ravage the earth and its people. All is to culminate in a final colossal battle—Armageddon—between the forces of evil, led by Satan's representative on earth—a world ruler called the anti-Christ—and the forces of good, led by a warrior Christ.

The fate awaiting us is so horrific in scope and kind that, as the Bible says, 'in those days men shall seek death, and shall not find it; and shall desire to die, and death shall flee from them' (Revelation 9:6). Calamity after calamity is described by John, with an imagery that is strange to our modern minds. But to provide some sense of the force of the vision, at one point, for example, John characteristically recounts:

> And I saw the seven angels which stood before God; and to them were given seven trumpets.
>
> And another angel came and stood at the altar, having a golden censer; and there was given unto him much incense, that he should offer it with the prayers of all saints upon the golden altar which was before the throne. . . .

And the angel took the censer, and filled it with fire of the altar, and cast it into the earth: and there were voices, and thunderings, and lightnings, and an earthquake.

And the seven angels which had the seven trumpets prepared themselves to sound.

The first angel sounded, and there followed hail and fire mingled with blood, and they were cast upon the earth: and the third part of trees was burnt up, and all the green grass was burnt up.

And the second angel sounded, and as it were a great mountain burning with fire was cast into the sea: and a third of the sea became blood. . . .

And the fifth angel sounded, and I saw a star fall from heaven unto the earth: and to him was given the key of the bottomless pit.

And he opened the bottomless pit; and there arose a smoke out of the pit, as the smoke of a great furnace; and the sun and the air were darkened. . . .

And there came out of the smoke locusts upon the earth: and unto them was given power, as the scorpions of the earth have power.

And it was commanded them that they should not hurt the grass of the earth, neither any green thing . . . but only those men which have not the seal of god in their foreheads.

And to them it was given that they should not kill them, but that they should be tormented five months: and their torment was as the torment of a scorpion, when he striketh a man. . . . (Revelation 8:2–8, 9:1–5; Authorized Version)

This passage, though typical, is also one of the milder and most comprehensible in the Book of Revelation, and the disasters it foretells are only a small part of a series of repeated assaults upon the earth. Since the eighteenth century some have believed that of the population of the world, 144,000 of the faithful are to be spared and taken up into heaven, in what is called 'the rapture'. Countless others, redeemed by their prolonged struggle with these calamities and the forces of the anti-Christ, will also eventually be blessed with eternal bliss here on earth. In the end, after many clashes, Satan and his earthly and spiritual minions are to be consigned to an eternity of torment in 'the lake of fire'.

The details of John's revelation, barely suggested here, have baffled, perplexed, and fascinated scholars and lay people alike for centuries. The obscure yet graphic imagery of John's apocalyptic vision has given rise to countless interpretations. For David Koresh and the Branch Davidians the decoding of the Book of Revelation was a pivotal concern. It obsessively occupied Koresh's thoughts while he struggled to resist the BATF and FBI

agents that had laid siege to his home. He tried to speak with the FBI nego-
tiators for hours about the need to understand the ways of God, as given in
the Book of Revelation and elsewhere, in order to understand his community and his own future course of action. At the time of his death he was
working on a manuscript in which he was deciphering the revelation and
his own role in the cosmic drama. He said he would surrender to the
authorities upon its completion, and as best we can tell it was almost complete. But the FBI agents had run out of patience. They had already cast
Koresh as a crazy man or a terrorist. They were not particularly interested
in nor very sympathetic to his religious monologues, which they dismissed
as 'Bible babble' (Tabor, 1995: 266; Sullivan, 1996: 221). Unable to turn
him from his endless preoccupation with religious concerns, they soon
stopped listening and decided to apply the tactics of 'psychological warfare'
to the Davidian compound. The power and water were cut off, communication with the outside world was blocked, and the men, women, and children in the compound were bombarded with bright lights and loud noises
such as Tibetan chants, sounds of rabbits and lambs dying, and rock music,
while helicopters hovered overhead throughout the day and night.

No effort was made to grasp and use the dynamics of biblical apocalypticism, by calling on the help of religious scholars, for example, to
address Koresh in the language with which he understood his situation.
From the perspective of the Davidians, then, surely the anti-Christ and his
minions were at the door, dressed in the tactical combat gear of the BATF and
FBI. The prophecies of the apocalypse were coming true! Perhaps a knowl-
edgeable dialogue about the texts with which he interpreted his world
could have led Koresh to think otherwise? We will never know, because the
FBI chose to ignore the advice of its own behavioural scientists from the
Criminal Investigative Analysis division of the National Center for the
Analysis of Violent Crime at the FBI Academy, who urged greater patience,
tactical withdrawal, and the opening of more channels of religious dialogue
(Wright, 1995a; Ammerman, 1995: 290–1; Sullivan, 1996: 219–20). They
chose instead to launch the final assault on the compound. Four tanks
spraying CS gas[7] were used to crash holes in the walls of the compound, and
though the FBI could see that the Davidians were using kerosene lanterns to
light their home, no fire trucks were on hand when a blazing fire soon
engulfed the fragile wooden structure, killing Koresh and almost all of his
followers, including sixteen children under the age of five.[8]

An apocalyptic world-view may, of course, stem from or largely incorporate materials from elsewhere than the Bible. The Solar Temple, for example, grew out of a very long and very complicated tradition of secret neo-
Christian mystical organizations based on ancient and medieval lore about

the quest for the Holy Grail and the teachings and tragic fate of a powerful twelfth-century ascetic order of warrior monks called the Knights Templar. To this already eclectic mixture of beliefs and practices the Solar Temple added a variety of occult notions 'ranging from Rosicrucianism to Egyptian thanatology to Luc Jouret's oriental folk medicine and ecological apocalypticism' (Palmer, 1996: 305). Through a complex manipulation of these diverse ideas, the core members of the Temple were prompted to believe that the time was right to protect the group from what appeared to be imminent collapse. This final act of self-defence took the form of a radical and final 'transit' of the membership, through the ritual orchestration of their physical deaths, to a higher level of spiritual existence in another part of the galaxy. The apocalyptic beliefs in question, in other words, were significantly different from those guiding the Branch Davidians or the Peoples Temple, but the consequences were much the same (as carefully reconstructed in the accounts of the events surrounding the tragedy provided by Introvigne, 1995; Palmer, 1996; and Hall and Schuyler, 1997).

Much the same can be said about Heaven's Gate. One need only read the advertisement that the group ran in *USA Today* in 1993, or the World Wide Web page they later created. In both places, Do (the leader previously known as Peep) issues the same warning: 'The earth's present "civilization" is about to be recycled—spaded under. Its inhabitants are refusing to evolve. The "weeds" have taken over the garden and disturbed its usefulness beyond repair' (*New York Post*, 1997: 179, 196). In the days immediately preceding their suicide, the group's Web page declared: 'Red Alert. HALE-BOPP Brings Closure.' Here and elsewhere, in line with their own synthesis of traditional religious themes and contemporary UFO mythology, they frankly announced their plans to soon leave their earthly 'containers' (that is, their bodies), to be carried by a UFO thought to be accompanying the comet Hale-Bopp to their new home in 'The Evolutionary Level Beyond Human (the "Kingdom of Heaven")' (*New York Post*, 1997: 207).

There can be little doubt, then, that the Branch Davidians were prepared to die for their apocalyptic beliefs, whether in fact they were ultimately responsible for their own deaths or not. And the members of the Solar Temple and Heaven's Gate acted on their beliefs with clear premeditation. So in what ways are these apocalyptic beliefs related to at least the potential for religious violence? A number of behavioural consequences logically follow from the belief that we may be living in the last days (see Robbins and Anthony, 1995: 239–41). First, for one anticipating the millennium of peace following Christ's return, conventional rules and norms, even the law itself, become relative. Of what good are the laws of humans, who are beings steeped in evil, in the face of the ultimate acts of divine justice and retribution? The righteous will not need the force of law to live in peace and joy, and the evil are destined to perish. Second, serious anticipation of the apocalypse entails preparing to deal with violent times and the persecution of the righteous by the Antichrist (before the return of Christ). Many of the saved will be forced to struggle long and hard with the forces of evil before their salvation; to that end weapons must be secured and defences prepared, for example, by building shelters, storing supplies, and generally training to be self-sufficient. This anticipation of violence sets the stage for its actual occurrence, as people look for evidence to confirm their fears and legitimate their preparations. In the process they will be inclined to try to identify their enemies in advance. This leads to a third behavioural consequence of apocalyptic beliefs: such an ultimate and emotionally volatile conception of one's situation greatly bolsters the common human tendency to 'demonize' our enemies. Opponents are portrayed as people who are capable of the most heinous acts, and thus they can be fairly resisted with the most extreme force. Fourth, the language and symbolism of Christian apocalypticism are steeped in what has been called 'exemplary-dualism' (Robbins and Anthony, 1979a, 1987; Anthony and Robbins, 1997). All is either good or evil, of God or of Satan, and this sharply dichotomized view of the world 'confers deep eschatological significance on the social and political conflicts of the day, thereby raising the stakes of victory or defeat in immediate worldly struggles. Thus communism, radical feminism, the papacy, and exotic cults have all been identified by some Protestant millenarians with the biblical Beast or the "Whore of Babylon"', other names for the Antichrist in the Book of Revelation (Robbins and Anthony, 1995: 243). From such a perspective, great importance can be attributed to relatively small events, precipitating a response that would appear to be disproportionate. Fifth and lastly, as can easily be appreciated, a life lived in serious expectation of the apocalypse tends to instil a level of enthusiasm for the cause that can blind a person's judgement on matters both great and small.

The role of apocalyptic ideas of diverse sorts in fostering extreme behaviour in new religions is readily documented. What is less easily realized is the depth of conviction and commitment that such ideas can inspire. This requires an act of considerable personal and sociological imagination. One might keep in mind, however, that more than a year after the original death of fifty-three members of the Solar Temple, sixteen more members chose to ritually kill themselves (21 December 1995). Then, even more surprisingly, five more members took their own lives on 22 March 1997. Exploring precisely why and how apocalyptic beliefs can have such a grip on people's consciousnesses goes well beyond the scope of what we can sensibly hope to address here (see Strozier, 1994). Robbins and Anthony (1995: 249) call our attention, though, to one obviously important factor: 'Millenarian-apocalyptic worldviews are most likely to be associated with volatility and violence when they are embodied in charismatic "messianic" leaders who identify the millennial destiny of humankind with their own personal vicissitudes.' Charismatic leadership is itself problematic; combined with an apocalyptic conception of the world it can be lethal—but only if the charismatic pattern of authority enacted in an apocalyptic group takes on a specific character.

In saying all this, however, we must recognize that even though there have been many world-rejecting apocalyptic groups, few of them have been implicated in any acts of violence, towards themselves or others (Hall, 1981; Robbins and Anthony, 1995: 243). At present, many millions of Americans take the apocalyptic prophecies of the Bible seriously.[9] But before those beliefs can lead to dangerous actions, many other things, including the charismatic leadership we are going to examine next, must come into play (see, e.g., Barkun, 1990; O'Leary, 1994).

Charismatic Leadership

'Prophecies', Robbins and Anthony dryly observe, 'presuppose prophets' (1995: 245), and most apocalyptic movements presuppose belief in at least two kinds of prophets: the original founders of the apocalyptic vision and contemporary figures who expound this vision to a new age. The presence of the latter is itself usually taken as a sign of the fulfilment of the original prophecy and, as such, a necessary constituent of continued belief in the prophecy. It is the destiny of the contemporary prophet to prepare the way for and to herald the completion of the original prophecy. Throughout history the relevance of apocalyptic lore to this world has been tied inextricably to the appearance of a prophet, a religious leader with charismatic authority.

Following Max Weber (1964: 324–92), sociologists have traditionally distinguished between three 'ideal types' of legitimate authority in society: traditional authority, charismatic authority, and rational-legal authority. Leaders are said to govern by tradition when their right to exercise authority over others is granted by the governed because it has simply always been so. Custom dictates that the nobility or others have the divine or natural right to rule. With rational-legal authority, however, the right to rule is identified with certain legally constituted offices, no matter who may occupy those public positions. The authority is invested in the position, not the person. For most of human history traditional authority has held sway, whereas the modern world is marked by the ascendency of different regimes of rational-legal authority, like those established by the English, American, French, Russian, and Chinese revolutions. History has repeatedly witnessed as well, though, the rise to power of those who are granted the right to rule by virtue of their 'supernatural, superhuman, or at least specifically exceptional powers or qualities' (Weber, 1964: 358–9). This is charismatic authority, rooted in the display of seemingly divine gifts. One need only think of such great military and political figures as Alexander the Great, Julius Caesar, Napoleon, Hitler, Stalin, and Mao. But of course one also thinks of the founders of the world's great religions, the Buddha, Moses, Jesus, Mohammed, and many other prophets, sages, and saints from Saint Francis to Madame Blavatsky.

True charisma, however, is not so much an attribute of someone's personality as it is a quality that people socially attribute to someone. No charisma exists in the absence of the recognition of a group, which then grants authority to the person on that basis. It is an inter-subjective phenomenon born of social interaction. Moreover, as social analyses consistently reveal, even the 'imputation of extraordinary qualities to the leader is a consequence of charismatic activities, not their foundation' (Couch, 1989: 274). Accordingly, many sociologists have begun to explore the ways in which charisma is acquired or 'socially constructed', how it operates, and how it can be lost (e.g., Wilson, 1975; Johnson, 1979; Wallis, 1982, 1984; Palmer, 1988; Couch, 1989; Bird, 1993). Being a charismatic leader need not be correlated with any particular virtues, exceptional intelligence, or even general competence. It undoubtedly is related to the possession of some special talents—but of a diverse kind difficult to specify. Bryan Wilson complains (1975: 6–7) that the modern tendency to equate charisma simply with the attractiveness or appeal of politicians, entertainers, and other media personalities unduly dilutes the magico-religious quality of charismatic leadership. Charismatic leaders, like the prophets of the Old Testament, Hitler, or David Koresh and Do, may often be less than attractive, admirable, or imposing.[10] Yet they are able, rather mysteriously, to galvanize the complete commitment of followers in ways unparalleled by other forms of authority. As Weber (1964), Wilson (1975), Wallis (1982), and many others commentators have stressed, the authority of the charismatic leader is founded in a deeply personal relationship with his or her followers, a relationship of extraordinary faith and trust. It is hard to say why this should be the case. But, without seeking to belittle the experience, we can say that the demand that persists in our societies for charismatic leaders undoubtedly stems, at least partially, from a simple origin: 'It is the easiest and perhaps the most natural recourse for [people] . . . in distress to believe that a father [or mother] will come and save them' (Wilson, 1975: 96; see also Chidester, 1988; Jacobs, 1989).

A crucial feature of charismatic leadership, which is of particular concern to us, is that it is non-institutional or even anti-institutional. Charismatic leaders, Wilson asserts (1975: 9–10), in line with Weber (1964), are neither merely the admired begetters of a new order nor merely gifted innovators (like President Abraham Lincoln or Bill Gates of Microsoft). As Weber classically presented them, charismatic leaders are romantic disrupters who abrogate and transcend social conventions. They tend to break the existing patterns of authority or harness even older ones to new circumstances. In the process they lift 'sanctions on previously proscribed behavior' (Wilson, 1975: 26). At the same time, of course, they impose new demands for obedience and new standards of service and sacrifice. But they do so within a highly personal, flexible, and emotionally charged framework of relationships and activities. This very personal style of leadership, inspired by some relatively utopian purpose or goal, is intrinsically precarious, particularly in the modern context where rational-legal forms of social organization tend to dominate. The resulting struggle of charismatic leaders with the precariousness of their authority can render this mode of leadership dangerous to the members of an NRM and to its opponents. It is dangerous because the external and internal dynamics of a charismatically led group can give rise to a feedback loop of 'deviance amplification' that can transform the charismatic relationship into tyranny (Wallis, 1977: 208; Couch, 1989: 274–5). Claims to charismatic authority can bring persecution from outside the group and lead to power struggles within the group, and both processes, we will see, merely heighten the very claims to charismatic authority that precipitated the persecution, instability, and so on in the first place.[11]

Outside their own groups, leaders of new religions in the contemporary West lack the conditions of social support that have traditionally existed for the prophets of old or that continue to exist for charismatic leaders in less developed countries (for example, in much of India): 'In modern times, charismatic leadership persists only in the interstices between institutional orders, in the narrow social space that remains for collective behaviour, spontaneous faith and unconstrained obedience and adulation' (Wilson, 1975: 2). By default, charisma is now often associated only with such trivial phenomena as rock idols and movie stars. More authentic charismatic leaders are forced to struggle against the endemic structural marginalization of their efforts by a society that neither understands nor respects the special deference granted to charismatic religious leaders. Through its inevitable interactions with the larger society, charismatically led groups attempt to bring their beliefs and practices into greater conformity with the values and systems of authority dominant in the rest of society. The constant struggle to resist this process of assimilation can infuse a dangerous paranoia into the dealings of charismatic leaders with outsiders. Such would seem to have been the case for Jim Jones and Jonestown (e.g., Johnson, 1979; Hall, 1981; Chidester, 1988); the chief lieutenants of Bhagwan Shree Rajneesh during the struggle to establish Rajneeshpuram (e.g., Milne, 1986; Palmer, 1988; Carter, 1990); and in the last months of the Solar Temple (e.g., Introvigne, 1995; Palmer, 1996; Hall and Schuyler, 1997) and Aum Shinrikyō (e.g., Kaplan and Marshall, 1996; Reader, 1996) groups.

Within the group, the precariousness of charismatic leadership is compounded by the paradoxical problems that are caused for this style of authority by the very success of some charismatic leaders. Some NRMs are able to find a niche in the larger rational-legal social order of today. But a measure of bureaucratization inevitably accompanies the longevity or growth of these successful new religious organizations. Charismatic leaders display a marked inclination to resist this process of institutionalization.[12] It would seem that they fear the 'routinization' of their charismatic authority, to use Weber's well-known phrase. Past a certain point, charismatic leaders can no longer maintain the personal contact with all their followers that is the hallmark of charismatic authority. They cannot even personally supervise all the essential activities of their group. As in any organization, authority must be delegated to others. It must be routinely associated with various designated positions or offices within the organization, and not with particular persons. But this shift towards a more rational-legal mode of authority is often felt by charismatic leaders to be an unacceptable diminution of their own power. In fact, with this shift 'some members will not be as emotionally dependent on the leader as others and thus will have less reason to grant total loyalty to the leader' (Johnson, 1979: 317).

Moreover, the delegation of authority may set in place the means for alternative sources of power to arise within these organizations. 'Large groups inevitably are more heterogeneous than small ones, and the effects of this heterogeneity compound the [leaders'] problem of maintaining firm or absolute control over all [their] followers' (Johnson, 1979: 317). And successful lieutenants may begin to usurp some of the prestige and power granted to the original charismatic leader.

Charismatic leaders are caught on the horns of a dilemma. They may wish to exercise ever greater control over an ever greater number of individuals and projects, but their continued charisma hinges on maintaining a delicate balance between exposure and secrecy. If too many people have too much contact with the leaders, their human frailties may show through.

Such exposure undermines the element of mystery and exaggeration essential to sustaining the tales of wonder, compassion, and extraordinary accomplishment commonly used to establish the aura of special authority around these leaders.[13]

To maintain this crucial element of mystery many charismatic leaders deliberately practise a measure of segregation from their followers. Access to the leader is restricted to those who are especially prepared, especially loyal, or very much in need of guidance, while occasions of mass exposure must be carefully managed to maximize their impact and minimize the chances of embarrassment. For the last twenty years of his life, for example, L. Ron Hubbard, the founder of Scientology, maintained a life of romantic secrecy and complete seclusion, sailing round the world on his yacht, accompanied by an élite body of followers called the Sea Org. In another instance, Bhagwan Shree Rajneesh separated himself from his followers by taking a vow of silence. He communicated to his followers through occasional and highly orchestrated audiences and meditation sessions in which he used his eyes, actions, and thoughts alone to inspire and guide his devotees. In these and similar circumstances in many NRMS, one can trace a pattern of concentric circles of delegated authority radiating out from the charismatic leader. Real power, however, tends to reside with an inner cadre that is in close daily contact with the leader. These individuals act as gatekeepers to others clamouring for access to the leader.

In discussing the prophetic claims of Moses David (David Berg), the extravagant and mysterious leader of the Children of God (now called the Family), Roy Wallis (1982: 37) highlights some of the ramifications of this organizational tendency:

> Few things can be more precarious than a conception of oneself as a direct agency and voice of a God whose present doctrine and approved practice is so much at variance with tradition. So precarious a situation must be protected by considerable milieu control. Only those who are completely committed can be permitted to remain in contact with the source of everyone's self-conception. Considerable care must therefore be taken over the selection of those permitted access to the leader. If his standing is upset or denied, not only is the leader's self-conception jeopardized, but also that of everyone around him. Thus, the élite, the 'charismatic aristocracy' . . . have a substantial incentive to protect his environment. They will seek to exclude from interaction with the prophet all who might see him in terms of some earlier identity, or who—by the nature of their interaction with him— undermine or discredit his identity as a prophet. Not only will likely sceptics and critics be excluded, but also those who might primarily view him

in terms other than his sacred status, for example, those who know and continue to treat him as father, husband, or mere expositor of the Bible.

But like the princes and viziers of old, 'the charismatic aristocracy' surrounding the cult leader may itself come to pose a threat to the sovereignty of the king, sultan, or religious leader. Day by day these élite followers may seize control of the real reins of power while conducting the daily business of the kingdom or religious empire. This is what appears to have happened to Bhagwan Shree Rajneesh, one of the most entrepreneurial and materially successful of the new gurus (see Milne, 1986; Palmer, 1988; Carter, 1990).

Sociologists who have studied the behaviour of charismatic religious leaders like Moses David, Jim Jones of the Peoples Temple and L. Ron Hubbard of Scientology, Bhagwan Shree Rajneesh, Chögyam Trungpa of Vajradhatu, Love Israel of the Love Family, or Shōkō Ashara of Aum Shinrikyō, have observed a marked tendency for these leaders to employ a common set of strategies to offset the external and internal pressures for change (see, e.g., Wallis, 1977, 1982; Johnson, 1979; Palmer, 1988; Mills, 1982; Van Zandt, 1991; Eldershaw and Dawson, 1995; Balch, 1988, 1995b; Reader, 1996). On the one hand, the charismatic leader seeks to resist the outside pressure that is constantly exerted to reduce the differences between an NRM and the rest of society. On the other hand, he or she wishes to circumvent the pressures from inside the group for the routinization of charisma. Of course the strategies in question are presented to the followers of these movements as ways of maintaining the purity, intensity, and quality of the vision and commitment of these groups; and in fact they often serve to do so. But frequently, with time, these strategies have other deleterious consequences for the solidarity and efficiency of the groups. It is these unintended, or at least unanticipated, consequences of the charismatic leaders' actions that may place the safety of the members of some NRMs in jeopardy. For these tactics tend to destabilize the movements, thereby increasing the dependence of the faithful on the symbolic power of the charismatic leader just when the leader's control is waning in the face of the organizational demands stemming from the group's very success.

There are at least six conspicuous strategies that many charismatic leaders use in different combinations to preserve their authority. These strategies are clearly interrelated, and the distinctions I have drawn are in some respects simply analytical. Their actual manifestation in NRMs is often a messy affair, subject to the caprice of the leader and the whims of fortune.

First, to keep followers off balance and their attention on the words and wishes of the charismatic leader, he or she may alter the doctrines and policies of the NRM, sometimes very suddenly. This may come about through the announcement of new visions or revelations or, more simply, with the claim that the group is ready to experience a deeper level of understanding of its beliefs and practices. Some leaders have proved to be most inventive in this regard, as two cases can illustrate.

Out of Dianetics, a psychological program of self-help, L. Ron Hubbard fashioned Scientology—a system of religious ideas and activities that kept expanding in scope and complexity for years. 'To be Clear', for example, was once the highest accomplishment for a Scientologist. But soon it was no more than an early, though foundational, qualification for progressing to a higher state of being, called the 'Operating Thetan' (see Wallis, 1977; Bainbridge and Stark, 1980; Bednarowski, 1989). Similarly, Chögyam Trungpa Rinpoche, the dynamic young leader of Vajradhatu, a new religion based on Tibetan Buddhism, attracted a large number of American adherents in the early 1970s with his highly approachable, casual, and Western style of presentation. In the mid-seventies, however, he sharply reversed course and imposed a much more austere, demanding, and traditional mode of Buddhist practice on his followers, chastising them for their laziness and counter-cultural appearance. Then, in the mid-1980s, just before his unexpected death, he just as suddenly switched gears again, initiating a plan to replace this tradition-bound and arduous path of enlightenment with a new system of meditative philosophy and practice called Shambhala Training. The new program was designed, once again, to present the truths of Tibetan Buddhism in a form more accessible to a wider Western audience (see Eldershaw and Dawson, 1995; Dawson and Eldershaw, 1997).

Shifts like these are intended to attract new members and tap new resources, but they are also used to force some of the old guard to the margins of the movements while elevating new people to the inner circle of devotees. The shifts have a levelling effect that reasserts the superiority of the leader to his or her followers. Meanwhile, the new structures of training, administration, and rewards that accompany the shifts fracture the patterns of influence and the personal and professional alliances that had been established within the organization. The change itself keeps the followers busy and diverted from challenging the prerogatives of the charismatic leader. In the face of new ways of doing things, all become equally dependent, once again, on the guiding wisdom of the leader.

Second, some charismatic leaders may need to seek constant reaffirmations of the loyalty of their followers. This leads to an escalation of the demands they place on members for personal service and sacrifice to the group. This, too, is what many of the shifts in doctrine, policy, and practices are about. Often the new views, procedures, and administrative structures are preceded or accompanied by new rituals or other acts of commitment.

In the most notorious instance, Jim Jones, for example, eventually asked his followers to undergo a series of 'White Nights' in which they rehearsed their final suicides. The members of the Peoples Temple never knew if the 'poison' they drank during these rituals was real. These 'White Nights' prepared them to really make the supreme sacrifice of their lives when Jones eventually decided that only an act of 'revolutionary suicide' could protect the symbolic integrity of the group and its beliefs (see Chidester, 1988). In the face of the inevitable dissolution of loyalty that comes with time or growth in size, charismatic leaders are sometimes challenged to devise ever more dramatic and overpowering rituals of commitment—rituals which by their very nature assure the leader of the sincerity and strength of the followers' devotion (Johnson, 1979: 319).

Third, like apocalyptic teachings, the socially precarious circumstances of charismatically led groups reinforce the tendency of the members to 'demonize' their enemies (real or imagined). Charismatic leaders may play upon a group's fears of persecution by inventing new and ever greater enemies and generally engaging in crisis mongering. By condemning the acts of others, the leaders can divert attention from their own failings and those of the group and provide a convenient excuse for the group's troubles. In the oldest political ploy known to humanity, the internal solidarity of the members is galvanized by the leader's call for unity in the face of new external threats.

Fourth, charismatic leaders will often call into question the inspired messages of all competitors for authority, both external and internal to the group. As a rule dissent is stifled through the careful control of information and the public use of ridicule and others means of peer pressure. Any apparent source of alternative leadership arising within the group is marginalized or simply ejected. Small and relatively inconsequential challenges to the authority of leaders are often seized upon as a pretext for fomenting a sense of crisis, effecting a shift in practices, justifying the movement of people in and out of the inner circle of the leader, and discrediting or expelling lieutenants who appear to be too popular or influential.

Fifth, similarly, many charismatic leaders seek to test the loyalty of their followers, heighten the emotional dependence of their followers, and generally disrupt potential sources of alternative authority by criticizing or actually physically separating couples or other close pairings within the religious groups. The bonds of romantic love or even just good friendship must not be allowed to take precedence over the affective tie of each individual to the charismatic leader. Of course, religious orders in almost all cultures have long recognized the need to regulate and suppress sexual attachments if higher spiritual ends are to be served. In our own culture one need only think of the monastic orders of the Catholic Church. But here the devotees enter with a fuller knowledge of what they are sacrificing. Such, too, is the case with prominent NRMs like the Unification Church and the Hare Krishna movement. Both groups require celibacy of their members until the leaders decide who will marry whom, and even then they exercise a regulatory control over conjugal relations (see Galanter, 1989; Rochford, 1985). Heaven's Gate insisted on strict celibacy and attempted to mask sexual differences by requiring everyone to wear the same loose-fitting clothing. Married couples were separated upon joining, and several members, emulating their leader Do, chose to have themselves surgically castrated.

In some instances, however, like the Peoples Temple, David Koresh at Waco, and to some extent the Children of God, the Solar Temple, Synanon, the Rajneesh movement, and other NRMs, the leaders' control of the sex lives of followers is only introduced, in a seemingly ad hoc manner, late in the history of the group. In an extreme instance, David Koresh eventually claimed a monopoly on sexual access to all the women in the Davidian compound. The commitment of the men to the apocalyptic world-view of the group was tested by the requirement to surrender their wives, lovers, and daughters (often at a quite young age) to Koresh. The women involved considered it an honour to be with Koresh, because he was believed to be the anointed messenger of God and the last of the prophets. His task, in part, was to populate the world with his godly children, both spiritual and biological.

Sixth, when all else fails, and sometimes earlier, some charismatic leaders have tried to consolidate their control and diminish countervailing influences by changing the location, and hence the operating environment, of their groups. Often these moves are to a more isolated spot. Jim Jones, for example, moved the Peoples Temple from Indianapolis to a rural and relatively secluded part of California, and then eventually to Jonestown, a settlement carved out of the jungle of Guyana in South America (Chidester, 1988). Moses David removed the Children of God, which he founded in southern California, from North America altogether. For years he and his followers lived and proselytized in Europe, South America, and the Far East (Davis and Richardson, 1976; Van Zandt, 1991). The Solar Temple, which began in Switzerland and France, attempted to establish itself in Quebec, with the hope of eventually fully relocating there (Palmer, 1988). The Church Universal and Triumphant moved from urban California to the Grand Teton Ranch in the relative wilds of Montana (Melton, 1992a: 201–9). The Rajneesh movement fled densely populated southern India for a ranch in the interior of Oregon (Carter, 1990). Bo and Peep moved the followers of their UFO cult from Texas to Oregon, and then into greater iso-

lation in Wyoming (Balch, 1995a). Over the protests of many of his followers, Chögyam Trungpa moved Vajradhatu from trendy Boulder, Colorado,
to the untrendy and provincial city of Halifax, Nova Scotia (Eldershaw and
Dawson, 1995).

By these and other means some NRMS may enter into a cycle of deviance
amplification. The attempt to resist the routinization of charisma can sometimes lead to a progressive intensification and aggrandizement of the
leader's power, along with the increased homogenization and dependence
of the followers, thereby setting the conditions for charismatic leaders to
indulge the 'darker desires of their subconscious' (a phrase used by Wallis
and Bruce, 1986; cited in Robbins and Anthony, 1995: 247). This in turn
may heighten the negative response of the surrounding society to the movement in question, and the resultant hostility fans the fears, anxiety, and
paranoia of the members of the NRM—a fear that charismatic leaders share
and also exploit to limit any further loss of authority. If a group subscribes
to an apocalyptic world-view, these beliefs help to justify and perpetuate
this entire vicious cycle of fear, resistance, increased homogenization, and
isolation.[14]

Social Encapsulation

New religious movements, Marc Galanter (1989) suggests, form small yet
fairly complete social systems. To survive, all social systems must satisfy certain requirements. Amongst other things, they need to receive and respond
to feedback and to maintain system boundaries. Interference with either of
these two requirements can lead to systemic dysfunction and perhaps violence. The increased isolation brought on by the spiral of deviance amplification characteristic of many apocalyptic and charismatically led groups can
have a disruptive effect on the functioning of NRMS as social systems. Isolation often prevents the groups from receiving sufficient feedback and
heightens the threat they feel from any incursions on their boundaries.[15]

The isolation and the boundaries of which I am speaking are both social
and physical. The members of the Solar Temple, for example, never ceased
to participate physically in the daily activities of life in Europe, Quebec, and
elsewhere. They had regular jobs, families, and homes, and they frequently
interacted with outsiders. But they also cultivated a profound sense of
themselves as a distinct community, a spiritual élite that while in this world
was symbolically set apart from it. Special and often secret knowledge and
rites were used to establish and maintain a clear social boundary around the
group. We now know that as the end drew near, the leaders and many of
the core members of the Temple had been striving for some time to tighten

and reinforce the boundary around the group. They were doing so to resist the inquiries of the governments of Switzerland, Quebec, and Australia into their affairs (see Palmer, 1996).

In the case of Koresh and his followers, the Davidians had built a compound in the countryside outside the city of Waco, Texas. They had purposefully chosen to segregate themselves physically, as well as to differentiate themselves socially and symbolically. Life in rural east-central Texas no doubt tends to remove people from many of the influences of urban North American society and from our pervasive pop culture, but the Davidians limited their contact with the outside world, the potentially contaminating world of Satan, even further. Since the community was not fully self-sufficient, many members still had to travel out to work, buy groceries, see doctors, and so on. But the communal life within the compound, as well as regular participation in Koresh's lengthy and strenuous Bible study sessions (often lasting all day or all night), welded the group together and established a symbolic boundary separating the Davidians from their neighbours. The identity of Koresh's followers, unlike that of most Americans, was shaped by their dedication to a transcendent cause (Tabor and Gallagher, 1995; Bromley and Silver, 1995).

The initial situation of the Peoples Temple was similar as well, especially during the prosperous years the group spent in Ukiah in northern California, and then in San Francisco. When things began to sour, however, the threat of persecution prompted Jim Jones to raise the physical barriers round his group and to tighten his control. He hastened his departure for Jonestown, which he had already begun to build, and persuaded many of his most loyal followers to move there with him. In the jungle of Guyana, the community was almost totally cut off from outside influences (Chidester, 1988), and the feedback that all systems require in order to maintain their integrity began to dwindle.

In fact, each of these groups found itself in circumstances where feedback, especially negative feedback, was suppressed. Negative feedback performs an important regulatory function in any social system, whether it comes from within the system or from outside. In NRMs, internal and external complaints and resistance exert a moderating effect on the pursuit of apocalyptic visions and the authoritarian proclivities of some charismatic leaders. Negative feedback is part of what helps a social system to maintain its equilibrium. Cut off from the outside world, socially and physically, it is quite possible that the Solar Temple, the Branch Davidians, the Peoples Temple, and, we might speculate, Heaven's Gate all lost an essential source of negative feedback. Without access to the reactions of outsiders, it may have become increasingly difficult for their members to gauge whether the behaviour of the group was becoming too bizarre and maladaptive. Turned in on themselves and feeling threatened, the members may have become preoccupied with hiding or destroying any signs of weakness. Thus individuals with complaints or simply alternative views may have been either suppressed or expelled. In each instance the resultant homogenization and social encapsulation of the members may have made the groups fairly paranoid about any apparent transgressions on their symbolic boundaries.

Ironically, in seeking to strengthen their boundaries against an apparent external threat, each of these groups may have become too rigid in its internal functioning and increasingly unrealistic in its dealings with the rest of the world. By being tightened, the boundaries may have become brittle and even more susceptible to symbolic violation. In most cases, however, we have too little detailed evidence to know exactly what happened.

Thinking of Jonestown, the most extreme and best-documented case, Galanter notes (1989: 124) that the mere 'arrival of Congressman Ryan and his entourage', which included several hostile ex-members of the Peoples Temple, was sufficient to precipitate the final act of mass suicide. Why? Because it 'portended the imminent disruption of the group's *control over its boundary*' (emphasis in the original).

> Ryan's visit jeopardized the system's integrity. The fact that four cult members chose to leave with him posed a challenge to the group's monitoring of the membership. Moreover, an intrusion by the U.S. federal government meant that suppression of negative feedback could no longer be absolute. On both counts, it was reasonable for Jones to fear that the cult could no longer operate in total identification with his will. In deciding to assault the Congressman, he realized that, 'They will try to destroy us.' Once it became apparent that his cult's boundary could no longer be secured, Jones chose to preserve its identity in spirit if not in living membership.

Did something similar happen to the members of Heaven's Gate, contributing to their unexpected deaths? At this time we cannot say, for we simply do not know enough about what happened during the last months, let alone days, of this group. Unlike Jonestown or Waco, there were no survivors to tell the tale.[16] But from the work of Robert Balch, the sociologist who studied this group in its earlier guise as the Bo and Peep UFO cult, it appears that a process of social encapsulation had began twenty years earlier. In 1976, Bo and Peep (also known as The Two, and later as Ti and Do) decided to impose a systematic policy of social and sometimes physical isolation on their followers, combined with a comprehensive regime of daily activities designed to breach the social customs and routines we all have learned so thoroughly. With little advance notice, Bo and Peep regularly moved their followers from one place to another, and from one kind of environment to another. As they moved from state to state in the American West, they lived in rugged campsites, inner-city homes, suburban homes, large and small farms and ranches, and finally a three-million-dollar mansion. In every locale, elaborate schedules of daily activities and training exercises were introduced that were followed meticulously for a time, only to be either gradually modified or suddenly abandoned altogether. By these means Bo and Peep sought to free their followers from their 'attachments to the human level' in preparation for moving to 'the level beyond human'.

By way of illustration, Balch offers some insights into the schedule prescribed for one woman who left the group in the early 1980s (1995a: 157–8):

> Her first of four daily rest periods began at 3:36 p.m. and ended exactly two hours later. At 5:57 she bathed. Twenty-four minutes later she took a vitamin pill, one of thirty-two consumed every twenty-four hours. At 6:36 she drank a liquid protein formula, and one hour later she ate a cinnamon roll. By 9:54 she was back in bed for another two hours. During her waking moments she wore a uniform at all times. Free periods were devoted to 'fuel preparation' (i.e., cooking), classes on astrology or 'brain exercises' such as working on jigsaw puzzles. Because she never left the house, the only way she knew what the weather was like was by watching the sky through a clerestory window—the only window in the house that wasn't covered. She wasn't sure how long this phase lasted because she lost track of time.

Was life in the group much the same years later when the members methodically poisoned themselves in three shifts? We have only a very incomplete record of the group's activities in the intervening years (see Balch, 1995a: 163–4). But the information provided by the news and police reports of their suicide is itself suggestive. Much also can be gleaned from the Heaven's Gate Web Page (http://www.heavensgate.com) and the video they left behind with a member who had recently defected. The eerily neat, uniform, and orderly condition of the bodies of the followers when they were found, the carefully arranged, spotless, and spartan interior of their mansion, and the fact that the group had only recently rented their new palatial home after living for some time on an isolated compound, surrounded by a twenty-foot walls of dirt-filled tires (fifty-five miles south-east of Albuquerque, New Mexico) all suggest that there had been little change in the basic beliefs and practices of the group. For the devoted core, however, some important symbolic threshold may have been crossed.

Conditioned by decades of patient training for the next level, isolated from external feedback by their elaborate routines, and sparked to action by the spectacular arrival of the comet Hale-Bopp, the thirty-nine committed members of Heaven's Gate may well have felt a strong collective urge to finally act upon their beliefs.

After their deaths it was reported that the leader, Do (that is, Marshall Herff Applewhite), had told some of his followers he was dying of cancer. We now know he was not. On the group's Web page, however, the sixty-two-year-old Do ominously says: 'I'm in a vehicle that is already falling apart on me, and I'm desperate to try to help you have a last chance to go.' Go where? To the Evolutionary Level beyond Human, of course. In 1985 Do's partner Ti (that is, Bonnie Lu Trusdale Nettles), to whom he was extremely close, had died of cancer, and the belief in his own illness may have helped to cultivate a 'now or never' attitude in Heaven's Gate.

For the Solar Temple, the final act was prompted by rising dissent and conflict within the group, combined with fears of persecution brought on by recent government investigations of the group's financial dealings. It is likely that Luc Jouret and Joseph Di Mambro, the leaders of the Solar Temple, thought there was a serious threat to the integrity of their group and to their personal authority (Palmer, 1996; Hall and Schulyer, 1997). In fact, Di Mambro, the true power behind the scenes, was dying of cancer. Was the murder-suicide he planned for those he thought were betraying him and for his most loyal followers the desperate act of a man intent on saving his reputation at all costs? We can never know.[17]

Was Do, after surviving the death of his beloved partner Ti, moved by similar concerns? The answer may well have died with the members of Heaven's Gate. Again, though, we can turn to the group's Web site and the advertisement they ran in 1993 to gain some insights. The language of both is more starkly apocalyptic than Balch (1995a) says was characteristic of the group at an earlier time. On the Internet, for all who cared to read, they had openly declared that the appearance of Hale-Bopp marked the culmination of their quest, the fulfilment of a prophecy from 'the Evolutionary Level Above Human (the "Kingdom of Heaven")' (New York Post, 1997: 207). They also revealed their fears that they might be persecuted for their beliefs. 'The powers that control this world', they warn, might seek to interfere with their plans, might attempt to 'incarcerate' them or 'subject [them] to some sort of psychological or physical torture (such as occurred at both Ruby Ridge and Waco)' (New York Post, 1997: 201–2). Did the internal dynamics of Heaven's Gate in its last days parallel those of the Solar Temple in its last days? So far there is so little evidence that we simply don't know.[18]

Other Helpful Insights from Social Psychology

To grasp better what may have happened in these groups, we can call upon some rather straightforward insights from social psychology. These ideas both reinforce and supplement the elements of the explanation offered above. Here I will limit my comments to a brief consideration of three relevant empirical generalizations about people's behaviour in groups, though others undoubtedly could be called upon as well. I will apply the principles of 'normative dissonance', 'groupthink', and 'shift-to-risk' to the behaviour of members of NRMs that have become violent.

With specific reference to Jonestown, for example, Edgar Mills Jr (1982) argues that 'the reduction of normative dissonance' in many NRMs impairs individual autonomy and sets the stage for more extreme, perhaps even violent, behaviour. To succeed, most NRMs must secure and maintain high levels of commitment from their members. But unless a certain balance is struck in the levels of commitment achieved, this intense commitment may actually prove detrimental. Many groups aim for nearly total commitment from their members. All must be surrendered to the group because of the transcendental and special character of its task (for example, to save the world now), and the apparent and often real hostility of the social environment in which it must operate. Cults are relatively small and vulnerable organizations, easily disrupted or waylaid if they do not cultivate unswerving obedience and sacrifice for the solidarity of the group. Too much obedience and commitment, however, can exert a destabilizing effect on these groups—it is detrimental to their long-term objectives and success. Why? The answer lies in the function of normative dissonance (that is, disagreement about fundamental values and norms) in moderating the actions of all groups in society.

In most social situations we live amidst a complex interplay of somewhat inconsistent values, norms, and conceptions of reality. Even in a family there are usually disagreements about what should be done, by whom, when, why, and so on. These differences are inevitable. They also serve as a constant reminder that we must be flexible in our dealings with others. We must always be ready to seek and live by compromises and to segment our roles and activities accordingly. (That is, under different circumstances we have different loyalties—for example, to school, work, and home.) On the whole this state of affairs has a moderating effect on our own actions and those of the groups to which we belong. The continual need to negotiate a path amongst differences imposes a crucial moment of critical distance between the impulse to act and the actions actually taken. Of course, a reduction in the normative dissonance in any situation will not necessarily result in impulsive, extreme, or violent behaviour. But it facilitates movement in that direction, and many NRMs engage in practices that systematically effect such a reduction of normative dissonance.

Most of the practices I have in mind we have addressed already. In the first place, many NRMs seem to attract relatively deprived or idealistic people, who often have a low tolerance for moral ambiguity or ambivalence. They want a higher than normal level of normative clarity and consonance in their lives. Second, the NRMs these people join commonly suppress or even expel dissenting members who offer an alternative source of authority. Third, there is a common tendency for charismatic religious leaders to surround themselves with sycophants. Fourth and lastly, the reduction of normative dissonance is intensified by the social isolation and encapsulation so commonly sought by these groups.

In general we know that people under pressure are susceptible to defective patterns of decision making. One such pattern was identified by Irving Janis (1972), who called it 'groupthink'. Janis examined a number of important political fiascos as test cases of faulty decision-making, decisions like that made by President Kennedy's advisory group to support the Bay of Pigs invasion of Cuba in 1961. In these groups Janis detected a common scenario that he thought accounted for their poor judgement. In these usually highly cohesive groups:

> Each member wants the approval of all the others, and this produces a strong tendency toward uniformity. No one wants to raise controversial issues, question weak arguments, or puncture unrealistic hopes. They sustain an illusion of invulnerability, marked by excessive optimism. They rationalize away any warnings and decline to reconsider past policy commitments that have brought them to this predicament. They take their own group's morality for granted and do not look carefully at the ethical consequences of their decisions. They assume that their enemies are too evil to warrant negotiation efforts, and too stupid or weak to stop whatever plans the group may devise. Each person censors his or her own doubts instead of voicing them. (Spencer, 1985: 171–2)

If this can be true of the advisers to the President of the United States, how much more is it likely to the case for such isolated and highly introverted, or even besieged NRMs as the Peoples Temple, the Branch Davidians, the Solar Temple, Heaven's Gate, and Aum Shinrikyō? Here we have truly homogeneous groups that fervently believe that the fate of the world ultimately depends on the cohesive front they can present to their enemies, real and presumed.

As other social-psychological experiments have shown, some groups are more inclined to entertain risky behaviour than the individual members would entertain on their own. Conditioned, perhaps, by the realities of normative dissonance in society, individuals leaning in a particular direction may believe that their own opinion is more extreme than that of other people, so they will refrain from acting on their beliefs. But if the other members of a group happen to share the individual's outlook, discussion often serves to validate these views and encourages the individual to express even more extreme opinions. Speaking out may, in turn, have a snowballing effect, radicalizing the views and behaviour of others in the group (Spencer, 1985: 172–3). This 'shift-to-risk' in some groups is, again, very likely in the NRMS that have become violent. The fatal combination of apocalyptic beliefs, unstable charismatic leadership, and social encapsulation has worked for years in these cases to select the membership of the groups in ways that would foster the emergence of ever more extreme views. Again, the homogeneity and solidarity that are necessary for the group's survival in a hostile social environment can become, paradoxically, the Achilles' heel that assures their abrupt demise.

Concluding Remarks

Do these kinds of social-psychological processes account for what happened at Jonestown and Waco and in the inner circles of the Solar Temple, Heaven's Gate, and Aum Shinrikyō? The analysis seems plausible, and even considering this possibility begins to dispel the needless mystery and fear created by talk of 'brainwashing' and 'mind control'. The argument for brainwashing, as we saw in Chapter 4, is intrinsically weak. Moreover, we do not really need it in order to understand what is really just normal human behaviour pushed by abnormal social circumstances to an extreme. In fact, the evidence compiled by the US Departments of Justice and the Treasury, as well as by two Congressional hearings into the Branch Davidian fiasco, suggests that it is equally likely that the consistently poor judgement exercised by the BATF and the FBI agents who laid siege to the Waco compound can be explained in the same terms (Barkun, 1994; Tabor and Gallagher, 1995; Ammerman, 1995; Wright, 1995a; Sullivan, 1996). The police officers experienced the consequences of a reduction of normative dissonance in their deliberations and fell prey to the faulty reasoning born of groupthink and a shift-to-risk.[19] The obvious and fatal insensitivity of the BATF and the FBI to the world-view of the Branch Davidians suggests that they were more interested in pursuing their own organizational agenda than achieving a peaceful end to the conflict. Why were the media, for example, invited to witness the original BATF assault? Once officers were killed and injured in that assault, the federal agents became preoccupied with defeating the challenge to their authority and power. Simply waiting for Koresh to surrender did not seem to be an acceptable option.

In any event, it is evident that the threat to life and limb from cult violence is not intrinsic to NRMs. Rather, it stems from processes of social interaction that would tend to foster extreme behaviour in all of us under the right circumstances. Admittedly, these tendencies are aggravated in important ways by the belief in apocalypticism, charismatic authority, and need for social segregation found in some NRMs. But each of these elements is perfectly understandable in its own right, and all have been common in other kinds of religious and secular organizations and movements throughout human history (e.g., see Robbins and Palmer, 1997). Students of religion, however, have barely begun to explore the ways in which our knowledge of these processes can really cast light on the tragic cases of cult-related violence that we have helplessly witnessed in recent years.[20]

A true understanding of these episodes will, of course, require even more. We should really seek to complement these kinds of social-psychological analyses with a sensitive exploration of the world-view of the members of the cults who have engaged in violence. What I have in mind are efforts like that of David Chidester (1988) in his remarkable book on the Peoples Temple and the Jonestown massacre, *Salvation and Suicide*. Drawing on interviews with former members and survivors of the Jonestown massacre, as well as the written record and over 900 hours of audiotapes of Jim Jones's sermons and other talks, Chidester takes us into the inner world of this group. He pieces together a picture of how these people had come to hold an alternative understanding of the nature of the time and space they occupied, as well as the distinctions they made between different kinds of people in this world. Giving us a glimpse into the distressing lot of the poor blacks that constituted the bulk of Jones's devoted following, Chidester allows us to grasp how suicide could appear to be a plausible response, perhaps the only acceptable response, to their plight as they saw it. By the end of *Salvation and Suicide* we realize that many of these people had come from a world that most of us can only vaguely imagine, of racial prejudice, social oppression, and moral bankruptcy. We have been allowed, at least partially, to see the simple but satisfying replacement they thought they had found with Jim Jones and their religious compatriots, a religio-socialist utopia that is equally foreign to our experience. We can appreciate how the souls that Jones had lifted to a new self-respect and vision of hope could decide that it was better to die for their beliefs, and with their community, than to stand by and witness the defeat of their dreams and the destruction of their new extended family. Operating with their definition of the situation in mind, the collective plunge into death becomes meaningful—though perhaps still not acceptable.

If possible, we need to acquire a similar grasp of the worlds occupied by the members of the Solar Temple and Heaven's Gate. Here the challenge is much greater, however, for the worlds most of these seekers left behind were quite conventional and comfortable—they were middle-class, white, and safe. The worlds they thought they were going to were quite fantastic. In these cases, the sociological imagination may be stretched thin, but as yet few have dared to stretch it in this way at all.

Chapter Six

Are the New Religious Movements Culturally Significant?

Our Skewed Perspective

We study NRMs because they are intrinsically interesting. Their beliefs and practices are often unusual and sometimes even fantastic. So we are curious about why people belong to these odd groups, who belongs to them, how they came to belong, and what the consequences of their involvement are. This natural curiosity became more urgent for the scholarly community when the anti-cult movement succeeded in turning the emergence of NRMs into a social problem. Many sociologists of religion (and others) recognized the need to replace the suppositions and rhetoric of the heated controversy surrounding the new religions with more reliable information. Scholars also paid attention to NRMs because they offered a good opportunity to study many of the essential elements of religious life in smaller and more manageable forums, where they might witness the processes by which new religious phenomena—doctrines, rituals, experiential practices, organizational structures, and so on—are born, live, and die. As yet, however, it would be difficult to claim that the significance of NRMs is due to their direct statistical impact on the religious economies of Western societies. No one, it is true, can put an accurate figure to the number of people involved in NRMs. The estimates offered by the anti-cult movement are certainly inflated; in fact, there is good reason to believe that the real numbers are relatively small. Contrary to the speculations of Stark and Bainbridge (see Chapter 1), it is unlikely any NRM is going to achieve the status of a truly world religion in the foreseeable future. In fact, membership in the most successful and hence most notorious NRMs founded in the 1950s, 1960s, and 1970s, groups like the Unification Church, the International Society for Krishna Consciousness, and perhaps even Scientology, seem to have declined sharply over the last decade. Moreover, there is also little reason to believe that the sheer number of new religions is growing appreciably, at least in North America and Western Europe. Yet, as I have tried to show throughout this book, scholars have turned to the study of NRMs to learn something about the larger society and culture from which these movements have sprung and to which they are reacting. Scholars in the field have been asserting for some time now that the significance of NRMs is 'cultural', though they rarely specify what they mean. We are told that they have a 'symbolic' importance out of proportion to their small numbers. In most cases NRMs are presented either as sites of spiritual, social, and cultural experimentation and innovation or as nodes of staunch resistance to certain changes overtaking our societies. These views are seen in many of the theories of the origins of today's NRMs that were surveyed in Chapter 2. Tipton's insightful analysis of the hybrid moral solutions offered by various NRMs to the disillusioned members of the counter-culture suggests the cultural experimentation model, whereas Hunter's analysis of NRMs as agents of de-modernization clearly calls to mind the resistance model. In either case, it is argued, NRMs may be studied as barometers of the larger social transformations occurring around us, to give us insight into what may lie ahead for us all (see Hammond, 1987; Robbins and Bromley, 1992).

This set of interpretive options is in some respects more apparent than real. A close reading of the literature reveals that the whole dialogue about the significance of NRMs is skewed by the persistent assumption that religion has become a largely reactionary phenomenon in the modern world. This assumption stems from the pervasive influence exerted by secularization theory on sociology as a whole. Social-scientific analyses, sometimes explicitly and more often implicitly, cast religious activity as intrinsically pre-modern, if not anti-modern. This tendency holds true even for Tipton's argument about the social functions fulfilled by NRMs. These groups strike innovative moral compromises between the expressive ideals of the sixties counter-culture and the need for authority and stable social order in people's lives. In form these compromises are relatively new to our society. But these new religions are presented primarily either as ways of sacralizing identities with an eye to putting a brake on social changes that the followers think are too chaotic and destructive (Mol, 1976), or as alternative ways of successfully reintegrating members into the dominant society (Johnson, 1961; Parsons, 1989). As 'religious' responses to changing social circumstances, as opposed to political, social, or psychological responses, that is, they tend to be viewed as essentially more conservative than either revolutionary or experimental phenomena. Let me explain further.

At the most basic and important level, people have turned to NRMs, like all other religions, to live in a meaningful and orderly world. In line with

Berger, and Stark and Bainbridge, it can still be said that being religious is about constructing a *nomos* that is highly resistant to the corrosive effects of the anomic elements of our lives, from loneliness through bad dreams and illness to death. Religion does this by anchoring that *nomos* in claims about some transcendent or supernatural aspect of our existence. On the whole, in this regard, we have encountered little evidence to suggest that the basic motivation of converts to NRMs differs from that of other religious people in our midst. It is their social circumstances, including the pervasive failure of conventional religions to keep a vibrant sense of the transcendent or supernatural alive in our societies, that seem to account for why certain people have become practitioners of Sōka Gakkai rather than rejoining their parents' Methodist church. The people who join NRMs are much like you and me. As shown in Chapters 2 and 3, however, they are distinguished by a higher sensitivity to moral, social, and cognitive ambiguity. They have a greater desire to live in a more coherent or at least meaningful world, as well as a good world. That is how scholars like Berger have helped us to understand these matters. But Berger's pessimistic reading of the future of religion, as expounded in his theory of secularization, does not necessarily follow from his theory of the fundamental nature and purpose of religion. In accepting the essential truth of the one, we need not accept the truth of the other.

Employing Berger's terms of reference, as discussed in Chapter 1, it can be said that the increased privatization and pluralism of the contemporary socio-religious environment need not, logically or empirically, result in the full de-objectivation of religious life. In a society in which many religions compete for our attention, including religions that literally come from around the world, the old and dominant religious certainties and monopolies must certainly give way. Religious ideas are being relativized as never before, and consequently religious life has increasingly become a matter of subjective conviction more than social consensus. But as Stark and Bainbridge propose, the passions of religious commitment may be stirred more deeply in this pluralistic context as religious activity becomes more a matter of individual expression and feeling, rooted in personal experience and intellectual experimentation, than mere social conformity or an ignorance of alternatives. The groups in which religious life finds expression may each be much smaller, and their nature may be markedly more diverse, but the life expressed may be as real and strong as religious life has ever been. The organizational character and the style of practice of the religions in question, however, have been transformed in ways that are better suited to the highly mobile and differentiated character of modern social life. This is achieved, in part, by making better use of the new means of communication available to us (for example, glossy publications, audio- and video-tapes, satellite radio and television, relatively cheap air fares, and the Internet), as well as modern systems of management, marketing, and so on.

Sociologists have tended to overlook this possibility because they have been theoretically captivated by at least one fundamental element of the dominant secularization thesis: the belief that the growing modernization (that is, rationalization) of our society is intrinsically antithetical to all kinds of religious activity. Like Berger, most sociologists of religion have tended to limit the options for all religions, new and old, to one of two. They can accommodate themselves to the modern, rationalized social order and achieve a stable but extremely modest existence as a component in the growing leisure or service economy. Or they can 'entrench themselves behind whatever socio-religious structures they can maintain or construct, and continue to profess the old objectivities as much as possible as if nothing had happened' (Berger, 1967: 153). In other words, they can either survive, yet more or less disappear as distinctive social entities with a unique purpose, or they can remain distinct but more or less disappear, surviving only at the very margins of society, where they will become more and more difficult to sustain, both economically and symbolically.[1]

In the face of this diagnosis, the prospects for attributing much in the way of real cultural significance to the continued emergence of NRMs is not very promising. At present it is too soon to tell whether the two limited options delineated by Berger, Wilson, and others will hold true for the future of NRMs in North America. But I would argue that a close reading of the literature on the possible significance of NRMs also reveals the elements of a third conception of the relationship between NRMs and the rest of society, one that may well prove to be more empirically and theoretically adequate. This more dialectical reading of the situation leads me to be more optimistic about the future survival, social role, and hence significance of NRMs. Aspects of this third alternative can be detected as far back as a series of insightful yet largely forgotten essays on the social significance of NRMs published by Stone (1978b), Westley (1978), and Colin Campbell (1978). Individually and collectively these articles suggest a more nuanced interpretation of the relationship between NRMs and modernity than the one proposed by scholars like Hunter, which identifies NRMs with processes of 'demodernization' (see Chapter 2). They present a different image of the very nature and hence significance of NRMs, one that highlights the compatibility of these new religions with the conditions of modernity, without necessarily subscribing to Berger's and Wilson's pessimistic accommodationist reading of the role of religion in a more secular age. The surprising convergence in these analyses has been independently corroborated by observations made much later in other innovative analyses by Parsons (1989), Lucas (1992), and Beckford (1989, 1992, 1996).

In reflecting on these matters, Beckford is one of the few prominent sociologists of religion to inquire directly whether the popular yet perplexing new concept of 'post-modernism' is of any help in clarifying the cultural significance of NRMs. If, as many social analysts declare, we are now living in post-modernist times, have there been qualitative changes in the nature of religion that parallel those detected in the arts, architecture, and some other aspects of social life (such as attitudes to sexuality)? I will use Beckford's brief but astute analysis, with which I agree, to assess and largely dismiss this fashionable though intriguing possibility. In its place I prefer to explore the relevance of Beckford's own novel suggestion that 'nowadays it is . . . better to conceptualize religion as a cultural resource or form than as a social institution' (1989: 171; 1992: 23).

The brief critical survey of some of the relevant literature undertaken in this chapter does not provide us with a fully formulated alternative view of the probable social and cultural significance of NRMs. To that end more focused theoretical and empirical research is required. In part, I am simply attempting to frame the interpretive options available, while also being somewhat provocative. Given the real constraints on our existing knowledge, at this juncture we are left with more questions than answers. But I am suggesting that it is time to rethink seriously the limited options with which sociologists have been working for so long.

Discerning a New Religious Consciousness

In some respects Stone (1978b), Westley (1978), and Campbell (1978) accept the veracity of Berger's and Hunter's analysis of the plight of modern people, and hence of their religious lives as well. None of the three, however, chooses to frame the adaptive response of religion, as manifested in NRMs, in the negative terms of reference implied by Hunter's 'anti-modernist' label. In their shared yet diversely based readings of the situation, they do not see the characteristics of NRMs as reactionary, but rather as symptomatic of the continued and healthy evolution of the forms of religious life. There is a more neutral, if not positive, cast to their comments and conclusions.

Despite some differences, there is a remarkable agreement between these three papers. In the first place, there are some strong similarities in their readings of the primary characteristics of the 'new religious consciousness' that each believes has emerged in the United States since the 1960s. I can detect at least six points of agreement. There is also considerable agreement on the likely social and cultural significance of these features of this new religious consciousness.

First, the new religions are marked by a pronounced religious individualism. The emphasis is decidedly on what the religious involvement can do for the individual and only secondarily on its broader implications or benefits for society or the group. People's participation is motivated by a preoccupation with the development of personal identity, and correspondingly the locus of the sacred is often seen to be within the individual and not outside (see Westley, 1978: 137). Immanence is stressed over transcendence. At least in daily practice, in meditation or chanting the names of God, for example, such is the primary experience of members.

Second, these religions are religions of experience: 'A common element that seems to characterize most of the participants of these groups is intense experiences of themselves and the sacred. The emphasis is on experience and faith rather than doctrine and belief' (Stone, 1978b: 124). As stipulated in Chapter 1, cults promise transformative experiences, and much of their activity is focused on the delivery or inducement of those experiences (see, e.g., Richardson and Davis, 1983).

This has meant, as Stone stipulates, that the new religious consciousness found in these groups displays a more pragmatic attitude to questions of religious authority and practice. This is the third feature of NRMs commonly noted by Stone, Westley, and Campbell. 'Gurus', Stone notes (1978b: 128), 'are followed for their expertise and proficiency in encouraging charismatic experience among their followers. Their authority is based on results first, then later perhaps scripture or divine revelation.' Or as Westley puts it, religious activity in these groups 'will involve skill development and skill testing of a progressive nature. As one becomes more ritually skilled, one will gain in authority' (1978: 138). This holds true, most obviously, for groups like Scientology and other NRMs born of the human potential movement, like Silva Mind Control, the organization Westley examines in her work. But in many respects it is equally as true for contemporary neo-paganism (Adler, 1986), a diverse range of New Age practices (see, e.g., Heelas, 1996; Hanegraaff, 1996; Brown, 1997),[2] the numerous groups based on various forms of Hindu and Buddhist yoga and meditation in America, and even the chanting, dancing, and the other rituals of members of Krishna Consciousness.

Fourth, the new religious consciousness is remarkably more syncretistic, accepting of relativism, and tolerant of other religious perspectives and systems than the religions dominant in the West in the past. Many of the new religions clearly borrow from a diverse array of traditions, both Eastern and Western, and most of them directly acknowledge the truth of other religions. In fact, many groups find no difficulty in admitting that their path to enlightenment or salvation is but one (though perhaps a most perfect one) among many. Campbell (1978: 154) comments that the spiritual and mystic religion of today's NRMs

> carries the principle of tolerance even further than the denomination, extending it not merely to all those of one's own faith or religion but to all people. An intensely personal religion of conviction in which truth is considered polymorphous in form necessarily involves the recognition that each and every human soul can be a vehicle for divine revelation in some form or other.

Fifth, the theology, or perhaps better just the world-view, of many of these groups is holistic, or as Campbell prefers, it is monistic (Stone, 1978b: 130; Campbell, 1978: 153). Almost every kind of dualism is rejected or diminished in scope and significance: the traditional dualisms of God and humanity, the transcendent and the immanent, humanity and nature, the spiritual and the material, the mind and the body, the subjective and the objective, male and female, good and evil, even cause and effect (see, e.g., Bednarowski, 1989). As Stone says (1978: 130), for instance: 'God language refers less to He and more to thou, we, it and I. God is neither spirit nor flesh, female or male. Cosmic "energy" is the image of God most universally used. Unlimited cosmic energy is not Wholly Other but open and accessible for all to tap into.'[3]

Sixth and last, each of the above features is compatible with what Stone calls greater 'organizational openness' (1978b: 129). In different ways Stone, Westley, and Campbell suggest the religions of the future, embodied in the NRMs of the present, will be increasingly like the 'client cults' of Stark and Bainbridge (1985). In Westley's Durkheimian turn of phrase (1978: 138), since new religions will be characterized increasingly

> by the respect and awe accorded the sacred *within* each individual, we may expect that this will be ritually expressed by each individual's private preoccupation with the relationship of the divine within to the external, everyday personality. While people may gather in groups to celebrate the cult, the source of sacred power (and of group integration) will be acknowledged by each individual turning inward as opposed to joining together with others to worship an external symbol of group unity.

Less effort will be made to attempt to address all aspects of followers' lives, to provide a truly encompassing world-view. More attention will be given to cultivating and serving certain crucial but socially segmented psychological and spiritual needs and desires. This will be done, moreover, within flexible organizational frameworks that allow for, or even foster, different ways of 'doing the religion'. Groups as diverse as Scientology, Vajradhatu, Transcendental Meditation, Kripalu Yoga, Wicca, Sōka Gakkai, and a host of expressions of New Ageism, and even some forms of Christian revivalism purposefully offer different modes of practice to their followers. Members may voluntarily select, according to their preferences, the type and intensity of their involvement from a set of options made available by the NRMs.

Contrary to the popular conception of cults, then, this perspective suggests that groups like the Unification Church and Krishna Consciousness, to the extent that they still demand a total commitment from their members, are the exception and not the rule in the new religious environment. This is not to say that they will not persist or have some social and cultural significance. Rather, as stipulated in the Introduction, up to a point it is still useful to think of NRMs as falling into two kinds or social forms. On the one hand, there are the more traditionally oriented new religions that tend to stress communal lifestyles and exclusive commitments, while, on the other hand, there are new religions that are more modern in their orientation, largely non-communal, and open to segmented and plural commitments. Too much emphasis has been placed in the past, however, by both scholars and popular observers, on the former category. The so-called totalistic cults have been in the spotlight precisely because they seem to be so out of step with the tenor of the times. They have become emblematic of the new religious life in our midst, and this misconception has helped to perpetuate the tendency to identify NRMs too exclusively with anti-modern tendencies (as Hunter does). The observations of Stone, Westley, and Campbell correct the balance somewhat. But what is more, they also make us think about the very adequacy of the pre-modern/modern dichotomy for talking about NRMs.

It is important to note, however, that Stone and Westley do not expect the communal character of religion to disappear. We are not on our way to a world of 'audience cults', to use Stark and Bainbridge's terms of reference once again. Somewhat paradoxically, the critical emphasis placed on religious experience over mere assent to doctrine is pivotal in this regard.

> When intense personal experiences are facilitated through the auspices of a religious or quasi-religious organization—*asanas* in a yoga group, an altar call in a revival service or a guided fantasy exercise in a human potential group—the experiences may become interpreted as religious ones. The newly awakened or reborn often attribute the source of the experience to a

charismatic leader or a group's gnostic power. They are further drawn into fellowship and identification with a group that positively interprets and appreciates experiences that the everyday world discredits as deviant. While intense personal experiences contain the germ of antinomian tendencies, their first-fruits are to stimulate an identification with a community that promotes similar experiences. Thus these experiences of individual effervescence bind communities together and encourage the perpetuation of the experiences. (Stone, 1978b: 126)

In line with the observations made in Chapter 2, we also must be careful to note that none of the six primary characteristics of the new religious consciousness outlined by Stone, Westley, and Campbell is unique or truly new. They are manifestations of trends that have been developing in American religion for centuries. But most observers would agree with Stone that 'their incidence never has been documented to be as strong or as widespread' (Stone, 1978: 127; see also Bednarowski, 1989).

The convergence in conceptions of the basic nature of the new religious consciousness is matched in Stone, Westley, and Campbell by a convergence in their estimation of the significance of this new religious consciousness. Two points of agreement stand out: the new religious consciousness embodied in so many new groups is markedly more compatible with science and the social sciences than conventional religions; likewise, it is more compatible with the new social order emerging around us, whether it is called advanced capitalism, late or high modernism, post-industrialism, or post-modernism.

Stone agrees with Wilson that most NRMs are too small and transient to be the basis for a new religious culture. But in a manner now characteristic of most students of NRMs, he argues that these groups may nevertheless 'serve as midwives for new sensibilities' (1978b: 131). Or in the words of Robbins and Bromley (1992: 4), the social and ideological innovations of NRMs 'may contribute to a subterranean cultural . . . resource pool', elements of which may move, in times of conflict and crisis, 'from [the] cultural background to [the] foreground'. Stone points to the evidence of the emergence in American society of a greater interest and trust in personal experience, intuition, holistic views, and syncretistic perspectives in fields of endeavour as diverse as medicine and business, not to mention the rapidly expanding market in humanistic and self-help psychological books on everything from being the first-born child to facing death with dignity.

He concludes that the emphasis placed by many new Eastern, human potential, and even Christian groups on one's 'inner voice' and personal experience and feelings as the best guide to truth and happiness, is part of a larger 'cultural drift' away from the austere legacy of the Protestant work ethic in America (Stone, 1978b: 131). There is more to life than work, Americans are increasingly discovering, and virtue is no longer to be measured primarily by wealth or worldly success. The ideal of rugged individualism is not as appealing as it once was. Yet the evidence from NRMs that points towards a rejection of the utilitarian legacy of America's Protestant past tends not to take the form, Stone insists, of 'otherworldliness or anti-rationalism'. Rather, the 'this-worldly asceticism' that sociologists since Weber (1958a) have attributed to the influence of the Protestant Reformation on the modern world is being slowly displaced by a kind of 'this-worldly mysticism' that is compatible with both the everyday demands of life in our hustle-bustle society and with non-reductionistic forms of science (Stone 1978b: 131). With the waning of the 'charisma of reason' in our day (p. 133), this new religious consciousness is geared to the promotion of a new kind of dominant scientism. The old belief in science, rooted in positivist conceptions of science, necessitated the war of science and religion. But the newer, more holistic models of science and of the universe, ranging from Bohm's theory of implicate order through chaos to Thomas Kuhn's theory of science, point to a more open-ended universe in which spiritual principles can find a place (Bohm, 1983; Gleick, 1987; Kuhn, 1970). A more holistic mode of scientism is emerging around us that is more receptive to the growth of many kinds of new religious activity.

Speculating further, Stone suggests that this this-worldly mysticism might even have a 'cultural survival value' because it is 'complementary to bureaucratic post-industrial society' (Stone, 1978b: 131). Giving a favourable interpretation to the diagnosis of modernity of Berger and Hunter, he comments:

> Finding satisfaction in religious experience may help accommodate late capitalism's characteristic separation of private life from vocational life, of finding meaning in consumption rather than production. . . . A mystical orientation is applied to the private sphere of life as individuals supply their own solutions to religious problems, are assured of a sense of self (or sequence of selves), and gain respite from the workaday world to return refreshed to support bureaucratic asceticism in their work-role. (Stone, 1978b: 132)

Thus, privatized religion, in the form of some this-worldly mysticism, may actually reinvigorate the role of religious beliefs and practices in the daily lives of contemporary Americans—fitting them, in a segmented but real way, into their busy schedules.

Westley likewise observes that 'the relationship of the new religions to science' need no longer be thought of as simply 'one of rejection, substitution and escape' (1978: 140–1; see also 142). New religions are not just explaining the meaning of life in a way that the scientific world-view fails to do. They are actively seizing on both the new cultural relativism promoted by the spread of social-scientific knowledge and some of the means and data of the natural sciences, with regard to brain states and psychological well-being, for example, to facilitate and legitimate their existence. Two decades later, turning to the comprehensive and meticulous analysis of Hanegraaff (1996: 62–76, 113–81), we can support this claim, pointing to a variety of more specific and important theoretical developments in the sciences that have since become foundational to the model of reality emerging from the 'new religious consciousness' (i.e., ideas like the holographic paradigm of David Bohm and Karl Pribram, the paradigm of self-organization associated with Ilya Prigogine, the theory of formative causation of Rupert Sheldrake, and the Gaia-hypothesis of James Lovelock). Similarly, NRMs can and do benefit from the increased modern awareness that humanity makes its own laws. Asian-based meditational practices in particular can turn theories of the social construction of reality to their epistemological advantage, using them to overcome charges of solipsistic and even narcissistic idealism. As Campbell (1978: 155) adds, the full-fledged 'rationalism, materialism and . . . self-concerned this-worldliness' of many people in contemporary society may be 'the focus of mystical opposition and scorn'. But 'there is no opposition to abstract, secular systems of thought in general . . . [and this] leaves many areas in the arts, philosophy and the sciences, where mysticism can draw on material syncretization.' In his view 'the monism, relativism, tolerance, syncretism, and above all, [the] individualism' of the new religious consciousness 'is clearly highly congenial to the ethos of contemporary society' (p. 153). Explaining why (see pp. 153–5), he echoes the insights of Westley, saying that, in comparison with the traditional churches and sects of our society,

> mysticism . . . benefits most from the 'shrinking' of the world and the increasingly pluralistic character of modern societies. As this brings religions into increased contact with one another it raises in an acute way the problem of inter-religious truth. The mystical solution is one of the simplest, avoiding the dangers of religious conflict and the difficulties of ecumenism by absorbing elements from various religions into a general mystical philosophy. (Campbell, 1978: 155)

These authors all associate the rise of the new religious consciousness they are describing with the advance of social differentiation with regard to institutions, the division of labour, and what Max Weber calls 'spheres of action' in general. Their discussion is quite general, however, and none offers a very complete explanation of how the new religious consciousness is actually related to the new, highly differentiated social order that is coming into being. They draw parallels between religious and social developments, but the grounds of the connection go unspecified. Is the new religious consciousness a mere epiphenomenon of larger social structural changes? Or is it both one of the mediums and the sources of the cultural and social changes we are experiencing? Because of the lack of causal specificity, it is very difficult to choose between the interpretations offered by Hunter, on the one hand, and by Stone, Westley, and Campbell, on the other. Are most NRMs just reactions to modernity, or do they represent some intrinsic adaptation of religious forms to the modern social world?

The consensus of Stone, Westley, and Campbell does make us think twice before too readily associating most NRMs with some counter-cultural reaction to, or compensation for, the social and psychological ills of modernity. It also shows that at least some thoughtful commentators on NRMs are not willing to accept the more pessimistic implications of the Berger and Wilson privatization thesis, which suggests that NRMs can be written off as cultural trivialities. Instead, with Stone, Westley, and Campbell, we get intimations that the changing face of religion as found in NRMs may represent just the continued dialectical adaptation of religion to society and society to religion. Religious institutions need not be the sole or even primary regulators of all aspects of social life for religion to continue to function as an important expression of cultural adaption to new social conditions. We would more readily recognize this possibility if we ceased to conceive of religion from within the overly narrow confines of a European, and probably Protestant and Enlightenment, point of view, for which 'religion' is a distinct set of institutions operating within a competitive hierarchy of other institutions. 'Religion' *per se* cannot be equated with the organizational form of the 'church' or even a constellation of competing 'churches'. Religion deals with a dimension of ultimate meaning that is relevant to all aspects of life, even in our scientific-technological age (see Beckford's comments below).[4]

Modernism and the New Religious Movements

Little direct attention has been given to the cultural significance of NRMs since the essays discussed so far were written twenty years ago (e.g., Hammond, 1987; Robbins and Bromley, 1992). But I have encountered two fascinating analyses that can be used to support the more generous reading of the significance of NRMs found in the essays of Stone, Westley, and Campbell. In a case study of the Unification Church—which is one movement that does not provide a strong case for the adaptive compatibility of NRMs with modernity—Arthur Parsons (1989) offers a further argument against too readily identifying NRMs with a demodernizing orientation. In fact, it is his argument that first led me to doubt the utility of even addressing the significance of NRMs in terms of a simple modern/anti-modern dichotomy. These doubts were reinforced by a little known yet innovative essay by Phillip Lucas (1992). In this analysis Lucas describes the marked similarities between two seemingly very different NRMs: the Pentecostal-Charismatic revival and the New Age movement. What these seemingly anti-modernist and modernist movements share, he suggests, may well prove to be more culturally important than their more obvious differences.

Parsons advances an alternative interpretation of the accommodations to secularity by NRMs on which Berger and Wilson tend to rely in casting doubt on the cultural significance of NRMs. He derives this alternative view from an application of the insights of Eisenstadt (1956). Eisenstadt observes, Parsons says (1989: 212),

> that, while innovative religious movements often appear to arise as responses to tensions within their secular host societies, they also tend to incorporate central cultural elements from those societies. He contends youth movements in modern societies, while they are a response to the disjunction between the expressive personalism of family life and the instrumental impersonalism of public life, also incorporate essential features of both of these realms. They provide contexts in which diffuse affectivity can be combined with universalistic or highly rationalized moral and cosmological principles.

On the one hand, concentrating on the means employed by NRMs, Wilson, and to a lesser extent Berger, tend to see evidence of the triumph of secularity in the attempt of many NRMs to harness the techniques of instrumental rationality to advance what they see as the essentially non-rational ends of religion. They are pessimistic about the chances of NRMs for success, both because they believe that the incongruity of the rational means and the non-rational ends will generate irresolvable tensions in the NRMs, and because they believe the congruity of rational means, within and outside the NRMs, will eventually lead to the dilution and dissipation of the non-rational ends that are the *raison d'être* of the NRMs (Wilson, 1976, 1982b). In crude terms, that is, they think that the growing preoccupation with the rational delivery of the message will suck the life from the message itself and hence from the groups. They will become routinized, bureaucratic entities, indistinguishable from the culture they oppose.

On the other hand, Parsons (1989: 213), following Eisenstadt in a slightly different direction, arrives at a more optimistic conclusion by focusing on the substantive ends promoted by many groups. NRMs, he observes, 'above all strive to rationalize culture in the name of the expressive values and emotional practices that are highly legitimate in contemporary society.' In other words, in the realm of ends as well as means, he finds that there is a marked element of cultural continuity between these supposedly deviant religions and the dominant culture, and as Rodney Stark (1987, 1996) has persuasively argued, the presence of such continuity weighs heavily in favour of the chances for success of various NRMs. Unquestionably, we can choose to emphasize the seemingly non-rational, or what Wilson calls the 'arbitrary', character of many of the beliefs of the NRMs, and hence set up a dichotomy between NRMs and modernity that sees all concessions to rationality as a loss of religiousness. In doing so, however, we are missing the true complexity of the situation.

> If the scholarly or public debate over specific prophetic movements becomes articulated in terms of their deviance from or rejection of conventional secular society, we fail to appreciate that their appeal and power are derived from the cultural and social fabric of their host societies. Indeed, at the core of innovative movements, in their fundamental moral principles and in their most ritualized social practices, we find components of secular society that have not been rejected but elaborated and intensified. Conformity and deviation are inextricably linked, not opposed, to each other: the more a group conforms to its host society, the more it simultaneously deviates from it. (Parsons, 1989: 223)

Mere conformity to its secular environment in means or ends, then, is not enough to determine whether an NRM is demodernizing or anti-modernist or not, and hence what its ultimate cultural significance might be, judged in these terms.[5]

A recognition of the real complexity of the situation cuts both ways, moreover, against the value of the heuristic dichotomy I set up (following Warner, 1993) in Chapter 1 to help define the factors that condition judgements of the possible significance of NRMs. For as Parsons (1989) further observes, this insight also undermines Stark and Bainbridge's view of secularization as a self-limiting process (see Chapter 1). To believe that 'too much worldliness automatically releases an other-worldly, religious counterrevolution' is to give an 'account of the relation between secular and religious forces [that] is too dualistic and mechanical; [when] in fact, their relation is much more dialectic and organic' (pp. 223–4).

Parsons's analysis, then, tends to invalidate some of the standard ways of differentiating anti-modernist from modernist NRMs and thereby defining NRMs as culturally inconsequential because they are either anti-modern or have sold out to modernity. It also makes it impossible to assess the cultural significance of NRMs by seeking to use data from the study of NRMs to support the superiority of Stark and Bainbridge's theory of secularization over that of Berger or Wilson. Lucas's analysis further calls such differentiations into question by demonstrating, on different grounds, how seemingly anti-modernist and modernist NRMs are as much alike in critical respects as they are different. He detects five points of similarity between the Pentecostal and Charismatic movements, on the one hand, and various New Age movements, on the other hand. As will become apparent, his points share much in common with the traits of NRMs identified by Stone, Westley, and Campbell.

The Pentecostal movement began within American Protestantism at the beginning of the twentieth century. It began as a small fringe movement that stressed the return of special spiritual gifts, recorded in the New Testament, to those who believed they had experienced a special baptism of the Holy Spirit, or the holy fire. The best known of the gifts is *glossolalia*—the gift of tongues. A person speaking in tongue utters a string of strange and continuous sounds in a kind of nonsensical language—sometimes when he or she seems to be in a trance induced by singing, praying, and occasionally even dancing. A second gift is the ability to interpret some of these utterances and make pronouncements to the congregation about their expression of God's will. Other gifts are those of prophecy and of healing by the laying on of hands. Pentecostal worship is exuberant, even somewhat disorderly at times. It represents a kind of permanent extension of the holy fervour often associated with the intense revivalist camp meetings of the nineteenth century. The return of the gifts is thought to be a sign that the end of days is approaching, and the Pentecostalists are seeking to prepare themselves and others by fostering the consciousness of being born again in Christ. Today such Pentecostalist denominations as the Assemblies of God, the Church of God in Christ, the International Church of the Foursquare Gospel, and many others constitute a major and rapidly growing segment of Christian culture in America and much of the rest of the world (Neitz, 1987; Cox, 1995). The Charismatic movement is more or less the expression of the same religious phenomena in organizations that have elected to stay associated with such traditional denominations as the Anglicans (Episcopalians) or the Catholic Church. Together, by some estimates, the Pentecostals and Charismatics constitute more than 20 per cent of American Christians. There may well be hundreds of millions of Pentecostals and Charismatics.

The New Age movement is much more amorphous. In fact, it is really just a convenient name for a clustering of similar organizations of the most diverse kind, ranging from groups practising witchcraft or neo-paganism to various experimental forms of almost secular psychotherapies. The movement as such is united by a common stress on the sacredness of the self and on various 'spiritual' processes of self-discovery that have either been invented or recovered from numerous traditional and usually pre-modern or marginalized cultures of the world (such as Native American, Celtic, or Tibetan). In these groups the inner path of spiritual development is linked to the salvation of the world from certain contemporary and grievous errors of humanity, ranging from the pollution of the environment to the suppression of our true psychic powers. The transformation of the self through spiritual enlightenment has the potential, it is believed, to bring about the collective and radical transformation of human nature itself, thereby ushering in a New Age. In the popular consciousness the New Age is associated with such beliefs and practices as yoga, meditation, the use of crystals for healing, macrobiotics, reincarnation, channelling, aroma-therapy, the reading of auras, telepathic contact with civilizations from other worlds, astral projection, and so on (Lewis and Melton, 1993; Heelas, 1996; Hanegraaff, 1996; Brown, 1997). There is no reliable way to even guess the number of people involved in this 'movement'. But the multi-million sales of James Redfield's New Age tale *The Celestine Prophecy*, which as I write was number one on the *New York Times* best-seller list for over a hundred weeks, suggests the pervasive appeal of these ideas. Throughout North America, moreover, centres of New Age activity and training, big and small, have been established in almost every city of any size.

With this brief introduction to the movements in hand, what is it that Lucas thinks these two seemingly very dissimilar 'religious' enthusiasms have in common?

First, both the Pentecostal-Charismatic and the New Age movements stress a rediscovery of the experience of sacred power in the daily lives of ordinary people (Lucas, 1992: 194–200). The experience in question is envisioned as intense, personal, ecstatic, and susceptible to being repeated. Both movements associate these experiences with the continuous presence in human affairs of spiritual energy, whether it be prana, mana, orgone energy, or the Holy Spirit. They believe in contact with spiritual beings, whether spirit guides and nature spirits, or angels and demons. They both believe in establishing various functional relationships with the spirit world, relationships that can lead to the acquisition of extraordinary powers or give special assistance in this world. Admittedly, in kinds of experiences and the means used to acquire them, these two movements differ in many important ways. But historically, socially, and culturally, each movement contributes to a new and marked democratization of numinous experience in society.

Second, both movements represent attempts to fashion new structures of social cohesion, under the guise of 'sacred communities' (pp. 200–1). In doing so, however, both are distinguished by a worldwide vision. In true globalistic manner they have consciously sought to transcend 'conventional denominational, national, and ethnic boundaries'. As internationalist movements they have adapted to 'current geopolitical realities and trends' and taken full advantage of new means of mass communication and travel, as well as mechanisms and forums for cultural exchange.

Third, at the heart of each movement is a strong emphasis on the task and means of spiritual healing, both of the mind and of the body (pp. 201–3). Underlying this preoccupation with the well-being of the individual is a common holistic belief in the interconnectedness of spirit and matter, the mind and the body, the individual and the community, and the sacred and the profane.

Fourth, both groups anticipate the arrival of a new age (pp. 203–5). Their beliefs and practices are all premised on elaborate eschatologies, though New Agers usually promote a kind of 'soft' apocalypticism by which the world will be suddenly changed for the better as a result of some collective spiritual effort, while the Pentecostal-Charismatic revival adheres to biblical prophecy and is thus 'far less sanguine about the prospects of the modern world'.

Fifth and last, both movements display an 'anti-institutional and decentralized character' (pp. 205–7). Loose organizational structures, resembling networks far more than traditional bureaucracies, are typical of both movements, and the primary locus of authority tends to be the individual and his or her interior experience, judged in the light of its pragmatic fruits for the individual and humanity.

Like Stone, Westley, and Campbell before him, Lucas notes how these features link both the Pentecostal-Charismatic and the New Age movements to some long-standing and pervasive themes of American religious life: a messianic view of the nation, an ethos of individualism and egalitarianism, a tradition of revivalism with its emphasis on personal religious experience, and a preference for pragmatism that entails belief in the reconciliation of the religious and the scientific world-views (pp. 207–11).

Where does this leave us? Are NRMs anti-modernist or modernist? Are some anti-modernist and others modernist? It is difficult to say. The latter appears initially to be more likely the case. NRMs do seem to divide into some kind of conservative and liberal, or traditionalist and experimentalist, clusters. Yet as Parsons's and Lucas's analyses suggest, it is not easy to decide which movements belong in which camp and why. Both the Moonies and the Pentecostal-Charismatics, seemingly very conservative or even pre-modern movements, display features commonly associated with the modernist label. Perhaps then we are faced with a single modernist continuum of more conservative or more liberal religions? Or do the ambiguities encountered indicate that the more accurate terms of reference are modern and post-modern, respectively? Will the introduction of a post-modernist category clarify matters?

Post-modernism and the New Religious Movements

In the essay 'Religion, Modernity, and Post-Modernity', James Beckford examines Berger's and Wilson's theories of the relationship between modernity and religion (amongst others) in the light of the data available on religion in contemporary Britain. He concludes that these approaches do not adequately capture the new realities of religious life:

> The most telling reason for questioning the received wisdoms is that none of the prevailing versions pays more than passing attention to what I believe to be the most important aspect of religious change in recent years. I am referring to the growth of parallel, yet contrasting, types of religion. On the one hand, Christian churches and Jewish groups with strict and very conservative outlooks are growing. And, on the other, a relatively new form of liberal and tolerant spirituality is spreading both inside and outside religious organizations. I shall refer to the latter as 'holistic' spirituality. The combination of these two contrasting developments wreaks havoc with prevailing ideas about religion and modernity. (Beckford, 1992: 17)

In describing some of the elements of the new spirituality that he has in mind, he strikes some familiar notes. Beckford (1992) specifies three 'major characteristics'. First, the new spirituality 'strains towards a holistic perspective which emphasizes the inter-connectedness between, for example, human and non-human, personal and public, physical and mental, or national and international' (p. 17). Hence its focus is not so much on the supernatural or the 'great transcendences' of the world religions as on the 'little transcendence' of the interests and limitations of the 'mundane world'. Second, there 'is the belief that the adoption of a holistic perspective can provide access to, or can release, new sources of power.' The extraordinary powers released are to be used, moreover, to fulfil a spiritually enlightened agenda of quite practical applications—improved health, food, natural environment, human rights, justice, and peace (p. 17). Third, this new spirituality is 'compatible with a wide range of specific ideologies and practices. . . . It represents a general shift in sensibility and ethos: not a specific programme of social change or a separate form of religious practice' (pp. 17–18).

It is true, Beckford admits, that the new spirituality is actively practised by only 'a tiny proportion of the population', and it 'lacks the sense of communal obligation and collective ritual attaching to public religion' (p. 18). It is not a phenomenon that can be equated with traditional conceptions of organized religion. Its influence can be detected, however, throughout contemporary life, in new ways of thinking about 'medicine, sport, leisure, education, peace, ecology, dying and grieving, self-help, gender, relations with non-human animals, social work, and even management training.' We are seeing, he says, a 'holistic shift' in society toward a kind of 'transcendent humanism'. Is this something like the new religious consciousness detected by Stone, Westley, and Campbell?

Instead of being more precise at this juncture, Beckford turns to a consideration of whether the now popular notion of post-modernity is of any help in understanding the changes he has in mind (p. 19). Given the complex and contested character of this concept, he is sceptical. If the term is merely being used to designate a period of time, say from the mid-1950s onward, then in some debatable yet trivial sense most NRMs are post-modern. But even then the application of the term denotes some shift in sensibility. Beckford summarizes the four themes most commonly associated with the new post-modernist sensibility and then considers whether they fit the new religious realities he has detected.

The concept of 'post-modernism' grew out discussions in the fields of art, literature, architecture, and philosophy about the emergence of certain rather radical new styles of thought. Philosophically the term is associated with the work of such French thinkers as Jean-François Lyotard (1984), Jean Baudrillard (1981, 1983), Michel Foucault (1972, 1982), and Jacques Derrida (1970, 1976). In their historical and philosophical analyses they have argued for a fundamental change in our intellectual agenda in the face of certain new social and cultural realities that they believed have been emerging over the last several decades. This new orientation entails the rejection, transcendence, or sometimes reversal of the guiding principles of the 'modernist' world-view, which had itself displaced the feudalistic world-view some four centuries earlier (see Rosenau, 1992). The hallmarks of the new post-modernist sensibility, Beckford suggests (1992: 19), are the following:

1. A refusal to regard positivistic, rationalistic, instrumental criteria as the sole or exclusive standard of worthwhile knowledge.
2. A willingness to combine symbols from disparate codes or frameworks of meaning, even at the cost of disjunctions and eclecticism.
3. A celebration of spontaneity, fragmentation, superficiality, irony, and playfulness.
4. A willingness to abandon the search for over-arching or triumphalist myths, narratives, or frameworks of knowledge.

These themes call to mind, Beckford acknowledges (1992: 19–20), 'a few New Age groups', particularly the Neo-Sannyassins of Bhagwan Shree Rajneesh and some other syncretistic Buddhist meditational groups in America (he names no specific groups, but I would argue that Vajradhatu/Shambhala is a candidate—see Dawson and Eldershaw, 1997). He is quick to insist, however, that these groups are only 'the glittering baubles on the exotic fringe of religion'. They do not represent the kind of religion that is thriving in contemporary Britain. Certainly these themes have little or no relevance for understanding the ideology and practice of the growing Christian fundamentalist, Pentecostalist, and Charismatic movements. These developments 'have been resolutely transcendental rather than immanent, serious rather than playful, in good faith rather than cynical, univocal rather than fragmented, and so on' (p. 20). More problematically, though, he also asserts:

> My assessment of the new spiritualities . . . is the same. . . . Their very holism locates them much more firmly in the traditions of modernity than of post-modernity. The stress on the inter-connectedness of all living things, the heightened awareness of 'the global circumstance' . . . the strong sense of evolutionary equilibrium and change, the belief in the possibility of personal and social transformation, and the affirmation of noninstrumental rationalities are all redolent of a revised 'Enlightenment project' with the emphasis more firmly placed on the human scale and spiritual implications of science, politics and State administration. (Beckford, 1992: 21)

It is true, he observes, that the sacred canopy of the past has been fragmented and the 'juxtaposition of formerly separate religions may have created the impression . . . of a patchwork quilt' (p. 21). But the new religions and the shift in sensibility they reflect are still concerned with the pursuit of 'the truth', and they have turned more to science (of a non-reductionistic kind), than away from it. The new religious leaders of today may be *bricoleurs*, that is, they may be using what is at hand to fashion something new, but they are not exponents of the religious equivalent of 'an art for art's sake' approach to life. In most cases the few links that can be made between post-modernism and specific religions are either sophistry or redundant, since the features addressed can be accounted for equally as well within the terms of reference of modernity.[6]

So let us ask once again, with Beckford's additional comments in hand: Are we closer to identifying the cultural significance of NRMS? I think we are making progress incrementally, though the question can never be definitively resolved. We should refrain from continuing to identify most, if not all NRMS, with some anti-modernist stance. The blend of traditional and modern elements, of religious and secular objectives and means, of conservative and liberal impulses, in every NRM I can think of is such that the anti-modernist label is bound to be misleading. Within a modernist framework, however, there would appear to be a significant division of NRMS into more traditionalist and experimentalist camps. More care must be taken to discern what the real points of variation are between these camps, with reference to detailed studies of specific religious groups.

Likewise, with Beckford, I do not see much advantage in labelling most NRMS post-modern. As I have argued elsewhere, the terms of reference of the post-modern are still more relevant for the fine arts, architecture, and literature than for the study of social action (e.g., Dawson and Prus, 1993a, 1993b; see also Rosenau, 1992). For scholars of NRMS, an awareness of the features of the post-modern is heuristically useful, but it does more to augment our descriptive vocabulary of some aspects of some new religions than to provide explanatory insights into the nature of NRMS as a whole.

In the conclusion of his analysis Beckford makes an interesting proposal that rings true and warrants more systematic investigation. This proposal accounts for many of the seemingly post-modern features of NRMS (for example, the combination of seemingly disparate codes or frameworks of meaning) without compelling us to accept, quite contradictorily, the post-modernist meta-narrative (in which all of life, including religion, has become playful). This simpler, more accurate proposal isolates an important feature of our new religious environment that is susceptible to empirical examination. It is in keeping, moreover, with aspects of the new religious consciousness as they are described by Stone, Westley, and Campbell. Today, Beckford proposes, 'it is . . . better to conceptualize religion as a cultural resource . . . than as a social institution' (p. 23; 1989 as well). The social-structural transformations wrought by the emergence of advanced industrial societies have undermined the communal, familial, and organizational bases of religion. As a consequence, in Beckford's evocative phrase, 'religion has come adrift from its former points of social anchorage' (p. 22). None the less, he argues (1992: 23) that

> Religious and spiritual forms of sentiment, belief and action have survived as relatively autonomous resources. They retain the capacity to symbolize, for example, ultimate meaning, infinite power, supreme indignation and sublime compassion. And they can be deployed in the service of virtually any interest-group or ideal: not just organizations with specifically religious objectives.

There is more merit in this suggestion than the attempts to fit the data on NRMs to the post-modernist grid.[7] Any effort, however, to explore its potential carries us well beyond the scope of this introductory book.[8]

Concluding Remarks

There is an abundance of literature on a wide range of NRMs. But to advance our knowledge of various NRMs and hence their probable cultural significance, sociologists of religion need to undertake even more, and far more careful, comparative studies of various features of specific NRMs.[9]

In the epilogue to their recent and detailed study of the Sōka Gakkai in Britain, for example, Wilson and Dobbelaere (1994) summarize what they discovered about the nature and the appeal of this very successful NRM from Japan. Many aspects of the group, as they describe them, are clearly in harmony with the observations made by Stone, Westley, Campbell, Parsons, Lucas, and Beckford on the primary characteristics of a new religious consciousness. But Wilson and Dobbelaere continue to hold staunchly to the traditional explanatory framework, linking the appeal of Sōka Gakkai to some compensatory or oppositional response to the disjunctures of modern life. Their analysis is a little vague in this regard, but it is hard to fault them seriously for reverting to this explanatory framework when we do not yet fully understand the possible causal connections between the presumed features of modernity and the features of various specific NRMs. We need to learn much more, by way of detailed case studies of individual NRMs, about the dialectical connections that exist between different social conditions and the presence or absence, success or failure, of certain religious beliefs and practices, before we can do much more than speculate about the cultural significance of NRMs.

Contrary to the assumption of some sociologists that the study of NRMs is already passé, much of the most important work has yet to be done. With almost three decades of research behind us, the promise offered by the emergence of contemporary NRMS for the direct testing and development of the most basic questions of the sociology of religion has yet to be fully realized. The need to know more has been, of course, a constant refrain of this text. But I hope it is now clear that we already possess the means to comprehend cults without indulging our fears or prejudices. Common sense recommends some vigilance about the cults in our midst, but for that vigilance to be wise it must be properly informed.

Notes

Introduction

[1] The *Toronto Star* and the *Globe and Mail*, respectively, for Thursday, 6 October 1994.

[2] By Friday, 7 October 1994, fifty-three bodies had been found and the Quebec and Swiss authorities declared that the deaths appeared to be the result of some combination of murders and suicides. Then, much to everyone's surprise, on 21 December 1995, sixteen more followers of the movement, which had been led by the Belgian Canadian Luc Jouret and the Swiss Joseph Di Mambro, committed ritualistic suicide in a French forest near the Swiss border. On 25 March 1997, five more members committed suicide at Saint-Casimir, Quebec.

To date there have been few studies of these events. Massimo Introvigne (1995) gives a history of the group, placing it within the long and complicated tradition of neo-Templar occult-esoteric movements in Europe. He also attempts an initial interpretation of the first tragedy in 1994. Susan Palmer (1996) and John Hall and Philip Schuyler (1997) also provide detailed and revealing analyses of the group's history, basic beliefs, and internal struggles. Palmer, in particular, offers a helpful theoretical framework for possibly understanding why the members of this group committed ritualistic murder and suicide. The most comprehensive study of this event, however, is probably to be found in the small book *Les Mythes du Temple solaire* by the Swiss historian of religions Jean-François Mayer (1996). Mayer studied the group before the tragedy and officially assisted the Swiss police in their investigation from the time the bodies were discovered.

[3] Danny Jorgensen (1980) gives an interesting analysis of the coverage of the Jonestown massacre in 1978 by the print media. He concludes that when the story was 'hot', in the days immediately following the tragedy, the newspapers gave an inordinate amount of selective attention to and emphasis on certain aspects of the event, decontextualized happenings, oversimplified processes, misinformed the public, and misused the comments of so-called 'experts' to make an unusual situation fit into a largely preconceived and commonsensical understanding of deviance. The distinguished historian of religion, Jonathan Z. Smith (1982: 109), is even more

scathing in his condemnation of the wholly 'pornographic' and 'polemical' character of the media coverage of the Jonestown massacre. The media treatment of the latest cult-related tragedies, the Tokyo subway gas poisonings (20 March 1995), perpetrated by the Aum Shinrikyō Buddhist sect led by Shōkō Asahara, and the Heaven's Gate mass suicide at Rancho Santa Fe, California (26 March 1997), do not suggest we can expect much improvement in this coverage soon (see, e.g., Richardson 1995a, 1996).

4 The Citizens Freedom Foundation is one example of many anti-cult organizations established in the United States in the late 1970s and early 1980s. After several unsuccessful attempts, it, along with many other small and regional anti-cult groups, helped to form the most national and prominent anti-cult organization, the Cult Awareness Network (CAN). The Council on Mind Abuse (COMA), located in Toronto, was the most prominent anti-cult organization in English-speaking Canada. The American Family Foundation is another prominent but less interventionist American anti-cult group. COMA has recently ceased to operate owing to lack of funding, and CAN was disincorporated by the courts and its assets put up for sale (21 June 1996) in order to satisfy a million-dollar judgement levied against it because of its involvement in the failed deprogramming of a Pentecostal boy in Seattle (the Scott case). Some other small anti-cult organizations, however, have come into being recently (for example, the Singer Foundation), and many of the leaders of CAN have simply transferred their activities to Europe, where popular and governmental interest in and actions against new religious movements have intensified since the Solar Temple tragedy.

5 E.g., Needleman (1970), Wallis (1977), Bromley and Shupe (1980), Barker (1984), Rochford (1985), Melton (1986), Ellwood and Partin (1988), Bednarowski (1989), and Van Zandt (1991).

6 For example, the articles published in such journals as *Sociology of Religion* and the *Journal for the Scientific Study of Religion*, or edited volumes of essays like Zarestsky and Leone (1974), Glock and Bellah (1976), Bromley and Hammond (1987), Robbins and Anthony (1990), Bromley and Hadden (1993), or book-length studies like Wuthnow (1976), Tipton (1982a), Westley (1983), Stark and Bainbridge (1985), Wright (1987), and Galanter (1989).

7 Ellwood and Partin (1988) provide some of this synthesis. But it takes the form of rather limited summary statements of social-scientific information that are confined to the introduction and conclusion of their book, while the body of the book is devoted to summarizing the beliefs of diverse 'emergent religions'. Thomas Robbins (1988) provides a most thorough and helpful review of the sociological literature on cults, upon which I will be drawing at several points. His book, however, is schematic and rather bibliographic.

8 Of course, there are many other important issues that could be addressed in a larger book. Some of these are (1) the fascinating history of the legal struggles involving 'cults' (e.g., Anthony, 1990; Anthony and Robbins, 1992, 1995; Richardson, 1991, 1995b, 1995d, 1996b); (2) the fund-raising activities of some NRMs and the conflicts they created both within and outside these groups (e.g., Richardson, 1988); (3) the

organizational structure and innovations of NRMS (e.g., Davis and Richardson, 1976; Richardson, Stewart, and Simmonds, 1979; Lofland and Richardson, 1984); (4) the factors affecting the success or failure of NRMS (e.g., Stark, 1987, 1996; Wilson, 1987; Stark and Iannaccone, 1997); and (5) the nature of the religious experiences, including altered states of consciousness, cultivated in many NRMS (e.g., Barker, 1984; Brown, 1997; Cox, 1977; Levine, 1984; Palmer, 1994; Preston, 1981; Puttick, 1997; Tipton, 1982a; Whitehead, 1987; Wilson and Dobbelaere, 1994; Wilson, 1984, 1990).

9   These are more or less the categories that Mary Farrell Bednarowski (1989) uses in her excellent study of the beliefs of various cults in *New Religions and the Theological Imagination in America*.

10 The magazine in question is *Maclean's*. The issue is 8 February 1993.

11 Let me give one fairly typical yet randomly encountered example. I recently found most of the negative stereotypes of cults repeated, without qualification, in a Canadian government report designed to help explode stereotypical ways of thinking about another social problem, namely, in the executive summary of a report by the Panel on Violence against Women, entitled *Changing the Landscape: Ending Violence-Achieving Equality* (Minister of Supply and Services Canada, 1993, cat. SW45-1/1993E). Cults, this report states, without qualification, are common sites of violence against women.

12 Even when consulted, most experts experience the frustration of seeing the careful distinctions and assessments they had laboured to convey in interviews with the press ignored or distorted in the resultant articles and media reports (for example, see the comments of Richardson in Van Driel and Richardson, 1988: 56, n. 12; Barker, 1993: 207; Beckford, 1994; Boyer, 1998). Barker (1995a: 301–6) presents an excellent discussion of both the necessity and the pitfalls of academics' seeking to address the cult issue publicly. Boyer (1998: 7) concludes his humorous reflections on his experiences with the media with a characteristic lament: 'For all the high-minded rhetoric about outreach, community service, and scholars' duty to educate and inform the public, the reality is often different. When academics venture into the realm of print or electronic journalism, we frequently play another role altogether: less as gurus and bearers of light than simply as fodder in the media's endless struggle to meet the one compelling, inexorable imperative of their existence: to cover all that blank paper with copy, to fill all those hours of air time with talk.'

13 Bromley and Shupe (1993: 194) recently explained a number of understandable reasons why scholars of religion tend to be more sympathetic to NRMS than to the anticult movement. But, as they stress, in the end every effort must be made to sustain a balanced perspective. We must try to avoid crossing the line separating the presentation of information from the rhetoric of interest groups vying for favour.

14 The British sociologist Bryan Wilson holds to a similar view, I have discovered (Wilson, 1982a: 133; and Wilson and Dobbelaere, 1994: 216–31), and there is a strong parallel with the general distinction made by Zald and Ash (1965) between inclusive and exclusive social movement organizations, as noted by Wallis (1984: 124–5).

[15] One of the strongest critics of the reductionism of social-scientific treatments of religion is the eminent historian of religions Mircea Eliade (e.g., 1963, 1969). His views and those of others of like mind have been the subject of long and complicated debates in religious studies (see, e.g., Garrett, 1974; Segal, 1983; Dawson, 1986, 1987; and Idinopulos and Yonan, 1994).

Chapter One

[1] Accurate estimates are hard to come by. On the basis of polls by Gallup and others, it is often suggested that in the 1970s about 1 per cent of Americans claimed to be involved with various Asian-based religions, though the figure for Transcendental Meditation is as high as 4 per cent (Wuthnow, 1988: 166). In Canada, Reginald Bibby (1987: 30) estimates the figure to be even lower. With such small percentages, though, the possible variation due to sampling error is great. In terms of actual numbers, however, these figures are not negligible. It must be remembered that 1 per cent of the population of the United States is still several million people.

The anti-cult movement and others, of course, give much higher estimates, suggesting sometimes that up to 10 per cent of the American population, or at least ten million Americans, have been involved with a cult at some time.

[2] There are broad similarities between the religious activities and orientations of Canadians and Americans. But as Canadians insist, and with some scholarly support (see Lipset, 1990; Handy, 1976; Mol, 1985), there are differences. Canadians, for instance, are simply a much less 'religious' people (see Bibby, 1987, 1993). Whereas church attendance remains relatively high in the United States, it is in sharp decline in Canada (as in Europe). However, the presence and influence of new forms of religious life in the two societies are similar enough to justify suspending consideration of such differences.

[3] Much to everyone's surprise, including those in the movement, the Unification Church officially changed its name, as of 10 April 1997, to 'Family Federation for World Peace and Unification'.

[4] A similar contrast of interpretive options could have been found by choosing any number of other prominent sociologists, like Bryan Wilson (1979 or 1982a) and Daniel Bell (1977). But the writings of Berger and of Stark and Bainbridge seem to have exercised a more direct influence on work in the field of NRMs.

[5] Less conventionally, but still in emulation of Weber (and others), Berger also argues that the roots of the secularization of society lie in the Christian tradition itself (Berger, 1967: 110–23, 157–68). The history and theology of Christianity, he proposes, carried the 'seeds of its own destruction' in its progressive commitment to the motifs of 'transcendentalization', 'historization', and the 'rationalization of ethics', a legacy of unique world-building themes dating from at least the times of the Old Testament. Fascinating as his discussion of that theory is, however, it does not bear upon our immediate subject, the study of NRMs.

[6] This same theory is presented in much greater complexity in Stark and Bainbridge (1987), resulting in a systematic deductive theory of religion framed in terms of 344 testable propositions.

7 Consult Dawson (1997) for an overview of the substantive and theoretical criticisms of church-sect-cult typologies found in the social-scientific literature of the last several decades, and a proposal for the reformulation of this mode of theorizing based on a return to the forgotten theoretical wisdom of Max Weber. Elements of this proposal will be used to justify the selective framework for the understanding of NRMs outlined in this chapter.

8 The concept and term 'denomination', while not part of the initial formulation of church-sect typology, dates from at least Richard Niebuhr's discussion of these matters in 1929. For a discussion of the concept, see David Martin (1962).

9 In part, as I specify elsewhere (Dawson, 1997), this is because in their other more generalized writings on church-sect theory Stark and Bainbridge have fallen prey to what Swatos (1976) calls the Troeltschian syndrome. In these writings they play upon the criterion of tension with the dominant society to differentiate churches from sects. There is an inconsistency or disjuncture, then, between the analytical frameworks they employ for distinguishing between cults and the one they employ for distinguishing between sects and churches; the net result is an incomplete typology of cults. I would argue that the measurement of tension with the dominant society used by Stark and Bainbridge and others to distinguish between churches and sects is far more complicated, problematic, and untested than the original Weberian criterion.

Chapter 2

1 This useful distinction is drawn from Machalek and Snow (1993), and hence in turn from Snow et al. (1980), Snow and Machalek (1984), and Rochford (1985). The idea of structural availability refers to the empirical generalization that the chances of joining an NRM increase the more one possesses certain social characteristics or is free of certain social constraints.

2 As indicated in the Introduction, the division of types of NRMs I have in mind is reminiscent of a distinction drawn by Wilson (1982a: 133). Likewise, it is similar to the contrasts drawn independently between types of new religions by Berger (1967), Stark and Bainbridge (1985), and Wallis (1984) that were discussed in Chapter 1. Here I wish to stress two things: (1) we are dealing with attributes indicative of the popular ends of a continuum, and with many mixed or intermediate forms of religious orientations and organizations found between these poles, and (2) we must avoid the inclination to reduce that continuum to the mere acceptance or rejection of modernity *per se*. What I have in mind and why is discussed in more detail in Chapter 6. The similarities between the distinctions drawn by several eminent commentators on contemporary religion suggests that we are dealing with more than a mere artefact of the analytic study of NRMs. But the distinction may become a mere artefact of analysis if it is used too cavalierly.

3 A related and, one might say, subsidiary aspect of arguments linking the emergence of NRMs to moral ambiguity advances the demise of American 'civil religion' in the 1970s as a causal factor. Robert Bellah has exerted a foundational influence on this interpretation as well. Those interested in this civil-religion thesis should read

Bellah (1967, 1975, 1981), Robbins et al. (1976), Johnson (1981), and Anthony and Robbins (1982b, 1990).

4 See Robbins, Anthony, and Curtis (1975: 59–61) for a more elaborate discussion of this and other methodological objections to this view of the emergence of NRMs.

5 Lynn Davidman (1990) argues as well for a strong correlation between the desire for a stable family life and the conversion of young professional women to more extreme religious groups, specifically Orthodox Judaism.

6 In *Revivals, Awakenings, and Reform*, McLoughlin actually expands the scope of his analysis by arguing that the American 'awakenings' should be conceptualized in terms of Anthony F.C. Wallace's well-known anthropological theory of 'revitalization movements' (Wallace, 1956, 1966). The latter refers to periodic movements of cultural upheaval and reform commonly effected through religious means that Wallace and others think have gripped many societies around the world throughout time. The rise of Islam, for example, can be interpreted in this manner. Eister (1974), Barker (1985), Hargrove (1988), and many others (including Eldershaw and Dawson, 1995) have tried to apply elements of this broader theory to the most recent wave of NRMs in the West. Considerations of space and complexity have prompted the omission of this discussion here.

7 For example, with regard to Buddhism in the United States, two very interesting books have recently been published: Thomas Tweed's *The American Encounter with Buddhism, 1844–1912* (1992) and Joseph Tamney's *American Society in the Buddhist Mirror* (1992).

8 Stephen Kent (1987) also calls attention to the parallels often drawn between the social, political, cultural, and religious unrest experienced by Americans in the sixties and seventies and that of the period in English history known as the Interregnum, the 1640s and 1650s. The Interregnum marks the time of the first phase of the English Civil War and its aftermath. As Kent meticulously documents, it too was a time in Western history when political disruption and eventual disappointment spurred the rise of sweeping and radical religious innovations—sectarian groups like the Diggers, Ranters, and Quakers whose behaviour and claims closely resemble those of many contemporary cults.

9 With this long tradition in mind, Werblowsky (1982: 35) asks playfully but fairly: 'How much of the "message" [of the NRMs] is new wine in old bottles, old wine in new bottles, old wine in old bottles, or new wine in new bottles?'

Chapter Three

1 Similar views are expressed in dozens of books: e.g., Patrick and Dulack (1976); Enroth (1977); Conway and Siegelman (1978); Hassan (1988: 48, 52); and Ross (1995).

2 Insight into why specific individuals do decide to join specific NRMs is often provided in such sources as Tipton (1982a), Levine (1984), Chidester (1988), Roof (1993), Lucas (1995).

3 In the other classic account of relative-deprivation theory, Aberle (1962) offers a similar typology: deprivations of possessions, social deprivation, behaviourial depriva-

tion, and worth deprivation. He also expands the reference for the comparisons leading to a sense of relative deprivation to people's perceptions of their past conditions (real or imagined) and expectations for the future.

4   Wilson (1990: 195) makes the same point most succinctly: 'The idea of relative deprivation as such might be seen as an iconoclastic challenge to pure religious motivation.'

5   Stark and Bainbridge (1996) have sought to integrate many of the points made in this chapter into one systematic theory, framed in terms of a large series of presumably testable propositions or hypotheses (e.g., see Chapter 7 of their book). Regrettably, however, little effort has been made so far by Stark and Bainbridge or others to actually test most of these propositions. Most sociologists have been preoccupied with other aspects of their theory, dealing with secularization and the structure of religious markets (e.g., Warner, 1993; Young, 1997).

6   Interesting clinical insights into the psychology of converts to NRMs can be found in Levine (1984), while Whitehead (1987) offers an intriguing psychological theory of conversion to Scientology by combining elements of psychoanalysis and Piagetian cognitive psychology (see Dawson, 1993). Many ethnographic studies of NRMs also contain valuable biographic accounts of certain members of these groups (e.g., Downton, 1979; Lucas, 1995).

7   Brock Kilbourne, 'Equity or Exploitation? The Case of the Unification Church', *Review of Religious Research* 28 (1986): 143–50, also documents the role of youthful idealism in predisposing people to joining the Moonies.

8   Lynn Davidman (1990) comes to remarkably similar conclusions about the young women converting to a strict form of Orthodox Judaism.

9   The similarity to Levine's theory is strengthened when Palmer calls upon a modified rites-of-passage hypothesis (using the work of Victor Turner, 1968) to account for the sexual innovations in NRMs in the final chapter of *Moon Sisters, Krishna Mothers, Rajneesh Lovers* (Palmer, 1994: 253–62). Limitations of space prevent consideration of this interesting theory.

10 Since the writing of this chapter an additional voice, that of Elizabeth Puttick (1997), has joined the debate. She discusses an even more diverse range of issues dealing with women and NRMs. Her primary empirical referent is the Rajneesh movement.

Chapter Four

1   Deprogrammers are those who have attempted, as Ted Patrick says (1976), to 'fight fire with fire' by physically removing young people, against their will, from NRMs and subjecting them, on behalf of their parents and others, to an often gruelling critique of the new religion they have joined until their confidence in their new beliefs is broken. Consult Shupe and Bromley (1980) for a history, description, and discussion of the first years of the anti-cult movement and deprogramming, and Shupe and Bromley (1994) for an updating of the situation.

2   At my own large and decidedly scientifically oriented university, for example, an affiliated Catholic college recently sponsored a public lecture entitled 'Cults: "Works of the Devil"' (7 November 1995). The speaker, previously employed by the Arch-

diocese of Toronto to 'educate' high school students about cults, presented the standard brainwashing scenario espoused by the anti-cult movement without qualification, other than the addition of the inflammatory supposition that NRMs are literally
the work of the Devil and his minions. Although many of the students in the audience were sceptical or even offended, many of the older members of the audience,
drawn from the larger non-academic community, seemed to accept much of what
was said, though little or no reliable evidence had been supplied. The scenario was
largely repeated, with only a little more sophistication, when a neighbouring university sponsored a lecture by Ron Loomis, a past president of the Cult Awareness
Network and long time anti-cult activist (27 February 1997).

3 The term conversion is often used rather loosely and this is not the place to rectify
this state of affairs. But a conversion is thought to entail an extensive 'reorganization
of identity, meaning, [and] life' rooted in a transformation of the 'informing aspect'
of one's biography (Travisano, 1981: 594, 600–1). In agreement with Bankston et al.
(1981), Heirich (1977), Lofland and Skonovd (1981: 375), and Snow and Machalek
(1984: 1970), I think a conversion is to be differentiated on this basis (by degree)
from such related phenomena as 'adhesion' (the renewal of an existing faith), alternation (the transitory adoption of an alternative orientation), or mere affiliation
(simply identifying with some group).

4 See Anthony and Robbins (1994) for an excellent overview of the emergence of the
brainwashing literature and the connection with Chinese POW camps.

5 In a limited sense Singer is using the term descriptively if, as she implies at points,
she is simply describing new religions that have proved to be harmful (such as Jim
Jones and the Peoples Temple and the Solar Temple) and then assigning the name
'cult' exclusively to them. But this approach is disingenuous and dishonest, since the
term 'cult' clearly has a much broader connotation in public usage. Moreover, her
more sweeping rhetoric at other points belies her claim to any restricted meaning.

6 Of course, if there is no brainwashing, then there also would be little or no need for
such largely self-proclaimed specialists as Hassan and Singer, 'exit counsellors' ready
to treat the 'victims' and advise the public.

Chapter Five

1 In *Cults in Our Midst*, for example, Margaret Singer (1995: 3) quite typically begins
her polemic against NRMs by highlighting the potential for cults to be violent:

> Twice in less than fifteen years we have been shown the deadly ends to which cult
> followers can be led. In 1978, aerial photos of 912 brightly clad followers of Jim
> Jones, dead by cyanide laced drinks and gunshots in a steamy Guyanese jungle,
> were shown in magazines and on television. . . . And in early 1993, television
> programs showed the Koresh cult's shoot-out, then several weeks later its flam-
> ing end on the Texas plains. How many more Jonestowns and Wacos will have to
> occur before we realize how vulnerable all humans are to influence? In the time
> between these two episodes, nearly a hundred cult children and mothers died
> from lack of care in Indiana and there were reports of numerous other children

and adults abused in cults. . . . Cult members who once were ordinary citizens have been persuaded by each of these and other groups to carry out group whims—including murder, suicide, and other violent acts—at the behest of the cult leader.

2 There are conflicting reports of the precise number of people who died at Jonestown; Singer, above, says 912, while Chidester (1988) says 914, and other sources cite both these and other slightly different numbers.

3 Fifty-three members died on 7 October 1994. Another sixteen took their own lives fourteen months later, and five more on 22 March 1997. See note 2 in the Introduction.

4 Of course the other major incidents of cult-related violence are the Aum Shinrikyō poison gas attack on the Tokyo subway (20 March 1995), which killed twelve people and injured thousands, and the Heaven's Gate mass suicide by thirty-nine people in California (26 March 1997). At the time of writing, however, very little reliable information was available on these groups and their recent activities. In the case of Heaven's Gate we must still rely, for the most part, on media reports. With regard to Aum Shinrikyō we have the brief and partial analyses of Mullins (1997) and Lifton (1997), as well as the much more detailed but rather sensationalistic account of two journalists, Kaplan and Marshall (1996). The best information is provided in Ian Reader's short book, *A Poisonous Cocktail? Aum Shinrikyō's Path to Violence* (1996). But this book is not readily available, and I have only just read it.

5 Of course, as specified in the Introduction, there are exceptions to every generalization about NRMs. For instance, the Church of Scientology instituted the infamous 'Fair Game Law' for one year. This 'law' stipulated that enemies of Scientology 'may be deprived of property or injured by any means by any Scientologist. . . . [They] may be tricked, sued or lied to or destroyed' (L.R. Hubbard, 'Penalties for Lower Conditions', *Hubbard Communications Office Policy Letter*, 21 October 1968, as quoted in Kent, 1996: 26). Though this policy was formally cancelled, many commentators continue to suspect that some retaliatory activities continue, in effect, to be condoned by at least some elements of the church. I can only say that my own dealings with the Church of Scientology have been most cordial and I have never been informed of any acts of violence perpetrated by members of this group.

6 Robbins (1986) contains a fascinating description of another apocalyptic group that committed suicide, the Russian Old Believers.

7 CS (O-chlorobenzalmalononitrile) gas is extremely irritating and even lethal to children; the military use of this gas was banned by the Chemical Weapons Convention signed by the United States (and ninety-nine other countries) in 1993 (Wright, 1995b: 168, 329).

8 For some detailed and very persuasive presentations of this reading of events, see Barkun (1994), Tabor (1995), Ammerman (1995), and Sullivan (1996). As Sullivan's analysis documents, neither the BATF nor the FBI made any effort to take the Branch Davidians' religious convictions seriously, let alone to understand their point of view. When they belatedly realized the error of their ways, officials systematically distorted the truth about their failure to consult religious experts (see Sullivan, 1996: 222–4).

9   The authoritative research of Roof and McKinney (1988) identifies 15.8 per cent of Americans as Conservative Protestants, and apocalyptic beliefs are pivotal to their self-understanding. To this number, of course, could be added many others from other religious orientations.

10   For an excellent account of the extraordinary charismatic powers of a decidedly plain and unobtrusive man, see Lucas's discussions of Earl Blighton, the founder and leader of a small but successful NRM (Lucas, 1995).

11   Both Palmer (1988) and Latkin (1992) offer insights into this process as it occurred in one particularly notorious instance: the ill-fated Rajneesh commune in Oregon (1981–5).

12   See Richardson, Stewart, and Simmonds (1979) for a good description of a battle between factions representing charismatic and rational-legal forms of authority in an NRM.

13   See, for example, the near hagiography of L. Ron Hubbard in *What is Scientology?* (1993: 25–55).

14   Once again, there are exceptions to every generalization about NRMs. Wallis (1982) presents Moses David of the Children of God as a classic illustration of the charismatic leader who tries to avoid the consequences of the routinization of charisma. But Davis and Richardson (1976; Richardson and Davis, 1983) argue that Moses David had purposefully introduced more organizational uniformity to the group homes around the world, from an early point in the movement's development, in order to make his followers less dependent on him and reduce his burden as leader. Richardson believes that the importance and influence of single charismatic leaders in NRMs is usually exaggerated, in part because we do not know enough about the organizational structure and daily operation of most NRMs. Nevertheless, in each of the prominent cases of cult violence discussed here, the influence of a strong charismatic leader does seem to have been crucial.

15   Ironically, of course, as Stark and Bainbridge point out (1996: 245): 'The realities of recruitment to high-tension sects and cults will favor social isolation.' As indicated in Chapter 3, the majority of converts to NRMs are not very attached to conventional society in the first place. They are also people who have chosen to accept a set of specific and general religious compensators in lieu of pursuing various scarce rewards in the larger society, precisely because the absence of these material, social, and psychological rewards made them feel deprived. The intrinsic tendency for these kinds of groups to become increasingly isolated and cut off from avenues of recruitment accounts, Stark and Bainbridge (1996: 243–54) think, for the short life of most NRMS.

16   One member had, however, left Heaven's Gate just a few days before. His account of events has yet to be published.

17   It seems that Jim Jones was also quite ill towards the end, though probably from his misuse of various prescription drugs (Reiterman and Jacobs, 1982).

18   Reader's (1996) excellent account of Aum Shinrikyō's path to violence, which I read too late to consider in this book, supports the three-factor model presented here.

[19] This interpretation receives support from the narrow-minded reactions of law-enforcement agents to the suggestion that they receive some formal instruction in dealing with religious issues, as recorded and reported by Sullivan (1996: 229–31).

[20] Catherine Wessinger is writing a book which describes and compares all of these and other instances of cult-related violence. It is entitled *How the Millennium Comes Violently* and from what I have read it will be of great assistance to scholars and students seeking more information about these events.

Chapter Six

[1] This rather pessimistic pattern of interpretation even slips into Robbins and Bromley's essay on social experimentation and the significance of the NRMs (1992). In this paper Robbins and Bromley argue that the experimentation of NRMs arises in response to various structural conditions in modern society. They then use Hunter's analysis along with Bromley and Busching's discussion of contractual and covenantal forms of social relations to delineate briefly the kinds of conditions they have in mind. Bromley and Busching depict NRMs as a reaction to the shift from pre-modern covenantal relations to modern contractual relations, and much like Berger, they propose that the religious response 'might take the form of either creating [new] pre-modern/covenantal social forms or adapting to the requisites of modern/contractual social forms' (Robbins and Bromley, 1992: 5). Once again we are faced with an either/or scenario that does not bode well for attributing any long-term positive significance to the NRMs of today.

[2] As Hanegraaff stresses throughout his detailed analysis of the literature of the New Age movement, 'the absolute primacy accorded to personal experience can be considered the central aspect of New Age beliefs about God' (1996: 185). 'The ultimate reality of the gods', he goes on to say, 'does not really matter as long as they can be addressed and their presence experienced. . . .' In the end, New Agers 'address the gods *because it works*. Whether the reality they contact is metaphysical or intrapsychic is felt to be of secondary importance' (emphasis in the original; 1996: 197).

[3] See Beckford's article, 'Holistic Imagery and Ethics in New Religious and Healing Movements' (1984), and Hanegraaff on New Age conceptions of holism and its identification with healing and personal growth (1996: 42–61, 119–58).

[4] I can think of few better illustrations of the view I am seeking to briefly describe than the movie *Contact* (1997), which stars Jody Foster and is based on a novel by the famous astronomer Carl Sagan.

[5] I have found this line of analysis to be most useful for an understanding of the nature and improbable success of Vajradhatu (now also known as Shambhala), a Western NRM based on Tibetan Buddhism (Eldershaw and Dawson, 1995; Dawson and Eldershaw, 1997).

[6] In a later essay Beckford (1996) extends this same critical line of analysis, examining Bauman's (1992), Giddens's (1991), and Beck's (1992) tentative discussions of post-modern religion.

[7] Robbins and Bromley (1992: 22) are taken with Beckford's suggestion as well.

Bibliography

Aberle, David
1962   'Millennial Dreams in Action'. Pp. 209–14 in S.L. Thrupp, ed., *Comparative Studies in Society and History*, Supplement II. The Hague, The Netherlands: Mouton.

Adams, R.L., and R.J. Fox
1972   'Mainlining Jesus: The New Trip'. *Society* 9(4): 50–6.

Adler, Margot
1986   *Drawing Down the Moon: Witches, Druids, Goddess-Worshippers, and Other Pagans in America Today*. Boston: Beacon Press.

Adorno, T.W., E. Frenkel-Brunswick, D.J. Levinson, and R.N. Sanford
1950   *The Authoritarian Personality*. New York: Harper and Brothers.

Aidala, Angela
1985   'Social Change, Gender Roles, and New Religious Movements'. *Sociological Analysis* 46(3): 287–314.

Alfred, H.R.
1976   'The Church of Satan'. Pp. 180–202 in C. Glock and R. Bellah, eds, *The New Religious Consciousness*. Berkeley, Calif.: University of California Press.

Ammerman, Nancy T.
1987   *Bible Believers: Fundamentalists in the Modern World*. New Brunswick, NJ: Rutgers University Press.
1995   'Waco, Federal Law Enforcement, and Scholars of Religion'. Pp. 282–96 in S.A. Wright, ed., *Armageddon in Waco: Critical Perspectives on the Branch Davidian Conflict*. Chicago: University of Chicago Press.

Anthony, Dick
1990   'Religious Movements and Brainwashing Litigation: Evaluating Key Testimony'. Pp. 295–344 in T. Robbins and D. Anthony, eds, *In Gods We*

Trust: New Patterns of Religious Pluralism in America. 2nd edn. New
Brunswick, NJ: Transaction.

Anthony, Dick, and Bruce Ecker
1987 'The Anthony Typology: A Framework for Assessing Spiritual and
Consciousness Groups'. Pp. 35–106 in D. Anthony, B. Ecker, and K.
Wilber, eds, *Spiritual Choices: The Problem of Recognizing Authentic Paths to
Inner Transformation*. New York: Paragon.

Anthony, Dick, and Thomas Robbins
1975 'The Meher Baba Movement: Its Effects on Post-Adolescent Social
Alienation'. Pp. 479–511 in I. Zaretsky and M. Leone, eds, *Religious
Movements in Contemporary America*. Princeton, NJ: Princeton University
Press.
1981 'New Religions, Families, and Brainwashing'. Pp. 263–74 in T. Robbins
and D. Anthony, eds, *In Gods We Trust: New Patterns of Religious Pluralism
in America*. 1st edn. New Brunswick, NJ: Transaction.
1982a 'Contemporary Religious Ferment and Moral Ambiguity'. Pp. 243–63 in
E. Barker, ed., *New Religious Movements: A Perspective for Understanding
Society*. New York: Edwin Mellen Press.
1982b 'Spiritual Innovation and the Decline of American Civil Religion'. Pp.
229–48 in M. Douglas and S. Tipton, eds, *Religion and America: Spirituality
in a Secular Age*. Boston: Beacon Press.
1990 'Civil Religion and Recent American Religious Ferment'. Pp. 475–502 in
T. Robbins and D. Anthony, eds, *In Gods We Trust: New Patterns of Religious
Pluralism in America*. 2nd edn. New Brunswick, NJ: Transaction.
1992 'Law, Social Science and the "Brainwashing" Exception to the First
Amendment'. *Behavioral Sciences and the Law* 10(1): 5–27.
1994 'Brainwashing and Totalitarian Influence'. Pp. 457–71 in *Encyclopedia of
Human Behavior*, Vol. 1. San Diego, Calif.: Academic Press.
1995 'Negligence, Coercion and the Protection of Religious Belief'. *Journal of
Church and State* 37(3): 509–36.
1997 'Religious Totalism, Exemplary Dualism and the Waco Tragedy'. Pp.
261–84 in T. Robbins and S. Palmer, eds, *Millennium, Messiahs and
Mayhem*. New York: Routledge.

Atwood, James D., and Ronald B. Flowers
1983 'Early Christianity as a Cult Movement'. *Encounter* 44(3): 245–61.

Austin, Roy L.
1977 'Empirical Adequacy of Lofland's Conversion Model'. *Review of Religious
Research* 18: 282–7.

Babbie, Earl, and Donald Stone
1977 'An Evaluation of the *est* Experience by a National Sample of Graduates'.
Bioscience Communications 3: 123–40.

Bader, Chris, and Alfred Demaris
1996   'A Test of the Stark and Bainbridge Theory of Affiliation with Religious
        Cults and Sects'. *Journal for the Scientific Study of Religion* 35(3): 285–303.

Bainbridge, William Sims
1978   *Satan's Power: Ethnography of a Deviant Psychotherapy Cult.* Berkeley, Calif.:
        University of California Press.

Bainbridge, William Sims, and Rodney Stark
1980   'Scientology: To Be Perfectly Clear'. *Sociological Analysis* 41(2): 128–36.

Balch, Robert W.
1980   'Looking behind the Scenes in a Religious Cult: Implications for the Study
        of Conversion'. *Sociological Analysis* 41(2): 137–43.
1988   'Money and Power in Utopia: An Economic History of the Love Family'.
        Pp. 185–221 in J.T. Richardson, ed., *Money and Power in New Religions.*
        Lewiston, NY: Edwin Mellen Press.
1995a   'Waiting for the Ships: Disillusionment and the Revitalization of Faith in
        Bo and Peep's UFO Cult'. Pp. 137–66 in J.R. Lewis, ed., *The Gods Have
        Landed: New Religions from Other Worlds.* Albany, NY: State University of
        New York Press.
1995b   'Charisma and Corruption in the Love Family: Toward a Theory of
        Corruption in Charismatic Cults'. Pp. 155–79 in D.G. Bromley, ed.,
        Religion and the Social Order, Vol. 5. Greenwich, Conn.: JAI Press.

Balch, Robert W., G. Farnsworth, and S. Wilkins
1983   'When the Bombs Drop'. *Sociological Perspectives* 26(2): 137–58.

Balmer, Randall
1989   *Mine Eyes Have Seen the Glory: A Journey into the Evangelical Subculture in
        America.* New York: Oxford University Press.

Bankston, William B., Craig J. Forsyth, and H. Hugh Floyd, Jr
1981   'Toward a General Model of the Process of Radical Conversion: An
        Interactionist Perspective on the Transformation of Self-Identity'.
        Qualitative Sociology 4(4): 279–97.

Barker, Eileen
1984   *The Making of a Moonie. Choice or Brainwashing?* Oxford: Basil Blackwell.
1985   'New Religious Movements: Theoretical Issues'. Pp. 36–57 in P.E.
        Hammond, ed., *The Sacred in a Secular Age.* Berkeley, Calif.: University of
        California Press.
1989   *New Religious Movements: A Practical Introduction.* London: Her Majesty's
        Stationery Office.
1993   'Will the Real Cult Please Stand Up? A Comparative Analysis of Social
        Constructions of New Religious Movements'. Pp. 193–211 in D.G.
        Bromley and J.K. Hadden, eds, *Religion and the Social Order,* Vol. 3, *The*

Handbook on Cults and Sects in America, Part B. Greenwich, Conn.: JAI Press.

1995a 'The Scientific Study of Religion? You Must Be Joking!' *Journal for the Scientific Study of Religion* 34(3): 287–310.

1995b 'Plus ça change . . .' *Social Compass* 42(2): 165–80.

Barkun, Michael

1990 'Racist Apocalypse: Millennialism on the Far Right'. *American Studies* 31: 121–40.

1994 'Reflections after Waco: Millennialists and the State'. Pp. 41–9 in J.R. Lewis, ed., *From the Ashes: Making Sense of Waco*. Lanham, Md: Rowman and Littlefield.

Bateson, C. Daniel, and W. Larry Ventis

1982 *The Religious Experience: A Social-Psychological Perspective*. New York: Oxford University Press.

Baudrillard, Jean

1981 *For a Critique of the Political Economy of the Sign*. St Louis, Mo.: Telos Press.

1983 *Simulations*. New York: Semiotext(e).

Bauman, Zygmunt

1992 *Intimations of Postmodernity*. London: Routledge.

Baumeister, Roy F.

1986 *Identity: Cultural Change and the Struggle for Self*. New York: Oxford University Press.

Beck, Ulrich

1992 *Risk Society: Towards a New Modernity*. London: Sage.

Beckford, James

1975 *The Trumpet of Prophecy: A Sociological Study of Jehovah's Witnesses*. New York: Oxford and Halsted Press.

1978 'Accounting for Conversion'. *British Journal of Sociology* 29(2): 249–62.

1984 'Holistic Imagery and Ethics in New Religious and Healing Movements'. *Social Compass* 31(2–3): 259–72.

1985 *Cult Controversies: The Societal Response to the New Religious Movements*. London: Tavistock.

1989 *Religion in Advanced Industrial Society*. London: Unwin Hyman.

1992 'Religion, Modernity and Post-modernity'. Pp. 11–23 in B. Wilson, ed., *Religion: Contemporary Issues*. London: Bellew.

1994 'The Media and New Religious Movements'. Pp. 143–8 in James R. Lewis, ed., *From the Ashes: Making Sense of Waco*. Lanham, Md: Rowan and Littlefield.

1996 'Postmodernity, High Modernity and New Modernity: Three Concepts in Search of Religion'. Pp. 30–47 in K. Flanagan and P.C. Jupp, eds, *Postmodernity, Sociology and Religion*. New York: St Martin's Press.

Beckford, James, and M.A. Cole

1988　'British and American Responses to New Religious Movements'. Pp. 210–24 in A. Dyson and E. Barker, eds, *Sects and New Religious Movements*. Manchester, UK: The Bulletin of the John Rylands University Library of Manchester.

Bednarowski, Mary Farrell

1989　*New Religions and the Theological Imagination in America*. Bloomington, Ind.: Indiana University Press.

Bell, Daniel

1977　'The Return of the Sacred: The Argument on the Future of Religion'. *British Journal of Sociology* 28: 419–49.

Bellah, Robert

1967　'Civil Religion in America'. *Daedalus* 96(1): 1–21.

1970　*Beyond Belief*. New York: Harper and Row.

1975　*The Broken Covenant*. New York: Seabury.

1976　'New Religious Consciousness and the Crisis of Modernity'. Pp. 333–52 in C. Glock and R. Bellah, eds, *The New Religious Consciousness*. Berkeley, Calif.: University of California Press.

1981　'Religion and the Legitimation of the American Republic'. Pp. 39–50 in T. Robbins and D. Anthony, eds, *In Gods We Trust: New Patterns of Religious Pluralism in America*. 1st edn. New Brunswick, NJ: Transaction.

Berger, Peter L.

1967　*The Sacred Canopy*. New York: Doubleday.

1969　*A Rumor of Angels*. New York: Doubleday.

Berger, Peter L., and Thomas Luckmann

1966　*The Social Construction of Reality: A Treatise in the Sociology of Knowledge*. New York: Doubleday.

Berger, Peter L., and Richard Neuhaus

1970　*Movement and Revolution*. New York: Doubleday.

Berger, Peter, Brigitte Berger, and Hansfried Kellner

1974　*The Homeless Mind: Modernization and Consciousness*. New York: Vintage.

Beyer, Peter

1994　*Religion and Globalization*. Thousand Oaks, Calif.: Sage.

Bibby, Reginald

1987　*Fragmented Gods: The Poverty and Potential of Religion in Canada*. Toronto: Irwin.

1993　*Unknown Gods: The Ongoing Story of Religion in Canada*. Toronto: Stoddard.

Bird, Frederick

1979　'The Pursuit of Innocence: New Religious Movements and Moral Accountability'. *Sociological Analysis* 40(4): 335–46.

Bird, Fred, and Bill Reimer

1982   'Participation Rates in New Religious Movements'. *Journal for the Scientific Study of Religion* 21(1): 1–14.

1993   'Charisma and Leadership in New Religious Movements'. Pp. 75–92 in D.G. Bromley and J.K. Hadden, eds, *Religion and the Social Order*, Vol. 3, *The Handbook on Cults and Sects in America, Part A*. Greenwich, Conn.: JAI Press.

Block, Fred, and Larry Hirschhorn

1979   'New Productive Forces and the Contradictions of Contemporary Capitalism: A Post-Industrial Perspective'. *Theory and Society* 7(3): 363–95.

Blumer, Herbert

1951   'Collective Behavior'. Pp. 208–10 in A.M. Lee, ed., *Principles of Sociology*. New York: Barnes and Noble.

1969   *Symbolic Interactionism: Perspective and Method*. Berkeley, Calif.: University of California Press.

Bohm, David

1983   *Wholeness and the Implicate Order*. London: Ark Paperbacks.

Boyer, Paul

1992   *When Time Shall Be No More: Prophecy Belief in Modern American Culture*. Cambridge, Mass.: Belknap Press of Harvard University Press.

1998   'Dealing with the Media Circus: Confessions of a "Cult" Expert'. *Bulletin of the Council of Societies for the Study of Religion* 27(1): 5–7, reprinted from the 18 April issue of *The Chronicle of Higher Education*.

Bromley, David G.

1988   'Deprogramming as a Mode of Exit from New Religious Movements: The Case of the Unificationist Movement'. Pp. 185–204 in D.G. Bromley, ed., *Falling from the Faith: Causes and Consequences of Religious Apostasy*. Newbury Park, Calif.: Sage.

Bromley, David G., and E. Breschel

1992   'General Population and Institutional Elite Support for Social Control of New Religious Movements: Evidence from National Survey Data'. *Behavioral Sciences and the Law* 10: 39–52.

Bromley, David G., and Bruce C. Busching

1988   'Understanding the Structure of Contractual and Covenantal Social Relations: Implications for the Sociology of Religion'. *Sociological Analysis* 49 (supp.): 15–32.

Bromley, David G., and Jeffrey K. Hadden, eds

1993   *Religion and the Social Order*, Vol. 3, *The Handbook on Cults and Sects in America, Parts A and B*. Greenwich, Conn.: JAI Press.

Bromley, David G., and Phillip E. Hammond, eds
1987   *The Future of New Religious Movements*. Macon, Ga: Mercer University Press.

Bromley, David G., and James T. Richardson, eds
1983   *The Brainwashing/Deprogramming Controversy: Sociological, Psychological, Legal and Historical Perspectives*. Lewiston, NY: Edwin Mellen Press.

Bromley, David G., and Thomas Robbins
1993   'The Role of Government in Regulating New and Nonconventional Religions'. Pp. 205–41 in J. Wood and D. Davis, eds, *The Role of Government in Monitoring and Regulating Religion in Public Life*. Waco, Tex.: Baylor University, Dawson Institute for Church-State Studies.

Bromley, David G., and Anson D. Shupe, Jr
1979a   'The Tnevnoc Cult'. *Sociological Analysis* 40(4): 361–6.
1979b   'Just a Few Years Seem like a Lifetime: A Role Theory Approach to Participation in Religious Movements'. Pp. 159–86 in L. Kriesberg, ed., *Research in Social Movements, Conflict and Change*, Vol. 2. Greenwich, Conn.: JAI Press.
1980   *The Moonies in America*. Beverly Hills, Calif.: Sage.
1986   'Affiliation and Disaffiliation: A Role Theory Interpretation of Joining and Leaving New Religious Movements'. *Thought* 61: 197–211.
1993   'Organized Opposition to New Religious Movements'. Pp. 177–98 in D.G. Bromley and J.K. Hadden, eds, *Religion and the Social Order*, Vol. 3, *The Handbook on Cults and Sects in America, Part A*. Greenwich, Conn.: JAI Press.
1994   'The Modern North American Anti-Cult Movement 1971–1991: A Twenty-Year Retrospective'. Pp. 3–31 in A. Shupe and D.G. Bromley, eds, *Anti-Cult Movements in Cross-Cultural Perspective*. New York: Garland.

Bromley, David G., Anson D. Shupe, Jr, and J.C. Ventimiglia
1983   'The Role of Anecdotal Atrocities in the Social Construction of Evil'. Pp. 139–60 in D.G. Bromley and J.T. Richardson, eds, *The Brainwashing/Deprogramming Controversy: Sociological, Psychological, Legal and Historical Perspectives*. Lewiston, NY: Edwin Mellen Press.

Bromley, David G., and Edward D. Silver
1995   'The Davidian Tradition: From Patronal Clan to Prophetic Movement'. Pp. 43–72 in S.A. Wright, ed., *Armageddon in Waco*. Chicago: University of Chicago Press.

Brown, Michael F.
1997   *The Channeling Zone: American Spirituality in an Anxious Age*. Cambridge, Mass.: Harvard University Press.

Calley, Malcolm
1965   *God's People: West Indian Pentecostal Sects in England*. London: Oxford University Press.

Campbell, Bruce F.
1978   'A Typology of Cults'. *Sociological Analysis* 39(3): 228–40.
1980   *Ancient Wisdom Revived: A History of the Theosophical Movement*. Berkeley, Calif.: University of California Press.

Campbell, Colin
1978   'The Secret Religion of the Educated Classes'. *Sociological Analysis* 39(2): 146–56.

Canada Panel on Violence Against Women
1993   *Changing the Landscape: Ending Violence Against Women*. Ottawa: Supply and Services Canada, cat. SW45–11, 1993E.

Carter, Lewis F.
1990   *Charisma and Control in Rajneeshpuram*. Cambridge: Cambridge University Press.

Cartwright, Robert H., and Stephen A. Kent
1992   'Social Control in Alternative Religions: A Familial Perspective'. *Sociological Analysis* 53(4): 345–61.

Chidester, David
1988   *Salvation and Suicide: An Interpretation of Jim Jones, the Peoples Temple, and Jonestown*. Bloomington, Ind.: Indiana University Press.

Church of Scientology
1993   *What Is Scientology?* Los Angeles, Calif.: Bridge Publications.

Clark, John, M.D. Langone, R.E. Schacter, and R.C.D. Daly
1981   *Destructive Cult Conversion: Theory, Research, and Treatment*. Weston, Mass.: American Family Foundation.

Coates, Priscilla D.
1994   'The Cult Awareness Network'. Pp. 93–101 in A. Shupe and D.G. Bromley, eds, *The Anti-Cult Movements in Cross-Cultural Perspective*. New York: Garland.

Cohen, Norman
1961   *The Pursuit of the Millennium: Revolutionary Millenarians and Mystical Anarchists of the Middle Ages*. Oxford: Oxford University Press.

Coleman, John
1984   'New Religions and the Myth of Mind Control'. *American Journal of Orthopsychiatry* 54(2): 322–5.

Conway, Flo, and Jim Siegelman
1978   *Snapping: America's Epidemic of Sudden Personality Change*. Philadelphia, Pa: J.B. Lippincott.

Couch, Carl J.

1989   'From Hell to Utopia and Back to Hell: Charismatic Relationships'.
        Symbolic Interaction 12(2): 265–79.

Cox, Harvey

1977   *Turning East: The Promise and Peril of the New Orientalism*. New York:
        Simon and Schuster.

1995   *Fire from Heaven: The Rise of Pentecostal Spirituality and the Reshaping of
        Religion in the Twenty-First Century*. Reading, Mass.: Addison-Wesley.

Davidman, Lynn

1990   'Women's Search for Family and Roots: A Jewish Religious Solution to a
        Modern Dilemma'. Pp. 385–407 in T. Robbins and D. Anthony, eds, *In
        Gods We Trust: New Patterns of Religious Pluralism in America*. 2nd edn.
        New Brunswick, NJ: Transaction.

Davidman, Lynn, and Janet Jacobs

1993   'Feminist Perspectives on New Religious Movements'. Pp. 173–90 in D.G.
        Bromley and J.K. Hadden, eds, *Religion and the Social Order*, Vol. 3, *The
        Handbook on Cults and Sects in America, Part B*. Greenwich, Conn.: JAI
        Press.

Davie, Grace

1994   *Religion in Britain since 1945: Believing without Belonging*. Oxford: Blackwell.

Davis, Rex, and James Richardson

1976   'The Organization and Functioning of the Children of God'. *Sociological
        Analysis* 37(4): 321–39.

Dawson, Lorne L.

1986   'Neither "Nerve" nor "Ecstasy": Comment on the Wiebe-Davis Exchange'.
        Studies in Religion 15: 145–51.

1987   'On References to the Transcendent in the Scientific Study of Religion: A
        Qualified Idealist Proposal'. *Religion* 17(4): 227–50.

1988   *Reason, Freedom and Religion: On Closing the Gap between the Humanistic
        and Scientific Study of Religion*. New York: Peter Lang.

1990   'Self-Affirmation, Freedom, and Rationality: Theoretically Elaborating
        "Active" Conversions'. *Journal for the Scientific Study of Religion* 29: 141–63.

1993   'Libido and Cognition: The Integrated Use of Freud and Piaget in the
        Study of Religious Experience'. *Journal of Psychology and Religion* 2–3:
        71–100.

1994a   'Human Reflexivity and the Nonreductive Explanation of Religious
        Action'. Pp. 143–61 in T.A. Idinopulos and E.A. Yonan, eds, *Religion and
        Reductionism—Essays on Eliade, Segal, and the Challenge of the Social Sciences
        for the Study of Religion*. Leiden, The Netherlands: E.J. Brill.

1994b 'Accounting for Accounts: How Should Sociologists Treat Conversion Stories?' *International Journal of Comparative Religion and Philosophy* 1(1 & 2): 46–66.

1996 'Who Joins New Religious Movements and Why: Twenty Years of Research and What Have We Learned?' *Studies in Religion* 25(2): 193–213.

1997 'Creating "Cult" Typologies: Some Strategic Considerations'. *Journal of Contemporary Religion* 12(3): 363–81.

1998a 'Anti-Modernism, Modernism, and Postmodernism: Struggling with the Cultural Significance of New Religious Movements'. *Sociology of Religion* 59(2): 131–51.

1998b 'The Cultural Significance of New Religious Movements and Globalization: A Theoretical Prolegomenon'. *Journal for the Scientific Study of Religion* 37(3): forthcoming.

Dawson, Lorne L., ed.

1996 *Cults in Context: Readings in the Study of New Religious Movements*. Toronto: Canadian Scholars Press. Reprint, New Brunswick, NJ: Transaction, 1998.

Dawson, Lorne L., and Lynn Eldershaw

1998 'Shambhala Warriorship: Investigating the Adaptations of Imported New Religious Movements'. Pp. 199–228 in B. Ouellet and R. Bergeron, eds, *Les Sociétés devant le nouveau pluralisme religieux*. Montreal: Fides.

Dawson, Lorne L., and Robert C. Prus

1993a 'Interactionist Ethnography and Postmodernist Discourse: Affinities and Disjunctures in Approaching Human Lived Experience'. Pp. 147–77 in N. Denzin, ed., *Studies in Symbolic Interaction*, vol. 15, Greenwich, Conn.: JAI Press.

1993b 'Human Enterprise, Intersubjectivity, and the Ethnographic Other: A Reply to Denzin and Fontana'. Pp. 193–200 in N. Denzin, ed., *Studies in Symbolic Interaction*, vol. 15, Greenwich, Conn.: JAI Press.

Deikman, Arthur J.

1990 *The Wrong Way Home: Uncovering the Patterns of Cult Behavior in American Society*. Boston: Beacon.

Dein, Simon

1997 'Lubavitch: A Contemporary Messianic Movement'. *Journal of Contemporary Religion* 12(2): 191–204.

Delgado, Richard

1980 'Limits to Proselytizing'. *Society* 17: 25–32.

1985 'Cults and Conversion: The Case for Informed Consent'. Pp. 111–28 in T. Robbins, W.C. Shepherd, and J. McBride, eds, *Cults, Culture, and the Law*. Chico, Calif.: Scholars Press.

Derrida, Jacques

1970 'Structure, Sign and Play in the Discourse of the Human Sciences'. Pp.

247–72 in R. Macksey and E. Donato, eds, *The Languages of Criticism and the Sciences of Man*. Baltimore: Johns Hopkins University Press.

1976   *Of Grammatology*. Baltimore: John Hopkins University Press.

Doress, Irvin, and Jack Nusan Porter

1981   'Kids in Cults'. Pp. 297–302 in T. Robbins and D. Anthony, eds, *In Gods We Trust: New Patterns of Religious Pluralism in America*. 1st edn. New Brunswick, NJ: Transaction.

Downton, James V.

1979   *Sacred Journeys: The Conversion of Young Americans to Divine Light Mission*. New York: Columbia University Press.

Durkin, John, Jr, and Andrew Greeley

1991   'A Model of Religious Choice under Uncertainty: On Responding Rationally to the Nonrational'. *Rationality and Society* 3(3): 178–96.

Ebaugh, Helen Rose Fuchs

1988   *Becoming an EX: The Process of Role Exit*. Chicago: University of Chicago Press.

Eisenstadt, S.N.

1956   *From Generation to Generation: Age Groups and Social Structure*. Glencoe, Ill.: Free Press.

Eister, Allan W.

1974   'Culture Crises and New Religious Movements: A Paradigmatic Statement of a Theory of Cults'. Pp. 612–27 in I. Zaretsky and M. Leone, eds, *Religious Movements in Contemporary America*. Princeton, NJ: Princeton University Press.

Eldershaw, Lynn, and Lorne L. Dawson

1995   'Refugees in the Dharma: The Buddhist Church of Halifax as a Revitalization Movement'. Pp.1–45 in *North American Religion*, Vol. 4. Waterloo, Ont.: Wilfrid Laurier University Press.

Eliade, Mircea

1963   *Patterns of Comparative Religion*. New York: Meridian.

1969   *The Quest: History and Meaning in Religion*. Chicago: University of Chicago Press.

Ellwood, Robert S., and Harry B. Partin

1988   *Religious and Spiritual Groups in Modern America*. 2nd edn. Englewood Cliffs, NJ: Prentice-Hall.

Enroth, Ronald

1977   *Youth, Brainwashing, and the Extremist Cults*. Grand Rapids, Mich.: Zondervan.

Erikson, Erik H.

1968   *Identity, Youth and Crisis*. New York: W.W. Norton.

Festinger, Leon, Henry W. Riecken, and Stanley Schachter
1956   *When Prophecy Fails*. New York: Harper and Row.

Fichter, Joseph H.
1983   'Family and Religion Among the Moonies'. Pp. 289–304 in W.V. D'Antonio and J. Aldous, eds, *Families and Religion: Conflict and Change in Modern Society*. Beverly Hills, Calif.: Sage.

Fields, Rick
1981   *How the Swans Came to the Lake: A Narrative History of Buddhism in America*. Berkeley, Calif.: Shambhala Publications.

Finke, Roger, and Rodney Stark
1992   *The Churching of America, 1776–1990*. New Brunswick, NJ: Rutgers University Press.

Foss, Daniel A., and Ralph W. Larkin
1978   'Worshipping the Absurd: The Negation of Social Causality among the Followers of Guru Maharaj Ji'. *Sociological Analysis* 39(2): 157–64.

Foucault, Michel
1972   *The Archaeology of Knowledge*. London: Tavistock.
1982   *This Is Not a Pipe*. Berkeley, Calif.: University of California Press.

Frankl, Razelle
1987   *Televangelism: The Marketing of Popular Religion*. Carbondale, Ill.: Southern Illinois University Press.

Freed, Josh
1980   *Moonwebs: Journey into the Mind of a Cult*. Toronto: Dorset.

Freud, Sigmund
1921   *Group Psychology and the Analysis of the Ego*. London: Hogarth.

Galanter, Marc
1980   'Psychological Introduction into the Large Group: Findings from a Modern Religious Sect'. *American Journal of Psychiatry* 137(12): 1574–9.
1989   *Cults: Faith, Healing and Coercion*. New York: Oxford University Press.

Galanter, Marc, and Peter Buckley
1983   'Psychological Consequences of Charismatic Religious Experience and Meditation'. Pp. 194–204 in D.G. Bromley and J.T. Richardson, eds, *The Brainwashing/Deprogramming Controversy: Sociological, Psychological, Legal and Historical Perspectives*. Lewiston, NY: Edwin Mellen Press.

Galanter, Marc, Richard Rabkin, Judith Rabkin, and Alexander Deutsch
1979   'The "Moonies": A Psychological Study of Conversion and Membership in a Contemporary Religious Sect'. *American Journal of Psychiatry* 136: 165–70.

Garrett, William
1974 'Troublesome Transcendence: The Supernatural in the Scientific Study of Religion'. *Sociological Analysis* 35(3): 167–80.

Gartrell, C. David, and Zane K. Shannon
1985 'Contacts, Cognitions, Conversion: A Rational Choice Approach'. *Review of Religious Research* 27(1): 32–48.

Giddens, Anthony
1991 *Modernity and Self-Identity: Self and Society in the Late Modern Age.* Cambridge: Polity Press.

Gitlin, Todd
1987 *The Sixties: Years of Hope, Days of Rage.* New York: Bantam.

Gleick, James
1987 *Chaos: Making a New Science.* New York: Penguin.

Glock, Charles Y.
1964 'The Role of Deprivation in the Origin and Evolution of Religious Groups'. Pp. 24–36 in R. Lee and M. Marty, eds, *Religion and Social Conflict.* New York: Oxford University Press.

Glock, Charles Y., and Robert N. Bellah, eds
1976 *The New Religious Consciousness.* Berkeley, Calif.: University of California Press.

Greil, Arthur L.
1993 'Explorations Along the Sacred Frontier: Notes on Para-religions, Quasi-religions, and Other Boundary Phenomena'. Pp. 153–72 in D.G. Bromley and J.K. Hadden, eds, *Religion and the Social Order*, Vol. 3, *The Handbook on Cults and Sects in America, Part A.* Greenwich, Conn.: JAI Press.

Greil, Arthur L., and David R. Rudy
1984 'What Have We Learned from Process Models of Conversion? An Examination of Ten Case Studies'. *Sociological Focus* 17(4): 305–23.

Gurney, Joan Neff, and Kathleen J. Tierney
1982 'Relative Deprivation and Social Movements: A Critical Look at Twenty Years of Theory and Research'. *The Sociological Quarterly* 23(4): 33–47.

Gurr, Ted
1970 *Why Men Rebel.* Princeton, NJ: Princeton University Press.

Gussner, R.E., and S.D. Berkowitz
1988 'Scholars, Sects, and Sanghas I: Recruitment to Asian-Based Meditation Groups in North America'. *Sociological Analysis* 49(2): 136–70.

Hall, John R.
1987 *Gone from the Promised Land.* New Brunswick, NJ: Transaction.

1990   'The Apocalypse at Jonestown'. Pp. 269–93 in T. Robbins and D. Anthony, eds, *In Gods We Trust: New Patterns of Religious Pluralism in America*. 2nd edn. New Brunswick, NJ: Transaction.

Hall, John R., and Philip Schuyler
1997   'The Mystical Apocalypse of the Solar Temple'. Pp. 285–311 in T. Robbins and S. Palmer, eds, *Millennium, Messiahs and Mayhem*. London: Routledge.

Hammond, Phillip
1987   'Cultural Consequences of Cults'. Pp. 261–73 in D. Bromley and P. Hammond, eds, *The Future of New Religious Movements*. Macon, Ga: Mercer University Press.

Hamnett, Ian
1973   'Sociology of Religion and Sociology of Error'. *Religion* 3(1): 1–12.

Handy, Robert T.
1976   *A History of the Churches in the United States and Canada*. New York: Oxford University Press.

Hanegraaff, Wouter J.
1996   *New Age Religion and Western Culture*. Leiden, The Netherlands: E.J. Brill.

Hannigan, James A.
1991   'Social Movement Theory and the Sociology of Religion: Toward a New Synthesis'. *Sociological Analysis* 52(3): 311–32.

Hardyck, A., and M. Braden
1962   'Prophecy Fails Again: A Report on a Failure to Replicate'. *Journal of Abnormal and Social Psychology* 65(2): 136–41.

Hargrove, Barbara
1988   'Religion, Development, and Changing Paradigms'. *Sociological Analysis* 48 (Supplementary issue): 33–48.

Harrison, Michael
1974   'Sources of Recruitment to Catholic Pentecostalism'. *Journal for the Scientific Study of Religion* 13(1): 49–64.

Hassan, Steven
1988   *Combatting Cult Mind-Control*. Rochester, Vt: Park Street Press.
1994   'Strategic Intervention Therapy: A New Form of Exit-Counselling for Cult Members'. Pp. 103–25 in A. Shupe and D.G. Bromley, eds, *The Anti-Cult Movements in Cross-Cultural Perspective*. New York: Garland.

Heelas, Paul
1996   *The New Age Movement: The Celebration of the Self and the Sacralization of Modernity*. Oxford: Blackwell.

Heirich, Max
  1977   'Change of Heart: A Test of Some Widely Held Theories about Religious Conversion'. *American Journal of Sociology* 83(3): 653–80.

Herberg, Will
  1955   *Protestant, Catholic, Jew.* New York: Doubleday.

Hine, Virginia H.
  1974   'The Deprivation and Disorganization Theories of Social Movements'. Pp. 646–61 in I. Zaretsky and M. Leone, eds, *Religious Movements in Contemporary America.* Princeton, NJ: Princeton University Press.

Hinkle, L.E., and Wolff, H.E.
  1956   'Communist Interrogation and the Indoctrination of "Enemies of the States"'. *American Medical Association Archives of Neurological Psychology* 76: 117–27.

Holt, John B.
  1940   'Holiness Religion: Culture Shock and Social Reorganization'. *American Sociological Review* 5 (Oct.): 740–7.

Hoover, Stewart M.
  1994   *Religion in Public Discourse: The Role of the Media.* Report for the Center for Mass Media Research, School of Journalism and Mass Communication, University of Colorado, Boulder.

Hubbard, L. Ron
  1975   *Dianetics: The New Science of Mental Health.* Los Angeles: Bridge. Originally published 1950.

Hunter, Edward
  1951   *Brainwashing in Red China.* New York: Vanguard Press.

Hunter, James D.
  1981   'The New Religions: Demodernization and the Protest against Modernity'. Pp. 1–19 in B. Wilson, ed., *The Social Impact of New Religious Movements.* New York: Rose of Sharon Press.
  1983   *American Evangelicalism.* New Brunswick, NJ: Rutgers University Press.

Huxley, Aldous
  1970   *The Perennial Philosophy.* New York: Harper and Row. Originally published 1944.

Iannaccone, Laurence R.
  1990   'Religious Practice: A Human Capital Approach'. *Journal for the Scientific Study of Religion* 29(2): 297–314.
  1995   'Voodoo Economics? Reviewing the Rational Choice Approach to Religion'. *Journal for the Scientific Study of Religion* 31(1): 76–89.

Idinopulos, Thomas A., and Edward A. Yonan, eds

1994   *Religion and Reductionism: Essays on Eliade, Segal, and the Challenge of the Social Sciences for the Study of Religion.* Leiden, The Netherlands: E.J. Brill.

Introvigne, Massimo

1995   'Ordeal by Fire: The Tragedy of the Solar Temple'. *Religion* 25(2): 267–83.

Introvigne, Massimo, and J. Gordon Melton

1997   'The Attack Upon Religious Groups in Present-Day Europe: A Special Report'. Paper presented to the American Academy of Religion, San Francisco.

Jacobs, Janet Liebman

1989   *Divine Disenchantment: Deconverting from New Religions.* Bloomington, Ind.: Indiana University Press.

Janis, Irving

1972   *Victims of Groupthink: A Psychological Study of Foreign Policy Decisions and Fiascoes.* Boston: Houghton Mifflin.

Johnson, Benton

1961   'Do Holiness Sects Socialize in Dominant Values?' *Social Forces* 39 (May): 309–16.

1977   'Sociological Theory and Religious Truth'. *Sociological Analysis* 38(4): 368–88.

1981   'A Sociological Perspective on New Religions'. Pp. 51–66 in T. Robbins and D. Anthony, eds, *In Gods We Trust: New Patterns of Religious Pluralism in America.* 1st edn. New Brunswick, NJ: Transaction.

Johnson, Doyle Paul

1979   'Dilemmas of Charismatic Leadership: The Case of the People's Temple'. *Sociological Analysis* 40(4): 315–23.

Jones, Constance A.

1994   'Church Universal and Triumphant: A Demographic Profile'. Pp. 39–53 in J.R. Lewis and J.G. Melton, eds, *Church Universal and Triumphant in Scholarly Perspective.* Stanford, Calif.: Center for Academic Publication.

Jones, Constance A., and George Baker

1994   'Television and Metaphysics at Waco'. Pp. 149–56 in J.R. Lewis, ed., *From the Ashes: Making Sense of Waco.* Lanham, Md: Rowan and Littlefield.

Jorgensen, Danny L.

1980   'The Social Construction and Interpretation of Deviance—Jonestown and the Mass Media'. *Deviant Behavior* 1(3–4): 309–32.

Judah, J. Stillson

1974   *Hare Krishna and the Counter-Culture.* New York: John Wiley.

Kanter, Rosabeth M.
1972   *Commitment and Community: Communes and Utopias in Sociological Perspective.* Cambridge, Mass.: Harvard University Press.

Kaplan, David E., and Andrew Marshall
1996   *The Cult at the End of the World.* New York: Crown.

Karr, Alphonse
1849   *Les Guêpes* VI, January.

Kent, Stephen A.
1987   'Puritan Radicalism and the New Religious Organizations: Seventeenth-Century England and Contemporary America'. Pp. 3–46 in R.F. Tomasson, ed., *Comparative Social Research*, Vol. 10. Greenwich, Conn.: JAI Press.
1988   'Slogan Chanters to Mantra Chanters: A Mertonian Deviance Analysis of Conversion to Religiously Ideological Organizations in the Early 1970s'. *Sociological Analysis* 49(2): 104–18.
1996   'Scientology's Relationship with Eastern Religious Traditions'. *Journal of Contemporary Religion* 11(1): 21–36.

Kilbourne, Brock
1986   'Equity or Exploitation? The Case of the Unification Church'. *Review of Religious Research* 28(2): 143–50.

Kilbourne, Brock K., and James T. Richardson
1982   'Cults versus Families: A Case of Misattribution of Cause?' Pp. 81–100 in F. Kaslow and M.B. Sussman, eds, *Cults and the Family*. New York: Haworth Press.
1989   'Paradigm Conflict, Types of Conversion, and Conversion Theories'. *Sociological Analysis* 50(1): 1–21.

Knox, Willem, Wim Meeus, and Harm't Hart
1991   'Religious Conversion of Adolescents: Testing the Lofland and Stark Model of Religious Conversion'. *Sociological Analysis* 52(3): 227–40.

Kuhn, Thomas
1970   *Structure of Scientific Revolutions.* 2nd edn. Chicago: University of Chicago Press.

Langone, Michael D., ed.
1993   *Recovery from Cults: Help for Victims of Psychological and Spiritual Abuse.* New York: W.W. Norton.

Latkin, Carl
1987   'Rajneeshpuram, Oregon—An Exploration of Gender and Work Roles, Self-concept, and Psychological Well-being in an Experimental Community'. Doctoral diss., University of Oregon, Eugene, Ore.
1992   'Seeing Red: A Social-Psychological Analysis of the Rajneeshpuram Conflict'. *Sociological Analysis* 53(3): 257–71.

Latkin, Carl, R. Hagan, R. Littman, and N. Sundberg
1987   'Who Lives in Utopia? A Brief Report on the Rajneeshpuram Research
        Project'. *Sociological Analysis* 48(1): 73–81.

Levine, Saul V.
1984   *Radical Departures: Desperate Detours to Growing Up.* New York: Harcourt
        Brace Jovanovich.

Levitt, Cyril
1984   *Children of Privilege: Student Revolt in the Sixties.* Toronto: University of
        Toronto Press.

Lewis, James R.
1986   'Reconstructing the Cult Experience: Post-Involvement Attitudes as a
        Function of Mode of Exit and Post-Involvement Socialization'. *Sociological
        Analysis* 47(2): 151–9.
1988   'Apostates and the Legitimation of Repression: Some Historical and
        Empirical Perspectives on the Cult Controversy'. *Sociological Analysis*
        48(4): 386–96.

Lewis, James R., and David G. Bromley
1987   'The Cult Withdrawal Syndrome: A Case of Misattribution of Cause?'
        Journal for the Scientific Study of Religion 26(4): 508–22.

Lewis, James R., and J. Gordon Melton, eds
1993   *Perspectives on the New Age.* Albany, NY: State University of New York Press.
1994   *Sex, Slander, and Salvation. Investigating the Family/Children of God.*
        Stanford, Calif.: Center for Academic Publication.

Lewy, Guenter
1974   *Religion and Revolution.* New York: Oxford University Press.

Lifton, Robert Jay
1961   *Thought Reform and the Psychology of Totalism.* New York: Norton.
1997   'Reflections on Aum Shinrikyo'. Pp. 112–20 in C. Strozier and M. Flynn,
        eds, *The Year 2000: Essays on the End.* New York: New York University Press.

Lippert, Randy
1990   'The Construction of Satanism as a Social Problem in Canada'. *Canadian
        Journal of Sociology* 15(4): 417–39.

Lipset, Seymour Martin
1990   *Continental Divide: The Values and Institutions of the United States and
        Canada.* New York: Routledge.

Lofland, John F.
1977   *Doomsday Cult: A Study of Conversion, Proselytization and Maintenance of
        Faith.* Enlarged edn. New York: Irvington.

Lofland, John, and James T. Richardson
1984   'Religious Movement Organizations: Elemental Forms and Dynamics'. Pp. 29–51 in L. Kriesberg, ed., *Research in Social Movements, Conflict and Change*, Vol. 7. Greenwich, Conn.: JAI Press.

Lofland, John, and Norman Skonovd
1981   'Conversion Motifs'. *Journal for the Scientific Study of Religion* 20(4): 373–85.

Lofland, John, and Rodney Stark
1965   'Becoming a World-Saver: A Theory of Conversion to a Deviant Perspective', *American Sociological Review* 30(6): 863–74.

Long, Theodore, and Jeffrey Hadden
1983   'Religious Conversion and Socialization'. *Journal for the Scientific Study of Religion* 22(1): 1–14.

Loomis, Ronald N.
1997   'Cults on Campus: The Appeal, The Danger'. Public lecture delivered at Wilfrid Laurier University, Waterloo, Ont., 27 February.

Lucas, Phillip C.
1992   'The New Age Movement and the Pentecostal/Charismatic Revival: Distinct Yet Parallel Phases of a Fourth Great Awakening?' Pp. 189–211 in James R. Lewis and J. Gordon Melton, eds, *Perspectives on the New Age*. Albany, NY: State University of New York Press.
1995   *The Odyssey of a New Religion. The Holy Order of MANS from New Age to Orthodoxy*. Bloomington, Ind.: Indiana University Press.

Lyotard, Jean-François
1984   *The Postmodern Condition: A Report on Knowledge*. Minneapolis: University of Minnesota Press.

Maaga, Mary McCormich
1998   *The Most Intimate Other: Hearing the Voices of Jonestown*. Syracuse, NY: Syracuse University Press.

Machalek, Richard, and David A. Snow
1993   'Conversion to New Religious Movements'. Pp. 53–74 in D.G. Bromley and J.K. Hadden, eds, *Religion and the Social Order*, Vol. 3, *The Handbook on Cults and Sects in America, Part B*. Greenwich, Conn.: JAI Press.

Martin, David
1962   'The Denomination'. *British Journal of Sociology* 13(2): 1–14.

Marx, John H., and David L. Ellison
1975   'Sensitivity Training and Communes: Contemporary Quests for Community'. *Pacific Sociological Review* 18(4): 442–62.

Marx, Karl
1972 'Contribution to the Critique of Hegel's Philosophy of Right: Introduction'. Pp. 37–52 in K. Marx and F. Engels, *On Religion*. Moscow: Progress.

Mauss, Armand
1993 'Research in Social Movements and in New Religious Movements: The Prospects for Convergence'. Pp. 127–51 in D.G. Bromley and J.K. Hadden, eds, *Religion and the Social Order*, Vol. 3, *The Handbook on Cults and Sects in America, Part A*. Greenwich, Conn.: JAI Press.

Mayer, Jean-François
1996 *Les Mythes du Temple Solaire*. Geneva, Switzerland: Georg.

McCarthy, John, and Mayer N. Zald
1977 'Resource Mobilization and Social Movements: A Partial Theory'. *American Journal of Sociology* 82(6): 1212–41.

McLoughlin, William G.
1978 *Revivals, Awakenings, and Reform: An Essay on Religion and Social Change in America, 1607–1977*. Chicago: University of Chicago Press.

Meerlo, Joost
1956 *The Rape of the Mind*. New York: Grosset and Dunlap.

Melton, J. Gordon
1985 'Spiritualization and Reaffirmation: What Really Happens when Prophecy Fails?' *American Studies* 26(2): 17–29.
1986 *The Encyclopedic Handbook of Cults in America*. New York: Garland.
1987 'How New Is New? The Flowering of the "New" Religious Consciousness Since 1965'. Pp. 46–56 in D. Bromley and P. Hammond, eds, *The Future of New Religious Movements*. Macon, Ga: Mercer University Press.
1992a *The Encyclopedic Handbook of Cults in America*. 2nd rev. edn. New York: Garland.
1992b 'Violence and the Cults'. Pp. 361–93 in J.G. Melton, *The Encyclopedic Handbook of Cults in America*. 2nd edn. New York: Garland.
1995 'The Changing Scene of New Religious Movements: Observations from a Generation of Research'. *Social Compass* 42(2): 265–76.

Miller, Donald
1983 'Deprogramming in Historical Perspective'. Pp. 15–28 in D.G. Bromley and J.T. Richardson, eds, *The Brainwashing/Deprogramming Controversy: Sociological, Psychological, Legal and Historical Perspectives*. Lewiston, NY: Edwin Mellen Press.

Miller, Timothy, ed.
1991 *When Prophets Die: The Postcharismatic Fate of New Religious Movements*. Albany, NY: State University of New York Press.

1995   *America's Alternative Religions.* Albany, NY: State University of New York Press.

Mills, Edgar W., Jr
1982   'Cult Extremism: The Reduction of Normative Dissonance'. Pp. 75–87 in K. Levi, ed., *Violence and Religious Commitment.* University Park, Pa: Pennsylvania State University Press.

Milne, Hugh
1986   *Bhagwan: The God That Failed.* London: Caliban.

Mol, Hans J.
1976   *Identity and the Sacred: A Sketch for a New Social Scientific Theory of Religion.* New York: Free Press.
1985   *Faith and Fragility: Religion and Identity in Canada.* Burlington, Ont.: Trinity Press.

Moore, H. Lawrence
1985   *Religious Outsiders and the Making of Americans.* New York: Oxford University Press.

Mullins, Mark
1997   'Aum Shinri Kyo as an Apocalyptic Movement'. Pp. 313–24 in T. Robbins and S. Palmer, eds, *Millennium, Messiahs and Mayhem.* London: Routledge.

Needleman, Jacob
1970   *The New Religions.* New York: E.P. Dutton.

Neitz, Mary Jo
1987   *Charisma and Community: A Study of Religious Commitment within the Charismatic Renewal.* New Brunswick, NJ: Transaction.

Nelson, Geoffrey K.
1984   'Cults and New Religions: Toward a Sociology of Religious Creativity'. *Sociology and Social Research* 68(3): 301–25.

New York Post
1997   *Heaven's Gate: Cult Suicide in San Diego.* New York: Harper Paperbacks.

Niebuhr, H. Richard
1929   *The Social Sources of Denominationalism.* New York: Henry Holt.
1951   *Christ and Culture.* New York: Harper and Row.

O'Leary, Stephen
1994   *Arguing the Apocalypse. A Theory of Millennial Rhetoric.* New York: Oxford University Press.

Palmer, Susan Jean
1988   'Charisma and Abdication: A Study of the Leadership of Bhagwan Shree Rajneesh'. *Sociological Analysis* 49(2): 119–35.

1994   *Moon Sisters, Krishna Mothers, Rajneesh Lovers: Women's Roles in New Religions*. Syracuse, NY: Syracuse University Press.

1996   'Purity and Danger in the Solar Temple'. *Journal of Contemporary Religion* 11(3): 303–18.

Palmer, Susan J., and Natalie Finn

1992   'Coping with Apocalypse in Canada: Experiences of Endtime in la Mission de l'Esprit Saint and the Institute of Applied Metaphysics'. *Sociological Analysis* 53(4): 397–415.

Parsons, Arthur S.

1986   'Messianic Personalism: A Role Analysis of the Unification Church'. *Journal for the Scientific Study of Religion* 25(2): 141–61.

1989   'The Secular Contribution to Religious Innovation: A Case Study of the Unification Church'. *Sociological Analysis* 50(3): 209–27.

Parsons, Talcott

1951   *The Social System*. Glencoe, Ill.: Free Press.

1963   *Societies: Evolutionary and Comparative Perspectives*. Englewood Cliffs, NJ: Prentice-Hall.

1971   *The System of Modern Societies*. Englewood Cliffs, NJ: Prentice-Hall.

Patrick, Ted, and Tom Dulack

1976   *Let Our Children Go!* New York: E.P. Dutton.

Penton, M. James

1985   *Apocalypse Delayed: The Story of the Jehovah's Witnesses*. Toronto: University of Toronto Press.

Pfeifer, Jeffrey E.

1992   'The Psychological Framing of Cults: Schematic Representations and Cult Evaluations'. *Journal of Applied Social Psychology* 22(7): 531–44.

Poling, T., and J. Kenny

1986   *The Hare Krishna Character Type: A Study in Sensate Personality*. Lewiston, NY: Edwin Mellen Press.

Preston, David L.

1981   'Becoming a Zen Practitioner'. *Sociological Analysis* 42(1): 47–55.

Pritchard, Linda K.

1976   'Religious Change in Nineteenth-Century America'. Pp. 297–330 in Charles Glock and Robert Bellah, eds, *The New Religious Consciousness*. Berkeley, Calif.: University of California Press.

Puttick, Elizabeth

1997   *Women in New Religions: In Search of Community, Sexuality and Spiritual Power*. New York: St Martin's Press.

Rambo, Lewis R.
1993   *Understanding Religious Conversion*. New Haven, Conn.: Yale University Press.

Raschke, Carl
1980   *The Interruption of Eternity: Modern Gnosticism and the Origins of the New Religious Consciousness*. Chicago: Nelson-Hall.

Reader, Ian
1996   *A Poisonous Cocktail? Aum Shinrikyo's Path to Violence*. Copenhagen: Nordic Institute of Asian Studies Books.

Reiterman, Tim, and John Jacobs
1982   *Raven: The Untold Story of Rev. Jim Jones and His People*. New York: Dutton.

Rescher, Nicholas
1988   *Rationality*. Oxford: Clarendon Press.

Richardson, James T.
1980   'Conversion Careers'. *Society* (March/April): 47–50.
1985   'The Active vs. Passive Convert: Paradigm Conflict in Conversion/Recruitment Research'. *Journal for the Scientific Study of Religion* 24(2): 163–79.
1991   'Cult/Brainwashing Cases and Freedom of Religion'. *Journal of Church and State* 33(1): 55–74.
1992a   'Public Opinion and the Tax Evasion of Reverend Moon'. *Behavioral Sciences and the Law* 10(1): 53–63.
1992b   'Mental Health of Cult Consumers: Legal and Scientific Controversy'. Pp. 233–44 in J. Schumaker, ed., *Religion and Mental Health*. Oxford: Oxford University Press.
1993a   'Definitions of Cult: From Sociological-Technical to Popular-Negative'. *Review of Religious Research* 34(4): 348–56.
1993b   'A Social Psychological Critique of "Brainwashing" Claims about Recruitment to New Religions'. Pp. 75–97 in D.G. Bromley and J.K. Hadden, eds, *Religion and the Social Order*, Vol. 3, *The Handbook on Cults and Sects in America, Part B*. Greenwich, Conn.: JAI Press
1993c   'Religiosity as Deviance: The Negative Religious Bias in the Use and Misuse of the DMS-III'. *Deviant Behavior* 14(1): 1–21.
1995a   'Manufacturing Consent about Koresh: A Structural Analysis of the Role of Media in the Waco Tragedy'. Pp. 153–76 in S.A. Wright, ed., *Armageddon in Waco*. Chicago: University of Chicago Press.
1995b   'Legal Status of Minority Religions in the United States'. *Social Compass* 42(2): 249–64.
1995c   'Clinical and Personality Assessment of Participants in New Religions'. *The International Journal for the Psychology of Religion* 5(3): 145–70.
1996a   'Sociology, "Brainwashing" Based Legal Claims, and Religious Freedom: A Personal Case History'. Pp. 115–34 in S. Kroll-Smith and P. Jenkins, eds,

Witnessing for Sociology: Reflexive Essays on Sociologists in Court. New York: Praeger.

1996b 'Journalistic Bias toward New Religious Movements in Australia'. *Journal of Contemporary Religion* 11(3): 289–302.

1996c '"Brainwashing" Claims and Minority Religions Outside the United States: Cultural Diffusion of a Questionable Concept in the Legal Arena'. *Brigham Young University Law Review* (4): 873–904.

Richardson, James T., ed.

1988 *Money and Power in New Religions*. Lewiston, NY: Edwin Mellen Press.

Richardson, James T., Robert Balch, and J. Gordon Melton

1993 'Problems of Research and Data in the Study of New Religions'. Pp. 213–29 in D.G. Bromley and J.K. Hadden, eds, *Religion and the Social Order*, Vol. 3, *The Handbook on Cults and Sects in America, Part B*. Greenwich, Conn.: JAI Press.

Richardson, James T., and David G. Bromley

1983 'Classical and Contemporary Brainwashing Models: A Comparison and Critique'. Pp. 29–45 in D.G. Bromley and J.T. Richardson, eds, *The Brainwashing/Deprogramming Controversy: Sociological, Psychological, Legal and Historical Perspectives*. Lewiston, NY: Edwin Mellen Press.

Richardson, James T., and Rex Davis

1983 'Experiential Fundamentalism: Revisions of Orthodoxy in the Jesus Movement'. *Journal of the American Academy of Religion* 51(3): 397–425.

Richardson, James T., Jan van der Lans, and Frans Derks

1986 'Leaving and Labeling: Voluntary and Coerced Disaffiliation from Religious Social Movements'. Pp. 97–126 in L. Kriesberg, ed., *Research in Social Movements, Conflicts and Change*. Greenwich, Conn.: JAI Press.

Richardson, James T., and Mary Stewart

1977 'Conversion Process Models and the Jesus Movement'. *American Behavioral Scientist* 20(6): 819–38.

Richardson, James T., Mary White Stewart, and Robert B. Simmonds

1979 *Organized Miracles: A Study of a Contemporary, Youth, Communal, Fundamentalist Organization*. New Brunswick, NJ: Transaction.

Robbins, Thomas

1984 'Constructing Cultist "Mind Control"'. *Sociological Analysis* 43(3): 241–56.

1986 'Religious Mass Suicide before Jonestown: The Russian Old Believers'. *Sociological Analyis* 47(1): 1–20.

1988 *Cults, Converts, and Charisma*. Newbury Park, Calif.: Sage.

Robbins, Thomas, and Dick Anthony

1972 'Getting Straight with Meher Baba: A Study of Mysticism, Drug Rehabilitation and Postadolescent Role Conflict'. *Journal for the Scientific Study of Religion* 11(2): 122–40.

1979a   'The Sociology of Contemporary Religious Movements'. Pp. 75–89 in A. Inkeles, ed., *Annual Review of Sociology*. Palo Alto, Calif.: Annual Reviews Inc.

1979b   'Cults, Brainwashing, and Counter-Subversion'. *Annals of the American Academy of Political and Social Science* 446 (Nov.): 78–90.

1982a   'Cults, Culture, and Community'. Pp. 57–79 in F. Kaslow and M.B. Sussman, eds, *Cults and the Family*. New York: Haworth Press.

1982b   'Deprogramming, Brainwashing and the Medicalization of Deviant Religious Groups'. *Social Problems* 29(3): 283–97.

1987   'New Religions and Cults in the United States'. Pp. 394–405 in Mircea Eliade, ed., *The Encyclopedia of Religion*. New York: Macmillan.

1995   'Sects and Violence: Factors Enhancing the Volatility of Marginal Religious Movements'. Pp. 236–59 in S.A. Wright, ed., *Armageddon in Waco*. Chicago: University of Chicago Press.

Robbins, Thomas, and Dick Anthony, eds

1981   *In Gods We Trust: New Patterns of Religious Pluralism in America*. 1st edn. New Brunswick, NJ: Transaction.

1990   *In Gods We Trust: New Patterns of Religious Pluralism in America*. 2nd edn. New Brunswick, NJ: Transaction.

Robbins, Thomas, Dick Anthony, and Thomas Curtis

1975   'Youth Culture Religious Movements: Evaluating the Integrative Hypothesis'. *The Sociological Quarterly* 16(4): 48–64.

Robbins, Thomas, Dick Anthony, Thomas Curtis, and Madaline Doucas

1976   'The Last Civil Religion: The Unification Church of Reverend Sun Myung Moon'. *Sociological Analysis* 37(2): 111–25.

Robbins, Thomas, and David Bromley

1992   'Social Experimentation and the Significance of American New Religions: A Focused Review Essay'. Pp. 1–28 in M. Lynn and D. Moberg, eds, *Research in the Social Scientific Study of Religion*, Vol. 4. Greenwich, Conn.: JAI Press.

1993   'State Regulation of Marginal Religious Movements'. *Syzygy: Journal of Alternative Religion and Culture* 2(3–4): 225–42.

Robbins, Thomas, and Susan J. Palmer, eds

1997   *Millennium, Messiahs and Mayhem*. London: Routledge.

Robertson, Roland

1985   'The Relativization of Societies, Modern Religion, and Globalization'. Pp. 31–42 in T. Robbins, W.C. Sheperd, and J. McBride, eds, *Cults, Culture, and the Law*. Chico, Calif.: Scholars Press.

Robertson, R., and J. Chirico

1985   'Humanity, Globalization and Worldwide Religious Resurgence: A Theoretical Exploration'. *Sociological Analysis* 46(3): 219–42.

Rochford, E. Burke, Jr

1985   *Hare Krishna in America.* New Brunswick, NJ: Rutgers University Press.

1988   'Movement and Public Conflict: Values, Finances and the Decline of Hare Krishna'. Pp. 271–303 in J.T. Richardson, ed., *Money and Power in New Religions.* Lewiston, NY: Edwin Mellen Press.

Rochford, E. Burke, Jr, Sherly Purvis, and NeMar Eastman

1989   'New Religions, Mental Health, and Social Control'. Pp. 57–82 in M. Lynn and D. Moberg, eds, *Research in the Social Scientific Study of Religion*, Vol. 1. Greenwich, Conn.: JAI Press.

Roof, Wade Clark

1993   *A Generation of Seekers: The Spiritual Journeys of the Baby Boom Generation.* San Francisco: Harper-Collins.

Roof, Wade Clark, and William McKinney

1988   *American Mainline Religion: Its Changing Shape and Future.* New Brunswick, NJ: Rutgers University Press.

Roof, Wade Clark, and Karen Walsh

1993   'Life Cycle, Generation, and Participation in Religious Groups'. Pp. 157–71 in D.G. Bromley and J.K. Hadden, eds, *Religion and the Social Order*, Vol. 3, *The Handbook on Cults and Sects in America, Part B.* Greenwich, Conn.: JAI Press.

Rose, Susan

1987   'Woman Warriors: The Negotiation of Gender in a Charismatic Community'. *Sociological Analysis* 48(3): 245–58.

Rosenau, Pauline Marie

1992   *Post-Modernism and the Social Sciences.* Princeton, NJ: Princeton University Press.

Ross, Colin A.

1995   *Satanic Ritual Abuse: Principles of Treatment.* Toronto: University of Toronto Press, 1995.

Saliba, John A.

1993   'The New Religions and Mental Health'. Pp. 99–113 in D.G. Bromley and J.K. Hadden, eds, *Religion and the Social Order*, Vol. 3, *The Handbook on Cults and Sects in America, Part B.* Greenwich, Conn.: JAI Press.

Sargent, William

1957   *Battle for the Mind.* London: Heinemann.

Schein, Edgar, I. Schneier, and C. Becker

1961   *Coercive Persuasion.* New York: Norton.

Schultze, Quentin J.

1991   *Televangelism and American Culture.* Grand Rapids, Mich.: Baker Book House.

Segal, Robert
1983   'In Defence of Reductionism'. *Journal of the American Academy of Religion* 51(2): 97–124.

Seggar, John, and Phillip Kunz
1972   'Conversion: Evaluation of a Step-Like Process of Problem-Solving'. *Review of Religious Research* 13(3): 178–84.

Selway, Deborah
1992   'Religion in the Mainstream Press: The Challenge for the Future'. *Australian Religious Studies Review* 5(2): 18–24.

Sherkat, Darren E.
1997   'Embedding Religious Choices: Integrating Preferences and Social Constraints into Rational Choice Theories of Religious Behavior'. Pp. 65–85 in L. Young, ed., *Rational Choice Theory and Religion: Summary and Assessment*. New York: Routledge.

Shinn, Larry D.
1993   'Who Gets to Define Religion? The Conversion/Brainwashing Controversy'. *Religious Studies Review* 19(3): 195–207.

Shupe, Anson D., Jr, and David G. Bromley
1980   *The New Vigilantes: Deprogrammers, Anti-Cultists and the New Religions.* Beverly Hills, Calif.: Sage.
1994   'The Modern Anti-Cult Movement, 1971–1991: A Twenty-Year Retrospective'. Pp. 3–31 in A. Shupe and D.G. Bromly, eds, *The Anti-Cult Movements in Cross-Cultural Perspective*. New York: Garland.

Singer, Margaret T.
1979   'Coming out of the Cults'. *Psychology Today* (Jan.): 72–82.
1995   *Cults in Our Midst: The Hidden Menace in Our Everyday Lives.* San Francisco, Calif.: Jossey-Bass.

Singer, Merrill
1988   'The Social Context of Conversion to a Black Religious Sect'. *Review of Religious Research* 29(4): 177–92.

Skolnik, Jerome H.
1969   *The Politics of Protest.* New York: Simon and Schuster.

Smith, Jonathan Z.
1982   'The Devil in Mr. Jones'. Pp. 102–34 in J.Z. Smith, *Imagining Religion: From Babylon to Jonestown*. Chicago, Ill.: University of Chicago Press.

Snow, David, and Richard Machalek
1984   'The Sociology of Conversion'. Pp. 167–90 in Ralph H. Turner and James F. Short, eds, *Annual Review of Sociology*. Palo Alto, Calif.: Annual Reviews Inc.

Snow, David A., and Cynthia L. Phillips
1980   'The Lofland-Stark Conversion Model: A Critical Reassessment'. *Social Problems* 27(4): 430–47.

Snow, David A., Louis A. Zurcher, Jr, and Sheldon Ekland-Olson
1980   'Social Networks and Social Movements: A Microstructural Approach to Differential Recruitment'. *American Sociological Review* 45(5): 787–801.

Society for the Scientific Study of Religion et al.
1988   *Brief Amicus Curiae*. Submitted in The Court of Appeal for the State of California, Fourth Appellate District, Division One, 29 Feb.

Solomon, Trudy
1981   'Integrating the "Moonie" Experience: A Survey of Ex-members of the Unification Church'. Pp. 275–95 in T. Robbins and D. Anthony, eds, *In Gods We Trust: New Patterns of Religious Pluralism in America*. 1st edn. New Brunswick, NJ: Transaction Press.

Spencer, Metta
1985   *Foundations of Modern Sociology*. 4th edn. Scarborough, Ont.: Prentice-Hall.

Stacey, J.
1990   *Brave New Families: Stories of Domestic Upheaval in Late Twentieth Century America*. New York: Basic Books.

Staples, Clifford L., and Armand Mauss
1987   'Conversion or Commitment? A Reassessment of the Snow and Machalek Approach to the Study of Conversion'. *Journal for the Scientific Study of Religion* 26(2): 133–47.

Stark, Rodney
1987   'How New Religions Succeed: A Theoretical Model'. Pp. 11–29 in D.G. Bromley and P.E. Hammond, eds, *The Future of New Religious Movements*. Macon, Ga: Mercer University Press.
1991   'Normal Revelations: A Rational Model of "Mystical" Experiences'. Pp. 239–51 in D.G. Bromley, ed., *Religion and the Social Order*, Vol. 1, *New Developments in Theory and Research*. Greenwich, Conn.: JAI Press.
1996   'Why Religious Movements Succeed or Fail: A Revised General Model'. *Journal of Contemporary Religion* 11: 133–46.

Stark, Rodney, and William Sims Bainbridge
1979   'Of Churches, Sects, and Cults: Preliminary Concepts for a Theory of Religious Movements'. *Journal for the Scientific Study of Religion* 18(2): 117–33.
1985   *The Future of Religion: Secularization, Revival and Cult Formation*. Berkeley, Calif.: University of California Press.
1987   *A Theory of Religion*. New York: Peter Lang, 1987. Repr. New Brunswick, NJ: Rutgers University Press, 1996.

Stark, Rodney, and Roger Finke

1993   'A Rational Approach to the History of American Cults and Sects'. Pp. 109–25 in D.G. Bromley and J.K. Hadden, eds, *Religion and the Social Order*, Vol. 3, *The Handbook on Cults and Sects in America, Part A.* Greenwich, Conn.: JAI Press.

Stark, Rodney, and Laurence R. Iannaccone

1993   'Rational Choice Propositions About Religious Movements'. Pp. 241–61 in D.G. Bromley and J.K. Hadden, eds, *Religion and the Social Order*, Vol. 3, *The Handbook on Cults and Sects in America, Part A.* Greenwich, Conn.: JAI Press.

1997   'Why the Jehovah's Witnesses Grow so Rapidly: A Theoretical Application'. *Journal of Contemporary Religion* 12(2): 133–57.

Stillson, Judah J.

1967   *The History and Philosophy of Metaphysical Movements in America.* Philadelphia, Pa: Westminster Press.

Stone, Donald

1978a   'On Knowing How We Know about New Religions'. Pp. 141–52 in J. Needleman and G. Baker, eds, *Understanding New Religions*. New York: Seabury Press.

1978b   'New Religious Consciousness and Personal Religious Experience'. *Sociological Analysis* 39(2): 123–34.

Straus, Roger

1976   'Changing Oneself: Seekers and the Creative Transformation of Life Experience'. Pp. 252–73 in J. Lofland, ed., *Doing Social Life*. New York: Wiley and Sons.

1979   'Religious Conversion as a Personal and Collective Accomplishment'. *Sociological Analysis* 40(2): 158–65.

Streiker, Lowell D.

1984   *Mind-bending: Brainwashing, Cults and Deprogramming in the 1980s.* Garden City, NY: Doubleday.

Strozier, Charles B.

1994   *Apocalypse: On the Psychology of Fundamentalism in America.* Boston: Beacon Press.

1997   'Apocalyptic Violence and the Politics of Waco'. Pp. 97–111 in C. Strozier and M. Flynn, eds, *The Year 2000: Essays on the End*. New York: New York University Press.

Sullivan, Lawrence E.

1996   '"No Longer the Messiah": US Federal Law Enforcement Views of Religion in Connection with the 1993 Siege of Mount Carmel Near Waco, Texas'. *Numen* 43(2): 213–34.

Swatos, William H., Jr
1976   'Weber or Troeltsch?: Methodology, Syndrome, and the Development of Church-Sect Theory'. *Journal for the Scientific Study of Religion* 15(2): 129–44.

Swatsky, Rodney
1978   'Moonies, Mormons, and Mennonites: Christian Heresy and Religious Toleration'. Pp. 20–40 in M.D. Bryant and H.W. Richardson, eds, *A Time for Consideration: A Scholarly Appraisal of the Unification Church*. New York: Edwin Mellen Press.

Tabor, James D.
1995   'Religious Discourse and Failed Negotiations: The Dynamics of Biblical Apocalypticism at Waco'. Pp. 263–81 in S.A. Wright, ed., *Armageddon in Waco*. Chicago: University of Chicago Press.

Tabor, James, and Eugene Gallagher
1995   *Why Waco?* Berkeley, Calif.: University of California Press.

Tamney, Joseph B.
1992   *American Society in the Buddhist Mirror*. New York: Garland.

Tipton, Steven M.
1982a   *Getting Saved from the Sixties*. Berkeley, Calif.: University of California Press.
1982b   'The Moral Logic of Alternative Religions'. Pp. 79–107 in M. Douglas and S. Tipton, eds, *Religion and America*. Boston: Beacon Press.

Tiryakian, Edward
1967   'A Model of Social Change and Its Lead Indicators'. Pp. 59–67 in S. Klausner, ed., *The Study of Total Societies*. Garden City, NY: Doubleday.
1972   'Towards a Sociology of Esoteric Culture'. *American Sociological Review* 78 (Nov.): 491–512.

Toch, Hans
1965   *The Social Psychology of Social Movements*. Indianapolis, Ind.: Bobbs-Merrill.

Travisano, Richard
1981   'Alternation and Conversion as Qualitatively Different Transformations'. Pp. 237–48 in G. Stone and H. Farberman, eds, *Social Psychology through Symbolic Interaction*. New York: John Wiley and Sons.

Troeltsch, Ernst
1931   *The Social Teachings of the Christian Churches*, Vol. I. London: George Allen and Unwin.

Turner, Bryan
1978   'Recollection and Membership: Converts' Talk and the Ratiocination of Commonality'. *Sociology* 12: 316–24.

Turner, Victor
1968   *The Ritual Process*. Chicago: Aldine.

Tweed, Thomas A.
1992   *The American Encounter with Buddhism, 1844–1912: Victorian Culture and the Limits of Dissent*. Bloomington, Ind.: Indiana University Press.

Underwood, Barbara, and B. Underwood
1979   *Hostage to Heaven*. New York: Clarkson N. Potter.

Van Driel, Barend, and James T. Richardson
1988   'Print Media Coverage of New Religious Movements: A Longitudinal Study'. *Journal of Communication* 38(3): 37–61.

Van Zandt, David E.
1991   *Living in the Children of God*. Princeton, NJ: Princeton University Press.

Wallace, Anthony F.C.
1956   'Revitalization Movements'. *American Anthropologist* 58: 264–81.
1966   *Religion: An Anthropological View*. New York: Random House.

Wallis, Roy
1977   *The Road to Total Freedom: A Sociological Analysis of Scientology*. New York: Columbia University Press.
1982   'The Social Construction of Charisma'. *Social Compass* 29(1): 25–39.
1984   *The Elementary Forms of New Religious Life*. London: Routledge and Kegan Paul.

Wallis, Roy, and Steve Bruce
1983   'Accounting for Action: Defending the Common Sense Heresy'. *Sociology* 17(1): 97–111.
1986   'Sex, Violence and Religion: Antinomianism and Charisma'. Pp. 115–27 in R. Wallis and S. Bruce, *Sociological Theory, Religion and Collective Action*. Belfast: Queen's University Press.

Warner, Stephen R.
1988   *New Wine in Old Skins: Evangelicals and Liberals in a Small Town Church*. Berkeley, Calif.: University of California Press.
1993   'Work in Progress toward a New Paradigm for the Sociological Study of Religion in the United States'. *American Journal of Sociology* 98(5): 1044–93.

Weber, Max
1949   *The Methodology of the Social Sciences*. Trans. and ed. E.A. Shils and H.A. Finch. New York: Free Press.
1958a   *The Protestant Ethic and the Spirit of Capitalism*. Trans. T. Parsons. New York: Charles Scribner's Sons.
1958b   *From Max Weber: Essays in Sociology*. Trans. and ed. H.H. Gerth and C.W. Mills. New York: Oxford University Press.

1963   *The Sociology of Religion*. Trans. Ephraim Fischoff. Boston: Beacon Press.
1964   *The Theory of Social and Economic Organization*. Trans. A.M. Henderson. Ed. Talcott Parsons. New York: Free Press.
1968   *Economy and Society*. Trans. and ed. Guenther Roth and Claus Wittich. New York: Bedminster Press.

Werblowsky, R.J. Zwi
1982   'Religions New and Not So New: Fragments of an Agenda'. Pp. 32–46 in E. Barker, ed., *New Religious Movements: A Perspective for Understanding Society*. New York: Edwin Mellen Press.

Westley, Frances
1978   '"The Cult of Man": Durkheim's Predictions and New Religious Movements'. *Sociological Analysis* 39(2): 135–45.
1983   *The Complex Forms of the Religious Life: A Durkheimian View of New Religious Movements*. Chico, Calif.: Scholars Press.

Whitehead, Harriet
1987   *Renunciation and Reformulation: A Study of Conversion in an American Sect*. Ithaca, NY: Cornell University Press.

Wilson, Bryan R.
1961   *Sects and Society*. Berkeley, Calif.: University of California Press
1970   *Religious Sects: A Sociological Study*. London: Weidenfeld and Nicolson.
1975   *The Noble Savages: The Primitive Origins of Charisma and Its Contemporary Survival*. Berkeley, Calif.: University of California Press.
1976   *The Contemporary Transformation of Religion*. Oxford: Clarendon Press.
1979   'The Return of the Sacred'. *Journal for the Scientific Study of Religion* 18(3): 268–80.
1982a   *Religion in Sociological Perspective*. Oxford: Oxford University Press.
1982b   'The New Religions: Preliminary Considerations'. Pp. 16–31 in E. Barker, ed., *New Religious Movements: A Perspective for Understanding Society*. New York: Edwin Mellen Press.
1987   'Factors in the Failure of the New Religious Movements'. Pp. 30–45 in D.G. Bromley and P.E. Hammond, eds, *The Future of New Religious Movements*. Macon, Ga: Mercer University Press.
1988   '"Secularization": Religion in the Modern World'. Pp. 953–66 in Stewart Sutherland et al., eds, *The World's Religions*. London: Routledge.
1990   *The Social Dimension of Sectarianism*. Oxford: Clarendon Press.
1993   'Historical Lessons in the Study of Sects and Cults'. Pp. 53–73 in D.G. Bromley and J.K. Hadden, eds, *Religion and the Social Order*, Vol. 3, *The Handbook on Cults and Sects in America, Part A*. Greenwich, Conn.: JAI Press.

Wilson, Bryan, and Karel Dobbelaere
1994   *A Time to Chant: The Sōka Gakkai Buddhists in Britain*. Oxford: Clarendon Press.

Wilson, Stephen R.
1984   'Becoming a Yogi: Resocialization and Deconditioning as Conversion Processes'. *Sociological Analysis* 45(4): 301–14.
1990   'Personal Growth in a Yoga Ashram: A Symbolic Interactionist Interpretation'. Pp. 137–66 in D. Moberg and M.L. Lynn, eds, *Research in the Social Scientific Study of Religion*, Vol. 7. Greenwich, Conn.: JAI Press.

Wood, Allen Tate, with Jack Vitch
1979   *Moonstruck: A Memoir of My Life in a Cult*. New York: William Morrow.

Wright, Stuart A.
1984   'Post-Involvement Attitudes of Voluntary Defectors from Controversial New Religious Movements'. *Journal for the Scientific Study of Religion* 23(2): 172–82.
1987   *Leaving Cults: The Dynamics of Defection*. Washington, DC: Society for the Scientific Study of Religion Monograph Series, no. 7.

Wright, Stuart A., ed.
1995a   'Another View of the Mt Carmel Standoff'. Pp. xiii–xxvi in S. Wright, ed., *Armageddon in Waco*. Chicago: University of Chicago Press.
1995b   *Armageddon in Waco: Critical Perspectives on the Branch Davidian Conflict*. Chicago: University of Chicago Press.

Wright, Stuart A., and William V. D'Antonio
1993   'Families and New Religions'. Pp. 219–38 in D.G. Bromley and J.K. Hadden, eds, *Religion and the Social Order*, Vol. 3, *The Handbook on Cults and Sects in America, Part A*. Greenwich, Conn.: JAI Press.

Wright, Stuart, and Helen Rose Ebaugh
1993   'Leaving New Religions'. Pp. 117–38 in D. Bromley and J. Hadden, eds, *Religion and the Social Order*, Vol. 3, *The Handbook on Cults and Sects in America, Parts A and B*. Greenwich, Conn.: JAI Press.

Wuthnow, Robert
1976   *The Consciousness Reformation*. Berkeley, Calif.: University of California Press.
1982   'World Order and Religious Movements'. Pp. 47–65 in E. Barker, ed., *New Religious Movements: A Perspective for Understanding Society*. New York: Edwin Mellen Press.
1985   'The Cultural Context of Contemporary Religious Movements'. Pp. 43–56 in T. Robbins, W.C. Sheperd, and J. McBride, eds, *Cults, Culture, and the Law*. Chico, Calif.: Scholars Press.
1988   *The Restructuring of American Religion*. Princeton, NJ: Princeton University Press.

Yinger, J. Milton
1957   *Religion, Society and the Individual*. New York: Macmillan.
1970   *The Scientific Study of Religion*. New York: Macmillan.

Young, Lawrence, ed.
1997   *Rational Choice Theory and Religion: Summary and Assessment*. New York: Routledge.

Zablocki, Benjamin
1996   'Reliability and Validity of Apostate Accounts in the Study of Religious Communities'. Paper presented to the Association for the Sociology of Religion, New York City.

Zald, Mayer, and Roberta Ash
1965   'Social Movement Organizations: Growth, Decay and Change'. *Social Forces* 44: 327–41.

Zarestsky, I., and M.P. Leone, eds
1974   *Religious Movements in Contemporary America*. Princeton, NJ: Princeton University Press.

Zaroulis, Nancy, and Gerald Sullivan
1984   *Who Spoke Up? American Protest against the War in Vietnam, 1963–1975*. Garden City, NY: Doubleday.

Zoma, Lois, ed.
1982   *The Apocalyptic Vision in America*. Bowling Green, Ohio: Bowling Green University Popular Press.

Zygmunt, J.F.
1972   'When Prophecies Fail: A Theoretical Perspective on Comparative Evidence'. *American Behavioral Scientist* 16(2): 245–67.

Index